# Writing the Orgy

# *Writing the Orgy:* POWER AND

## PARODY IN SADE

---

### LUCIENNE FRAPPIER-MAZUR

translated by GILLIAN C. GILL

PENN

University of Pennsylvania Press
Philadelphia

Library of Congress Cataloging-in-Publication Data

Frappier-Mazur, Lucienne.
    [Sade et l'écriture de l'orgie. English]
    Writing the orgy : power and parody in Sade / Lucienne Frappier
–Mazur : translated by Gillian C. Gill.
        p.    cm.
    Includes bibliographical references and index.
    ISBN 0-8122-3251-8 (cloth). — ISBN 0-8122-1590-7 (pbk.)
    1. Sade, marquis de, 1740–1814.   Histoire de Juliette.
2. Dominance (Psychology) in literature.   3. Eroticism in
literature.   4. Sex in literature.   5. Parody.   I. Title.
PQ2063.S3F7313   1996
843'.6—dc20                                              96-2111
                                                          CIP

To François and
His Father

# Contents

*Translator's Note. While preparing this translation I had the pleasure of working in constant contact with Professor Frappier-Mazur and she was kind enough to take responsibility for the text in its final stages.*

—*Gillian C. Gill*

# Preface and Acknowledgments

Contemporary interest and fascination with Sade's work is quite understandable. The orgy scene—the narrative kernel of his major novels—extends the limits of what can be put into words and explodes boundaries and ideologies. Yet the orgy scene *represents* not only the subversion but, just as much, the re-creation of a social order and hierarchy, under a phallic, unifying economy. The same ambivalence between convention and tradition on the one hand and transgression on the other, exists at the textual level. Sade's text does not function as an organic whole and seems deliberately to leave contradictions open. Why would someone who so clearly illuminates the mechanisms of class exploitation through those of sex exploitation want to perpetuate any form of exploitation? What, then, is the significance of Sade's misogyny, which no one would think of denying, and of his hatred of the female body?

In the first part of this study, I show the erotic body as both represented and representing through the ritualistic scenario of the orgy scene. The second part addresses the intricate relation between the erotic and the textual body.

The present volume bears the mark of a collective effort. I am deeply grateful to Carroll Smith-Rosenberg and Phyllis Rackin for providing me with intellectual inspiration, advice, and support throughout the writing of this book. My warmest thanks go to my translator, Gillian Gill, who spent the better part of several months in the company of a subject matter she did not always find truly congenial. To Frank Bowman, who gave so generously of his time and learning for both the French and the English versions, my debt extends far beyond the limits of this book, as he well knows. My son François and my friends and colleagues Lance Donaldson-Evans, Alvia Golden, Lynn Hunt, Carlos Lynes, Henri Mitterand, Nicole Mozet, Judith Schlanger, Gretchen van Slyke, and Françoise van Rossum-Guyon all have contributed to the final shaping of this *Sade* and I thank them for their generosity and critical acumen. I also wish to thank my research assistant, Guillemette Bolens, who did impeccable work researching bibliographical citations and translations, and Alison Anderson, Ridley Hammer and Jerome Singerman, at the University of Pennsylvania Press, whose professional advice and assistance have been invaluable.

I am indebted to the American Council of Learned Societies for a fellowship in 1984–85 and to the Mellon Foundation for a grant during the summer of 1985, both of which enabled me to write the first part of this book. The publication in English was made possible through the financial support of the French Ministry of Culture, and of the School of Arts and Sciences and the Research Foundation at the University of Pennsylvania. To all my sincere gratitude.

Chapter 3 incorporates material previously published in "The Social Body: Disorder and Ritual in Sade's *The Story of Juliette*, in *Eroticism and the Body Politic*, ed. Lynn Hunt (Baltimore: Johns Hopkins University Press, 1991), reprinted by permission of the publisher. Chapters 5 and 7 incorporate material previously published in "A Turning Point in the Sadean Novel: The Terror," *Pli. Warwick Journal of Philosophy* (1994, issue on "The Divine Sade," ed. Deepak Narang Sawhney), reprinted by permission of the journal.

# Introduction

Donatien-Alphonse-François de Sade is a cult hero for many of our contemporaries; yet he is also accused of being repetitive and boring, and this criticism may let the reader, especially the female reader, avoid grappling with the intolerable aggression of the text. There is no denying that in one work after another, and especially in the major novels, we find the same speeches, the same orgy scenes, the same sado-erotic inventiveness, and again and again the same paroxysms. But this overdetermined repetition itself needs to be understood. How does it function? What does it correspond to? The *Histoire de Juliette* (*The Story of Juliette*) marks the coming of age of the Sadean novel and the culmination of the fictional model founded by *Don Quixote*. Written, unlike *Don Quixote*, as a first person narrative, the *Histoire de Juliette* exaggerates the parody and self-reflexivity of Cervantes's text, and offers an extreme instance of literary intertextuality. Seemingly the first novel that Sade conceived entirely after the French Revolution, *Juliette* to a large extent represents his definitive ideas; it is characterized both by a new political awareness and by changes in form. Politics are set at the heart of the orgy through the politicization of the sexual and the sexualization of the political, and the work successfully weaves parody, power relationships, and the orgy scene into one fabric. Less than four years after the women's political clubs were closed, less than two years after women were banned from assembling and taking part in public life—two of the ways in which the Convention reacted to the disturbances and noisy revolutionary zeal of a few women—*Juliette* is, together with Defoe's *Moll Flanders*, one of the rare eighteenth-century novels to be narrated from beginning to end (except for two interpolated stories) by a heroine who has *freedom* of movement,[1] a freedom which at this period was inseparable from libertinism and transgression.

The *orgy* scene may be defined as the presentation of a *collective* act focusing on excess—be it of sex, of food or of language—and on confusion: mingling of bodies, hybrid foods (such as fish and fowl), blurring of the line between natural and artificial decor. At one and the same time, orgy connotes the hybrid, repetition, and equivalence, and constitutes a *scene*. *Parody*, which may reflect admiration as much as censure, is distinguished from other forms of imitation by its heterogeneous diction. It imitates and burlesques a discourse or code which it weds to other discourses, without muffling the discord between them. Parody can be defined in two essential ways: it can either reinscribe some classic discourse, and thus have limited relevance, or else convey a subversive, innovative, and plural discourse. Sade's novel falls largely under this second definition, even though passages of it are borrowed or collaged or parodic in the narrow meaning of the word. The text is overwhelming and yet elusive, and this phenomenon is not to be accounted for uniquely by the not inconsiderable dimension of self-parody. *The essence of the text is parodic because the Sadean imaginary doubles the parodic structures characteristic of the orgy motif*, that is, circularity and specularity, transgression, inversion, heterogeneity.[2]

These are also the structures of carnival, and the popular, ribald strain running through the orgy in the novel can be linked to carnivalesque literature. More clearly than this tradition, however, the Sadean orgy seems, if we discount the difference in social levels, directly to inscribe the violence of the brutal real-life charivaris, which, as Emmanuel Leroy-Ladurie shows in *Carnival in Romans*, turned at times into blood baths.[3] Conversely, even if the Sadean scene does preserve certain elements of carnival, it lays much greater stress on pessimism and death. And yet Sade is even closer to the eighteenth-century libertine novel in which the orgy, while maintaining its connection to pornography, binds philosophy and eroticism together in a line that goes back to Plato's *Symposium*. Admittedly, the Roman Saturnalia—the term reappears in several eighteenth-century titles—linked orgy and carnival, but the differences between the two are far deeper and more important than the similarities. The literature of carnival is not necessarily centered on eros. More particularly, carnival is a public event, democratic in appearance if not in function, whereas the orgy is for the elite and performed behind closed doors. Most of the actors who take part in the orgy are aristocrats, and the action is played out amidst luxury and abundance, all of which distorts the inversion of the class relations characteristic of Saturnalia.[4] Readers are never in doubt as to the aristocratic status of orgy, and any disproportion in rank among those involved never poses a threat to social hierarchy. The only representatives of the lower classes with whom the nobles consort are servants or prostitutes. The stereotype of the marquise granting her favors to a valet could more properly be described as the valet rendering his mistress a sexual service.[5]

The Sadean orgy exacerbates power relations and thus at times refers back to this pre-revolutionary type of class relations. Almost all the orgy's victims are chosen from among the nobility or the wealthy, and yet the masters of the orgy are able to renew their crimes indefinitely without fear of punishment. The private setting and the unrealistic disproportion of forces suggest that we need to attempt a socio-symbolic reading, which, starting with *La Philosophie dans le boudoir*, would be pertinent for both the Ancien Régime and the Revolutionary period. Moreover, to take up a distinction made by Michel Foucault, Sade's novel unites features of an *ars erotica* with those of a *scientia sexualis*, though indeed the balance tips heavily toward the latter.[6] In Part 3 of the first volume of his *History of Sexuality*, Foucault argues that the *scientia sexualis* has progressively invaded the discourse on sex. At some point in the seventeenth century there "emerges a political, economic, and technical incitement to talk about sex" as something "to manage" in public speech, to control by means of a kind of policing that would not necessarily be repressive (see Foucault, pp. 24, 33, 34). The discourse of Sade reflects this general urge even as it exceeds it in every direction.

From the *ars erotica*, Sade retains the idea of the search for pleasure as the only absolute possible and perhaps, that of the subject's particular relationship to the master and initiator (who in his novels is often a woman). But he takes over the whole of the sexual science, since this "power-knowledge," as Foucault calls it, is based on the procedure of confession, itself founded on the notion of sin, two elements which in Sade take the inverted forms of proclamation and transgression. His characters loudly lay claim to each and every criminal and sacrilegious act, and this claim to a sexuality inseparable from violence forms the basis of the whole aesthetic, sociopolitical, and philosophical structure of Sade's thought. For Sade can no more envision a text outside a science of the sexual than he can a social state, and for him the representation of the sexual is also a representation of the social.

The narrative plot of the Sadean novel develops certain modes of symbolic representation, with the phantasy of the erotic body at their center. A psychoanalytic reading is required here, but not in isolation. Instinctual drives alone cannot account for the elaboration of the symbolism—and the techniques—of the body. In large measure, sexual behavior itself is something learned and socially determined, something that fits into much larger symbolic systems.[7] This basic point is in no way contradicted by the fact that Sadean practices seem to diverge from the norm. These practices may still be read in the context of the social upheaval experienced by their author—beginning, under the Ancien Régime, with the thirteen years he spent in prison, a punishment he could neither accept nor understand. Sadean practices trace a parallel between the erotic body and society, between erotic body and textual body. At times Sadean discourse posits an anteriority for the body and the drive, and a causal relationship between the body and the social and textual, which would mean that the body directed the perception of the social and gave rise to the textual. At other times, quite to the contrary, Sade posits language as the source of erotic experience, and implies that an imaginary which is already socially determined organizes the relation to the body. In the constant oscillation between these two positions, resulting questions of causality and anteriority are never resolved. If shared modes of symbolization characterize different systems of representation in the same era, is this because there is some causal relation between the social and economic reality and its symbolic representation in ideology? Such would be the (pre-Althusserian) Marxist thesis, but I prefer to envisage a continual process of exchange and interaction in which no clear-cut priorities can be set up. Anthropology, which moves between the two viewpoints, interprets things in this way: how indeed could one conceive of a social reality that was not already comprehended and perceived from within a system of symbolic representation?[8]

If, moreover, an author tends to subvert distinct symbolic systems according to common processes, this phenomenon presupposes a homology not only among these different systems but also between the social and the individual. In his "anthropological" essays, Freud returns several times to this point and establishes a parallel between the development of the individual and that of civilizations and social formations, tracing the same idealization processes in all of them. He argues that the individual superego and the idealization of the father correspond to the development of a collective superego—both the national cult of great men and the totemic system.[9] The parallels Freud draws are sketchy and he makes no claim to account for the whole social dimension,[10] but his approach turns up again in some anthropological interpretations of symbolic systems that also assume a homology between the cultural and the individual unconscious. And the anthropological interpretation of social rituals often intersects with psychoanalytic interpretations of the symbolism of dreams and phantasies,[11] even if this convergence is not always acknowledged. Thus psychoanalytical theory will serve to refine and complete the anthropological approach when we come to analyse the erotic body and its social and textual symbolism in Sade's work.

# PART 1

# Erotic Body, Social Body: Disorder and Ritual

*T*
*he rituals of the Sadean orgy* have been described and interpreted over and again. Still, their status should not be taken for
granted and much remains to be said about their social symbolism.
To adopt the point of view of social symbolism is not to strip the rituals of their private character or to deny their relation to Sade's own
sexuality. His temperament, childhood, family situation, and physiological peculiarities[1] must all have played a determining role, but all
these factors are themselves inextricably tied to social origin and to
the events of history. The Sadean phantasies are not merely a matter of
psychic content and congenital cause. They were violent to begin with
but their violence was exacerbated by the exceptional constraints and
punishments that society set against the brutal and sacrilegious fancies
of this nobleman of the Ancien Régime. In the threatening political
climate of the years before the Revolution, Sade's violent phantasy is
a reaction to his arbitrary imprisonment under the lettre de cachet, to
the death sentence levied on him, and to the sexual abstinence prison
imposed on him and the compensatory practices he then indulged
in. Sentenced to death on two occasions, first by the Parlement of
Aix in 1772 and then under the Terror in 1794, he was incarcerated
under the Ancien Régime briefly from 1772 to 1773 and then from
1777 to 1790, imprisoned again during the Terror from December
1793 to October 1794, and then again during the Consulate and the
Empire from 1801 to his death in 1814. Sade experienced much more
in his body than the ever imperfect realization of his sexual tastes. He
knew social upheaval and the very real poverty that resulted. He suf-

fered under a succession of different political powers who locked him away in physical conditions that were close to unbearable in the early period, though becoming quite mild under the Terror. How could Sade not have made a connection between the accumulation of physical and moral trials he experienced, and indeed somatized through obesity and other ailments,[2] and the social state which caused them? Not enough attention has been paid to life in prison as an assault on the body. The violence of the Sadean phantasy increases as a result of the violence directed against him over many years. Writing allows Sade to master that double reality, both social and private, within the erotic imaginary, through the ritual of the orgy scene.

In fact, ritual, whether individual or collective, as it aims to "re-formulate past experience,"[3] does so by directing it: that is to say, it "converts the obligatory into the desirable."[4] This is why Victor Turner describes the ritual symbol, like the dream, as "a compromise formation between two main opposing tendencies," one that permits a compromise between "the need for social control and certain innate and universal human drives whose complete gratification would result in a breakdown of that control."[5] Even as they play this role of compromise, however, certain rites are very violent. Conversely, even though the Sadean phantasy can hardly be called moderate, it acquires a ritual character by being methodical and organized.

The parallel Turner draws between ritual and dream refers implicitly to phantasy, a widely accepted Freudian term that would in fact suit his argument even better. In *The Interpretation of Dreams*, Freud actually describes phantasy as a compromise formation and shows that "its structure is comparable to that of dreams."[6] In the case of Sade, the term phantasy can be justified in the sense of "day-dreams, scenes, episodes, romances or fictions which the subject creates and recounts to himself in the waking state" and figuring "in a manner that is more or less deformed by defensive processes a wish fulfilment and, in the last resort, an unconscious desire."[7] Freudian theory distinguishes among "conscious phantasies or day dreams; unconscious phantasies which analysis reveals to be structures underlying a manifest content; primary phantasies."[8] At first sight, the Sadean phantasy, since it is verbalized, seems by definition to be conscious, an obsessional declaration of the desire it figures, that is, the desire for a polymorphous sexual practice, the desire to supplant the father and to tear out the mother's womb. Nonetheless, behind these conscious desires there is a glimpse of "primal phantasies" such as castration anxiety (and its adult avatars on the level of society) or incest with the mother, as well as "underlying structures" such as repetition or the masochistic reversal of the sadistic position.[9] On the whole, the general question of how far phantasy and/or desire in Sade can be considered conscious is only tangential to our interest in the social and textual symbolism of the orgy. Highly relevant, on the other hand, is the link between ritual and phantasy.

The ritualism of the Sadean phantasy reveals an attempt to come to terms with the real in a way shared by both the individual and the collective symbol. And the reality principle, for Sade, is confused with political and social imperatives. The exceptionally wide gap between his desire and the constraints that bound him explains both the violence of his phantasies and their heavy ritualization. The ritual symbol, says Victor Turner, refers to two poles of signification, the one ideological, the other sensorial; the first located in the social and moral order, the second in the natural and physical order. It is the content of the latter that comes closest to the external form of the symbol.[10] Thus the text as a whole suggests a parallel between the erotic body, whose symbolism is particularly easy to read, and the social body.

As a general rule, according to Mary Douglas, "the social experience of disorder is expressed by powerfully efficacious symbols of impurity and danger. . . . A social structure which requires a high degree of conscious control will find its style at a high level of formality in stern application of the purity rule, denigration of organic process, and wariness towards experiences in which control of consciousness is lost."[11] This double description helps to identify one of the ambivalences of the Sadean symbol, which associates the ritualistic protocol with the violence and rupture of the rule of purity, and thus reproduces the strong social structuration of the Ancien Régime as well as its collapse, the willed character of the Cartesian ego as well as the instinctual force of desire. Mary Douglas takes her inspiration from Marcel Mauss when, in the following passage, she traces the major outlines of the social geography of power, as materialized in the corporal space:

> The human body is always treated as an image of society and (. . .) there can be no natural way of considering the body that does not involve at the same time the social dimension. Interest in its apertures depends on the preoccupations with social exits and entrances, escape routes, and invasions. If there is no concern to preserve social boundaries, I would not expect to find concern with bodily boundaries. The relation of head to feet, of brain and sexual organs, of mouth and anus are commonly treated so that they express

the relevant patterns of hierarchy. Consequently I now advance the hypothesis that bodily control is an expression of social control—abandonment of bodily control in ritual responds to the requirement of a social experience which is being expressed. Furthermore, there is little prospect of successfully imposing bodily control without the corresponding social forms. And lastly the same drive that seeks harmoniously to relate the experience of physical and social, must affect ideology. Consequently, when once the correspondence between bodily and social controls is traced, the basis will be laid for considering co-varying attitudes in political thought and theology.[12]

Although Mary Douglas's analyses refer to traditional cultures in which individuals still live in a continuum with their environment, the principle of their bodily symbolism owes something to her observations of certain sectors of her own culture, as evidenced by some of the comparisons she makes. This principle is further confirmed when we look at Sade's symbolizations. The symbols' content and their social implications may vary by social group, but the types of insights afforded by their configuration do not. In the case of Sade, and therefore on the level of the individual, this type of symbolization must surely have been reactivated by his prison experience—by reduced space and somatization. The eroticization that affects all intense perceptions of social disorder also comes into play. Gilles Deleuze attributes "eroticism's aptness to serve as a mirror to the world, to reflect the world's excesses and extract its violences" to the fact that "anything excessive in a stimulus is, in some manner, eroticized."[13] Sade himself often returns to this second point. These different factors establish a correlation between the Sadean experience of the social and the constitution of the orgiac body. Therefore my approach in Part I will be to analyze the figures and schemata of the Sadean orgy first as sexual symbols and then to try and locate the isomorphism of the erotic body and the social body (as Sade understands it), an isomorphism that develops along the semantic axis of disorder and order. Two methodological problems arise as a result. First, the question arises as to whether the social symbolism of the Sadean novel evolved with the succession of political regimes. I shall show that the experience of the revolutionary years did indeed introduce quite noticeable changes both in Sade's symbolism and in his textual practice. Furthermore, even though the outline of *Les Cent-vingt journées de Sodome* (*The 120 Days of Sodom*)[14] already includes all the phantasies of violent destruction to be developed later, the overall plan, the details of tortures, and the section of the plan that was actually drafted obey an exclusive principle of order that will never be equaled in later years. The second problem raised by my approach relates to the ambivalence of the figures and symbols for the orgy, and to the difficulty of assigning them as a unit either to order or to disorder. Thus the reader will find them reappearing under different rubrics. Within this symbolization, every difference is translated into sexual difference and absorbed into the suppression of sexual difference. Sade seeks to abolish differences, sometimes drowning them in heterogeneous indistinction (Chapter 1), or at other times eliminating them by reducing everything to a masculine sameness. (Chapter 2). He reaffirms and recreates differences in the utopic imaginary by reinscribing them according to the ideal hierarchy of the orgy (Chapter 3).

# 1. Indistinction and the Hybrid

I shall use the term "heterogeneity" to refer to an absence of unity, to the effects of exteriority and rupture that are aroused by bodily phantasies, effects that will be found in turn in the order of signifiers. Here they appear as a symbolic manifestation of heterogeneous drives, that is to say of a destructuring process which cannot at the outset be assimilated to signification, but which makes sense through symbolization. Moreover, it must be emphasized that the hybrid, surplus nature of the symbols of heterogeneity tends to dissolve into orgiastic indistinction. The latter remains nonetheless the antithesis of ordering. All the symbols of the hybrid and of indistinction belong to the maternal axis. Whether serving to recall or violently to deny the mother-child fusion, these symbols escape the law of the father in so far as they oppose any form of order, of placement, and separation.[1]

## Flux and Emissions from the Body

Together with sweat, urine, vomit, and even tears, the major signifiers in the repertory of body products are *sperm*, *shit*, and *blood*. Sometimes the stress is on their flux and flow, but these products take on their most virulent meaning when reintroduced into the body.

Although sperm gushes out on almost every page of the *Histoire de Juliette*, it achieves greater socio-symbolic interest when it is retained.[2] "Shit" appears as a unit of generalized heterogeneity, and brings into play "within a *single set up* the noble and valorized body (as represented by the sexual and nervous apparatus) and the vile, depreciated body (as represented by the digestive and defecatory apparatus)."[3] Given what Lacan felicitously termed the hagiographic[4] tendencies of Sade's critics, it is scarcely surprising that most have been content to deplore, or even ignore this especially troubling aspect of his work. More recently, Janine Chasseguet-Smirgel has offered an extremely detailed psychoanalytic interpretation of Sade's coprophilia.[5] She argues that the function of co-prophilia is to "*fecalize* the universe, or, more precisely, to eliminate the universe of differences (the genital universe) in order to install in its place the anal universe, in which all units are interchangeable" (p. 203). This function is indeed very important, Chasseguet-Smirgel goes on, but it is not the only one. Take for example the roll of the manuscript of *Les Cent-vingt journées*, "this strange bowel whose form was closely wedded to content" (p. 208) and which was probably hidden by Sade in one of the "prestiges" or "étuis" he used for anal masturbation.[6] To take another example, a parallel can be drawn between the different parts of the digestive system (intestine, mouth, anus) and its products, on the one hand, and, on the other, the Sadean topography and its enclosed places—castles with their secret, inner chambers, their underground cells, their narrow winding corridors like "bowels" (Chasseguet-Smirgel, p. 189).

Chasseguet-Smirgel says that the sexual pleasure of the pervert is "aroused by the rupture of what Sade called 'barriers' and 'brakes' which leads him into the universe of the undifferentiated" (p. 236) that is constituted by the regression to the maternal. It must be added, however, that the subject who frees himself from the law thereby runs a risk—the risk of being swallowed up and losing his identity. Thus the phantasied realization of perverse desire represents both sexual pleasure and its danger. One should not underestimate the anguish the subject feels when he turns back toward the undifferentiated,[7] or the silent threat that reappears in the social symbolism of Mary Douglas and serves as its underpinnings. In Sade, the ingestion-excretion loop, from mouth to anus and back to mouth, entirely skirts the digestive process per se and concentrates on the body openings common to both sexes and on the constant to-ing and fro-ing between inside and outside the body, or one body and another, that is set up by coprophagia. In Sade we see the fragility of the limits that have been transgressed as well as the indefinitely repeated paroxystic regression toward the maternal archaic which Julia Kristeva has termed *abjection* and which corresponds to that stage of primary narcissism in which no clear difference is made between the inside and the outside of the body, between self and other. The exchange of pain and pleasure between agents, or between agents and victims, untiringly shows that the boundary can be crossed "in both directions"[8] and that the places of sexual pleasure mark the zone of danger.

Taking the "known dangers of society" as our point of departure in the search for the themes of body pollution and the potential concordance of these agencies,[9] we may ask against whom the defilement is directed, or, in other words, who is in danger? Who commits the defilement, and who are the endangerers? What is the reason for, and what is the nature of the dangerous act?[10] The answer to these questions no doubt evolved over the course of Sade's career, but its nature never changed. It is obviously Sade who is in danger, both as an individual and as an aristocrat. His rank did not offer him protection and his imprisonment demonstrated that his social class was threatened before[11] and even more after 1789. Between 1763 and 1776, the time of his sexual escapades as well as of several sessions in prison, he feels secure in his privileges and his immunity to punishment, as we see clearly in the indignation he expresses in 1776 when the father of one of the young girls he had commandeered for the orgies at La Coste aims a pistol at his head. Sade brings suit against the man, but, well aware of his notoriety since his condemnation to death: in 1772, the courts take no action. Sade writes to his agent: "Today a stranger armed with a pistol comes to demand his daughter, tomorrow a peasant armed with a shot-gun will come to demand his day's pay."[12] The endangerers (that is, in the scene, those guilty of defilement, with whom the scriptor[13] identifies) are in the first place the magistrates who dared to convict him; his mother-in-law who had him locked up; the successive prison officials; and the rioting "people" whom he observed and harangued from the Bastille during the first days of July 1789, an act that led to his transfer to Charenton just be-fore the Bastille was taken and its prisoners freed. As for the dangerous act, this can be attributed to Sade himself and to his persecutors. Throughout his life Sade will move in transgression. With regard to this antisocial be-havior (criminal debauchery and excessive sumptuary expenditures) and the lettres de cachet Sade's mother-in-law obtained against him, Pauvert is right to remark: "I should just like someone to explain to me what else his mother-in-law could have done."[14] When compared to a criminal trial, the lettre de cachet was a lesser evil. During the Terror, Sade's republican ac-tivity offered him no protection. Under the Consulate, Bonaparte had Sade interned because of his writings. After the Revolution, his mother-in-law could no longer serve as scapegoat, and Sade was obliged to correlate the dangers in the outside world with the changes in regime and the abolition of privilege for the nobility. Sade is the victim both of institutional power and of the endangering classes. The social universe he faces, whether from his prison or during his years of freedom, threatens him from every side.

It is easy to establish a relationship between this ceaseless threat and the violence unleashed in his work, but the violence is only the most general aspect of Sade's body symbolism. Following Mary Douglas, let us posit that bodily margins, in particular the orifices, stand for the most vulnerable points in the social entity. When secretions and body waste cross these barriers, the survival of the group is threatened and a dangerous defilement is created. Filth itself is always perceived as the remains of matter in transit which has strayed from its appointed place. All body waste retains some power, but the most dangerous wastes are those readmitted into the body after they have been purged.[15] Once this notion is accepted, certain parallels necessarily emerge, especially because this type of symbolism tends to manifest itself when there is a failure of social sanctions against those guilty of social unrest,[16] as in the case of that vassal of Sade who aimed a gun at him with impunity.

At this point, the comparison between *Les Cent-vingt journées de Sodome*, *La Nouvelle Justine* (*The New Justine*), and the *Histoire de Juliette* becomes significant. Between the first work and the other two, the relation between emission and reingestion varies, as do the very characteristics of that reingestion. In *Les Cent-vingt journées*, where the narrative structure is as rigidly organized as the social order of the Ancien Régime, the very mention of disordered flux is far less frequent than in *Justine* and *Juliette*, whereas coprophagia invades the whole text; it is more detailed, better regulated, organized on a vast scale, and evoking more disgust than in any other work. Often coprophagia is doubled by the ingestion of vomit. Thus it appears that *Les Cent-vingt journées* not only represents Sade's experience of imprisonment as a rupture of social boundaries but is also his clearest attempt to establish order and mastery symbolically by maximally systematizing the process of reingestion. This process is still dominant in other works, but it takes place on a smaller scale, as each individual operation demands. What is more, the effect of disorder increases with allusions to an uncontrolled flux that is not always limited to the mouth or the anus: "Both girls had to shit at the same time and while the one inundated the mouth of the rake with shit, the other did as much to his face" (8: 160, 162).[17] Similarly Juliette allows Saint-Fond "to shit on her bosom, spit, and piss on her face" (8: 210, 218). A blow from a mace spatters a victim's brains into Saint-Fond's nose and his face is covered with brain (8: 326, 338). Sperm and blood are even more apt to spring up in fountains: "The blood, thrown in every direction, spurted out like a fine rain scattered by strong winds." (8: 327, 338); "Fuck, the ejaculate from the dildoes, and blood flooded us from every side; we were swimming in the waves of it all" (9: 378, 975).

Despite all this, the three works are chiefly characterized by reingestion — particularly of excrement but also of sperm, blood, and even sometimes tears: "He filled her mouth with sperm, while I filled his own with the food he loved so much" (8: 163, 165); a duke drinks the blood streaming over the thighs of Juliette who has been rigged out in a crown of thorns and given two hundred strokes of the rod (8: 191, 197); "and as (Mme de Noirceuil) was in tears as a result of all the ills she had suffered in the last quarter of an hour at the hand of Saint-Fond, it is her tears that the libertine devours and dries with his tongue" (8: 214–215, 223). Blood is often sucked up along the edge of wounds,[18] Clairwil rubs "her clitoris over the bloody wounds" she has inflicted on one "unfortunate man" (8: 352, 364); blood pours forth when the hymen is broken (8: 97, 91; 350, 362), when flesh is bitten (8: 321, 332), more rarely from male organs (8: 354, 366), or when the heart is torn out (8: 525, 544). Blood is especially enjoyed when it pours out from buttocks and anus (8: 351, 362; 9: 93, 687; 94, 688; 219, 815). Every page records "the interest felt in the openings of the body" — usually mouth and anus — an interest that reflects what Mary Douglas called "the preoccupation with social exits and entrances, escape routes and invasions." The controlled collapse of social barriers is represented in phantasy, as well as, perhaps, the alternation of freedom and enclosure which can be linked directly to Sade's prison ordeal.

The reader may have noted that, despite what certain critics have claimed, many details allow us to *see* concretely the blood which, without equaling the flow of shit, pours out in "floods" or in "great gushes." Blood can further be distinguished from excrement. Produced by the body but not as a waste product, blood never appears to be vitiated; and even though its uncontrollable flux and association with the openings of the body make it a part of orgiastic indistinction, it still belongs within the ambit of the paternal metaphor. In fact, blood is indissolubly linked to the absolute power of the masters of the orgy since it offers a constant proof of that power. Inversely, menstrual blood plays almost no part in Sade's world.[19] In the orgy, blood is the sovereign blood of the old order, of "blood symbolism" and lineage, which seeps down even into the blood of torture.[20]

In every case we find, if not an exact correspondence between the orgiastic figures and a given external event, at least a correlation between the erotic staging and social conditions, between the disruptive force of the mouth-anus-mouth loop and of other forms of ingestion and the violence of political upheavals — the invasion of the body of the aristocracy by the brute force of the "people" which refuses to remain "in its place." As it breaks down demarcations, coprophiliac heterogeneity blends in with orgiastic indifferentiation. The ingestion of shit translates the extremity of the danger (reintroduction after expulsion)—class hierarchy is being destroyed and Sade himself is socially impotent—and at the same time constitutes an attempt to neutralize that danger. To the permeability of the body's boundaries, which refers back to primary narcissism, corresponds the group's vulnerability to attack at its frontiers; to the lack of self-identity, the loss of identity the Sadean phantasy inflicts on the aggressor from without. Sade frequently has recourse to this type of acting out: rather than deny danger, he masters it through a ritual representation which, by ascribing defilement to the masters of the orgy, acts as an exorcism. In the perverse scenario, "the subject thus escapes the danger of finding himself the object and victim" and seeks rather "to control and master the partner erotically."[21]

## Polymorphous Sexuality and Dismemberment

All the figures of the orgy hint at the (Lacanian) phantasy of the "fragmented body." Here this phantasy will be considered as an element of heterogeneity, of disorder and rupture. Later in this book it will be linked to the basic procedures that organize the Sadean scene. Sade oscillates between the rosy and the black sides of this phenomenon, but black predominates, demonstrating the relation between polymorphous pleasure and partial object. Everywhere we find the modes of sexual pleasure associated with different parts of the body and a mixture of animate (human and animal) and inanimate partners. In a few great scenes, there is a collective moment in which the orgy seems to progress automatically, and body parts, which are not even named, function like robots.

> All was activity, all was arousal, all was accommodation. All that could be heard were cries of pleasure or pain, and the delicious murmur of the rods. All was nakedness; all presented lubricity in its most scandalous aspects. (9: 520, 1124)

The absence of names makes this euphoric moment the paroxysm of confusion. A like indistinctness can be seen in sentences like "let us be whores in all the parts of our bodies" (9: 70, 664; see also 33, 624; 87, 681). But as soon as naming appears, however briefly, the fragmentation moves into the foreground: "Noirceuil is surrounded: asses, cocks surround him on all sides; he is frigged, fucked, sucked" (9: 578, 1184).

This link between polymorphous pleasure and the dismembered body is the very one that Freud, in his discussion of partial drives, sets up between auto-eroticism and organ pleasure. At this stage in infantile pleasure, all that counts is the subject's various erogenous zones, and each of these can function in isolation (auto-erotic function). Partial drives can also be directed at partial external objects—breast, food, feces, penis. Thus phantasies of the fragmented body are not limited to the subject's own person and, inversely, it is not rare for a subject to identify a whole person with a partial object, in particular the phallus.[22] Phantasies of dismemberment, auto-eroticism, and a libidinal relation to partial objects continue into adulthood, becoming the basic elements in all pornography and directing the gestures of the orgy.[23] In crime, there is a correspondence between the fragmented eros and the attacks on erogenous zones and partial objects, particularly female ones. Whether reality or phantasy, this aggression acts as a defense reaction against the fear of dismemberment which occurs in the mirror phase, and serves the masculine subject as a means of deflecting the threat hanging over his own body.

Already at the beginning of the *Histoire de Juliette*, deflorations by dildo are so brutal as to cause death (8: 97, 91), and, from the first half of the book, the agents enjoy assaulting the vagina. Starting with Juliette's journey to Italy, a frenzy of torture is unleashed against the female sex: the vagina is bitten into, pricked with pins, whipped, and stabbed with daggers, the anus is ripped, the clitoris torn off, all in one uninterrupted crescendo:

> Then he had pincers brought in, and while I frigged him and while one of the torturers held the victim down and she was ringed by asses, the barbarian had the sang froid to tear away, piece by piece, all that young girl's breast flesh, and flatten her bosom so well that soon not a trace could be seen of the snowy orbs that had adorned her only a few hours before.
>
> Once that first operation was complete, the victim is presented in another manner; she is held by four persons, her legs stretched as far open as possible, and with her cunt immediately facing him. "Very well," said the cannibal, "I shall now set to in the workshop for the human race." I was sucking him this time; for a quarter of an hour his pincers root about, and he thrusts them right into the womb.
>
> "Turn her over!" he cried furiously. The most beautiful buttocks in the world are presented to him, his cruel iron is thrust into her anus, and this delicate part is treated with the same frenzy as the other. (9: 465–466, 1068)[24]

This quotation links the fragmented eros to the destruction of the organs of pleasure. Massacre is the end result of a hatred of procreation, in particular of its most concrete form, gestation, a process peculiarly outside the empire of the male. The bellies of pregnant women are routinely stamped upon and the hatred such women arouse is apparent when the bodies of mother and fetus are torn apart in scenes of ferocious inventiveness:

> —He puts on a shoe studded with iron spikes, leans on two men, and, with all the strength of his back, launches a kick right into the belly of the young woman who, bursting open, torn, bloody, sags under her bonds and lays before us her unworthy fruit, which the ruffian immediately waters with his seed.
> —Ferdinand was operating upon a girl; he was tearing pieces out of her with hot pincers; he was being sucked and as he reached the point of coming, the rascal took hold of a scalpel, cut off her teats, and threw them in our faces.
> —The last two girls are seized; they are tied up on two iron slabs, placed one on top of the other, in such a way that the bellies of the two women fit together perpendicularly . . . The two slabs, one rising, one falling, smash together with such force that the two creatures crush each other and both they and the fruit of their wombs are ground into powder in a moment. (9: 409–410, 1009–1110)
>
> —Drunk with rage and lubricity, he rushes upon the other two victims. Using nothing but his claws, he tears the child out of the mother's womb, cracks it against the skull of that unfortunate woman, throws himself upon the other girl, smothers, rends, and massacres them both. (9: 502, 1105)[25]

The attack on the maternal body is as exactly targeted as it is concrete. In *La Philosophie dans le boudoir* (*The Philosophy in the Boudoir*), the mother's womb is infected, and, in the *Histoire de Juliette*, they repeatedly proceed to empty out, tear, and open the uterus, while extracting the fetus.

Insight into the phantasies of aggression against woman can be gained from Melanie Klein's theory of envy: the Sadean libertine will insatiably reiterate that there is nothing to envy in the female organs. The link between denigration and disavowal must be emphasized. Envy appears to originate, "beyond a defense linked to the castration complex," in the narcissistic wound inflicted upon the child by the omnipotence of the mother. This gives rise to the desire to "degrade all attributes of femininity, everything that differentiates the mother from the son or the father, in order to eliminate the child's inadequacy."[26] Hence the displacement of vagina to anus, and "the horrible abortions which the libertines" inflict upon women.[27]

A related kind of phantasy—a distortion of the mother-child dyad—

makes it even clearer that envy and jealousy are the source of Sade's hatred of generation. At the end of a series of tortures and incestuous crimes inflicted on a mother and her three adolescent, almost adult children, the four victims are bound "abdomen to abdomen so that they form, it might be said, one single body" (9: 322, 920). This is a strange simulacrum of a pre-natal, mother-child grouping. The four are untied after they have been tortured, and the rest of the episode traces two intertwined performances, a furious return to the maternal breast and a brutal phantasy of pregnancy. At the end only the son is spared, thus intensifying the misogynistic implications:

> Borchamps wishes Ernelinde (the younger of his two daughters) to open up her mother's womb with the scalpel. The child refuses: she is threatened. Terrified, beaten black and blue, aroused by the hope of saving her own life if she agrees, her hand, guided by that of Carle-Son, yields to the barbarous impulses lent her.
> —"Here is where you received your life," says this cruel father as soon as the slit is made, "you must go back in from whence you came." She is garrotted, tied up so tightly that, by force of art, she is thrust living between the thighs that once expelled her forth.—"As for that other one," says the captain, referring to Christine (the elder daughter), "she must be tied to her mother's back. . . . You can see," he says when this is all finished, "that it is possible to reduce three women to such a small volume." (9: 323, 920–21)[28]

To put back into the womb the daughters who should never have come out of it,[29] to reduce them all to the smallest volume possible (we have already seen that another torture consists in pulverizing pregnant women) is a way of reversing the process of generation and punishing woman in the place where she sins. It is also a way to take on the capacity to give birth vicariously. This scene represents a phantasy of pregnancy which becomes denaturalized through the anarchic character of the operation, the size of the children, and the hatred shown for their sex.

In another scene, the very person of the father is linked to the phantasy of pregnancy, preceded by a castration-incorporation that provides an inverted realization of a father-child fusion: the children are forced to swallow the father's organs, then the father is forced to swallow his daughters' breasts. In this manner, the crime of incest results in a male pregnancy, this time assigned to the stomach not the womb:

> We then sought to oblige the father to enjoy each of his children; but since, despite our efforts, it proved impossible to get him up, we castrated him, and force-fed his cock and balls to his progeniture; then we cut off the daugh-

ters' breasts, and forced the father to swallow the still throbbing flesh that he himself had created. (9: 296, 894)

Here, on the father's side, is the counterpart scene of the one quoted a little earlier. It is no less anarchic. Anthropophagic ingestion suggests a symbolic acting out of impregnation-gestation, and in these two scenes there is no mistaking the double transposition of the bodily communion of mother (or father identified as mother) and child, nor the ambivalence of envy and denial the maker of the phantasies thereby betrays.[30]

The subject is seized not just by envy but by a dizzying attraction to the abject, a fascination with the "desirable and terrifying . . . inside" of the mother's body, with the attempt to enjoy "what manifests [a devouring mother] . . . : urine, blood, sperm, excrement."[31] This dizzying attraction is inseparable from the breakdown of corporeal boundaries represented by figures of heterogeneity (the body dismembered, eviscerated, emptied out), the most uncommon of which (such as coprophagia, or a grown child forced back into its mother's womb) function in reverse. All these symbols generate a hybrid/*hybris* hubris—mixture and excess—a term that unites the heterogeneous to the will-to-power of the masters of the orgy.[32] It seems that the disproportion between the strength of the child and the adult is what gives the quality of *hybris* to the symbols of heterogeneity, for, should the son return as he desires into the mother's body, she might end up triumphant over him: this he cannot accept. Therefore limits are smashed, the mother is killed according to the archaic imaginary scenario, and the agents' regressive ambition is realized: the dream of recreating an anal universe, determining its population (and depopulation) and making children in the digestive tract.

The aggression is so extreme that it again evokes the symbolism of social threat. Freud perceived "the crisis related to castration as the model for subsequent panic attacks when the feeling that 'Throne and Altar are in danger' arises," and the formula is surely most fitting for the case before us.[33] To counter the instinctual violence which he attributes indiscriminately to women and the lower classes, the Sadean agent brings to bear his studied and yet visceral violence, and thus reaffirms the hierarchy of power. The destruction of the other's body in the phantasy serves as a basis for the symbolic representation of a social body which is poised to unleash its strength [34] and from which every flicker of identity is willed to disappear. Mother and child represent not just defilement but danger. The terrible power attributed to the fetus—yet another sign of the interest shown in the body's orifices and boundaries—can be extended to the social. Still incomplete, of indeterminate sex, on the margin between being and non-being, the fetus is seen as a danger in many cultures.[35] Lacking an assigned place in society, the fetus presents the same connotations of "displacement" as defilement.

Furthermore, it is not just a question of the "people" seeking to usurp the exercise of power, but also, inversely, of citizen Sade who is unable to find his place either in prison or in the new regime, even as he rejects the old and phantasizes a utopic return to an anarchic and predatory system.[36] And the double rout of the instinctual subject and the ideological subject crystallizes whenever possible in the woman and her fetus.

# 2. An Ordered Indistinction: The Protocol of the Orgy and the Reduction of the Feminine

Sade's text alternates between activity and passivity, but active aggressiveness predominates. The desire for mastery is already inherent in the gesture of writing, but it dominates the staging of the orgy and imprints on it the most rigorous order. The paradox of the hierarchy of head over body is that the head gives orders to the agents as well as to the victims, but only in the service of sexual pleasure. In this way, hierarchy disciplines the orgy, but with no loss of heterogeneity.

The erotic figures and motifs that contribute to this protocol fall into four types of operation, the last three of which serve to suppress the feminine: substitution and equivalence, associated with money and directly modeled on currency (prostitution, masturbation, and theft); serialization and parcelization, both associated with number and machines; reduction to the masculine Same or sexual reduction (bisexuality and theories of reproduction); and enclosure (incest, common ownership of women, sodomy, and cannibalism).

## The Monetary Model

It will come as no surprise that money is an ordering principle for the orgy. As a closed system, money was bound to fascinate Sade. Understood as both the means to sexual pleasure and its symbol, money shares the ritual character of orgy and possesses semi-magical qualities. As Mary Douglas puts it, "money provides a fixed, external, and recognizable sign for what would be confused, contradictable operations or internal states." Ritual mediates experience and money mediates transactions. "Money provides a standard for measuring worth, and ritual standardizes situations," and both make a "link between the present and the future. . . . Money is only an extreme and specialized type of ritual," Douglas concludes.[1] Thus this kind of symbolism occupies a median place between the economic conception of money (as "measure") and the psychoanalytical interpretation of it (as an "external sign of internal states"). Like ritual, money functions as a symbolic compromise between the need for social control and the strength of the instinctual drive. This is quite clear in three of the orgy motifs which Sade explicitly associates with money: *prostitution, masturbation, theft*.

## SEXUAL PLEASURE AND MONEY

As a system of circulation and enrichment, *prostitution*, for the Sadean libertine, constitutes the ideal form of sexual exchange since it grafts sex onto money. Unlike masturbation and theft, prostitution does not demand any special staging. Even though it least resembles ritual, it still relates to it through its character of necessity and obligation and its ordering function. It also symbolically signifies.

Prostitution, as it is still practiced today, constitutes the most obviously mercantile form of the exchange of women which men engage in and which, together with marriage, structures the organization of society. No other institution, perhaps, more tightly links the instinctual and the economic domains. Through the intermediary of the prostituted woman—and the passive form is important here—two people, typically two men, trade gold for sexual pleasure, but do not have access to both at the same time. The prostitute herself is to receive only a small part of the monetary gain and none of the pleasure.[2] Sade partially subverts this common model. He also radicalizes it, and thus exhibits what the model represses.

First, Juliette and her female friends freely engage in prostitution. As a form of immediate exchange, prostitution offers them an inexhaustible source of gold in return for a limitless compliance. Thus Juliette, who has long been rich enough to forsake prostitution, tells the Italian cardinals: "As you know, each of us lives by his own trade. Chewing little wafer idols is worth five or six hundred thousand livres in income for you. Pray allow me to make as much from my own line of work which is equally meritorious and infinitely more agreeable to society" (9: 88, 680). Second, at least in the best of cases, Sade's female libertines who engage in prostitution are compensated in pleasure as well as money. Barthes cites the most extreme instance of this double inversion: "The poor must be robbed and the rich must be prostituted: Verneuil will agree to sodomize Dorothée d'Esterval only if she demands a great deal of money from him."[3] Yet this example also uncovers something that is usually repressed in the relationship of man to prostitute. The reciprocal exclusion of pleasure and money in the prevailing model of prostitution veils another, deeper, exclusion—the incompatibility of pleasure for the two partners. "What Sade proclaimed loud and clear (and that we pretend to ignore) is that jouissance cannot be concordant. . . . Thus, in prostitution, man imposes two conditions: his sexual equipment shall take precedence and the woman shall be frigid."[4] Sade makes this point energetically: "Seek to give pleasure to the object which serves your pleasures: you will soon learn that it is at your expense" (8: 257, 269). For him, even if the woman is taking pleasure and if she is wealthy (inversion of the model), the man must still pay her if he is to feel pleasure (conformity to the model): "Bernis and his companion . . . would taste no pleasure if they did not pay you: I am sure that you can appreciate this" (9: 79, 673).

In his turn, Saint-Fond also inverts the content of the exchange but in a different way, for by prostituting Juliette he is compensated with pleasure, not money: "Saint-Fond takes his pleasure when he knows you are in the arms of another, he places you there and seeing you there hardens his prick; you will multiply his pleasures by the extension you give to your own (8: 249, 260). But he thereby exemplifies a second layer of the repressed content in prostitution—the homosexual bond that presides over the exchange of women. Sadean symbolism draws attention to the habitual implications of prostitution even more than it subverts them.

Thus the game the libertine woman plays with prostitution is often subject to restrictive rules. It is true that Juliette and her women friends proceed to exchange men as well as women among themselves, and that in this way they go against cultural norms. However, whereas Juliette sells her women into prostitution (9: 454, 1059) she does not sell her men (her valets) but merely lends them out, an act which seems to afford her no particular sexual pleasure. Even more obviously, she grants Noirceuil and Saint-Fond the right to prostitute her, but neither she nor Clairwil thinks of making these two men part of the erotic exchange. Finally, even though the Society of Friends of Crime does recommend prostitution as a duty to the women who seek to join, it follows the prevailing model in dissociating pleasure and gain, even while allowing the woman to profit monetarily (8: 414, 432). As these details indicate, Sade only partially blurred the sexual hierarchy inherent in prostitution. There are even moments when the most cliched *doxai* of his work rest upon this hierarchy. For example, he writes, "The greatest mark of scorn one can lay upon a woman is to prostitute her to someone else" (6: 431; ****). Despite all this, prostitution remains the mode of exchange which Sade's libertine woman herself prefers. In her own mind, Juliette never separates prostitution from theft (9: 435, 1037) and gives up neither.

The compromise function of ritual can be seen more clearly in the alliance of gold and *masturbation*, which is never practiced independently of the concept of gold as means. Clairwil and later Juliette, gloat over their gold in a solitary ceremony in which jouissance occurs merely by thinking of the many crimes and pleasures the gold will make possible. Thus this ritual has a dynamic dimension that relies on exchange value. The gold throws out a bridge into the future:

> (Clairwil) I so idolize gold that I have often frigged myself as I beheld the immensity of louis d'or I have amassed, and this through *the idea that the wealth before my eyes will allow me to do anything I want*. (8: 312, 286)

> (Juliette) More than four million, two of them in my casket, and at times, like Clairwil, I have frigged my cunt and discharged at this singular notion: *I love crime, and here I have all the means for crime at my disposal*. (8: 394, 410)

> How divine it is to swim in gold and be able to say as you count out your money: *here is the means to all the crimes and all the pleasures; with this, I can realize all my illusions . . . the law itself will yield to my gold and I will be a despot at my ease*. (8: 312, 324)[5]

Solitary masturbation is clearly homologous to gold here as a general equivalent, but it is presented only as a way station between two orgies. The jouissance intrinsic to contemplative accumulation is always justified by the explicit hope of *realizing* the exchange value, and all the figures of the orgy fulfil this role which thus becomes a form of, admittedly warped, socialization.[6] Everything in Sade is done in common, if not in harmony, and he provides innumerable versions of the transition from thought to act founded upon exchange, or rather on the perversion of exchange.

*Theft* already implies the participation of two persons, and the gesture of stealing, given a higher value than simple possession, becomes a vitiated form of erotic exchange. Dorval cites to Juliette the example of the great lord who cheated at the gambling tables in order to get an erection (8: 126, 124). Juliette for her part is sexually stimulated by the mere idea of theft, and even more by its execution: "When I steal I feel the way a normal woman does when she is frigged," she says to Clairwil. "Here, you see this diamond, Charlotte wished to give it to me. I refused: as a gift, it gave me no pleasure; stolen, it is delightful to me" (9: 414, 1015). Even when she has become immensely rich, Juliette never ceases to steal.

In the Sadean catalogue, theft does not stand apart merely because it is less monstrous than other transgressions, hence more easily observed, as Bataille argues.[7] Indeed, the ultimate form of theft is the theft of sperm, and this materially seals the bond between jouissance and transgression. The Dorval episode is the one that most tightly binds money, theft, and jouissance. Dorval, a thief by trade, employs Juliette and another prostitute in his scams and gives them the task of stealing from two rich clients, one after the other, while he voyeuristically observes both the sexual act and the theft. After this opening sequence, he leaves his post, and, in the second phase of the operation, he *steals* (8: 116, 113, Sade's italics) with his mouth the sperm contained in the two women's vaginas, before he himself penetrates them. The essential point to note here is the coincidence established between theft and the act of sex, as well as the identification of sperm with money as theorized by Freud.[8] Sperm is a principle of life and may become the object of cannibalism. The same is true of money. Saint-Fond likens money to the blood of nations because it is the substance of life: "If I thought gold flowed in their veins, I would bleed them one after the other, and then gorge myself on their substance" (8: 225, 234).

## JOUISSANCE AS STANDARD

From the economic angle, prostitution, masturbation, and theft obviously combine money and sexual pleasure and thus show that both function in the same way. Exploiting the currency model, jouissance functions as a universal measure for the acts of the orgy: prostitution offers money and pleasure to the libertine alone; masturbation is the response to the promise of pleasures concealed in the heap of gold; and sperm is equated with the money obtained by theft. Simultaneously, jouissance establishes a second series of equivalences, among the functions of the different parts of the body. The procuress Duvergier explains this exchange theory to Juliette. It matters little which part of the body you use to produce pleasure, she says—and enumerates eight such parts—providing that it earns you money (8: 131, 129). Jouissance and money together guarantee the equivalence among the parts of the body that is needed to effect the disorder characteristic of orgy, but the monetary model imposes some orderliness upon the heterogeneity of organ pleasure and of partial objects.

If the abstract model of money as a leveler that can be glimpsed behind the pleasure standard were to be applied, it might be possible to talk here of a form of rudimentary capitalism. It seems dangerous, however, to push the parallelism with complex forms of capitalist economics[9] except perhaps in one respect: the role of the imaginary in the production of jouissance, which is founded on the idea of crime and indistinguishable from it.[10] "I have come while committing theft, murder, and arson, and I am perfectly sure that it is not the object of libertinism that drives us on, but the idea of evil" (13: 164, 363–64), says the duke in *Les Cent-vingt journées*. The libertine is above all concerned to ensure that the loop between desire and execution remains unbroken. As soon as satisfaction is achieved, desire must be aroused anew, the imaginary must be solicited. In the same way, a consumer society can continue only by creating new demands, that is, by using the imagination to arouse desire. In this last case, desire is conformist whereas the equivalence of the figures in the orgy is based on the imaginary of transgression. We must therefore refer to a transgression-jouissance, against which all crimes are measured, and which functions as a gold standard even when dissociated from money. Juliette expounds to the executioner Delcour a unitary theory of the moral vices that eroticizes them all equally by submitting them to a process of mental representation:

> In that case, said Delcour, you must be of the opinion that all the passions may be increased or nourished through lust?"—Lust is to the other passions what nervous fluid is to life: it sustains them all, it gives strength to all, as we can see from the fact that a man *without balls* [Sade's italics] could never have passions. "—So you fancy that one may be ambitious, cruel, miserly, vengeful, with the same motives as with lust?" —Yes, I am convinced that all these passions excite us, and that a lively, well organized mind may be as aroused by any passion as it would be by lust. I tell you nothing here that I have not experienced myself; I have frigged myself, I have fully discharged merely by thinking about ambition, cruelty, avarice, and vengeance." (8: 299, 310)[11]

Whether actualized or not, the money model structures all the erotic practices, reduces them all to one functional principle, and thereby tends to erase all differences among them. To continue giving details of the homology with money would be both superfluous and monotonous. Let us simply take it as given. The homology can be discerned quite plainly behind the serial schemata of numeration and machines. It is also hinted at behind the sexual reductiveness of the actors in the orgy.

## Parcelization: Numbers and Machines

The fragmented body, now ordered and mastered, can also be detected at the basis of parcelization.

### NUMERICAL ORGANIZATION

Even the casual reader cannot help but be struck by Sade's obsession with various numerical classifications.[12] There is no break in continuity between the dismembering of the body and organ pleasure, on the one hand, and numerical organization on the other. The obsession with numbers and classification, which originates in anality, is linked to coprophiliac obsession, and heterogeneous elements are replicated by serial schemata. The episode in the Carmelite convent, which Clairwil stage-manages, goes as far as possible in this regard. Not many critics have noted the simplicity of the principle underlying the choice of numbers: a playful use of the multiplication table; multiples of six; or else groupings of sixteen, or eight; multiples of four, eight, sixty-four—there will be sixty-four monks—in order to arrive at first 128 and then 256 sexual acts.[13] The same principle lends itself to more complex combinations:

> We accommodated eight men at the same time: we had a cock under each armpit, one in each hand, one between our breasts, one in the mouth, the seventh in the cunt, the eighth up the ass. (8: 467–68, 488)[14]

The serial tableaux grow more numerous; a lesbian and sodomist chain in the convent at Bologna, and in Minski's chateau a room hung with skeletons, the "living furniture" (women whose bodies are designated by some perverse logic to serve as chairs and tables), and serial murders.[15] Usually backed up by hard numbers, the quantitative model always regulates these inventions which highlight the ordered anarchy of despotism:

> At the back of this room was a vast alcove surrounded with mirrors and decorated with *sixteen* black marble columns, *to each of which* was bound a young girl, presented rear on. By means of *two* cords . . . he could inflict on *each of the asses* facing him a different punishment . . . *Quite apart from these sixteen young girls, there were six others and twelve young boys,* either agents or patients, who waited in the *two* neighbouring apartments and attended to their master's libertine pleasure during the night. *Two duennas* supervized all of this while he slept. (8: 566–67, 588–89, my italics)

Such scenes may be read as a mocking mystification, but the numerical groupings betray the leveling impulse of the erotic imaginary which sees polymorphous sexuality as an indiscriminate blur of organs and entities.

## SYSTEMS AND MACHINES

Mechanical inventions act as agents and amplifiers for sexual polymorphism. Although fragmentation of the body sustains these inventions, they nonetheless, like numeration, serve to create equivalences and to level everything, without giving primacy to either of these two goals. It has been said that the Sadean machine sets forth the relation between time and production, and serves to increase the erotic output of the body. Somewhat akin to La Mettrie's Machine-Man, the Sadean machine serves to suppress all transcendental agency, to deny interiority, and to ensure the anonymity of the erotic group,[16] without excluding the voluntarist stance of the Sadean libertine. This concept of human mechanics can be understood once it is placed in the larger context of those power procedures that Foucault defines as an *anatomo-politics of the human body*, procedures that started to develop in the seventeenth century. Hence the appearance of *disciplines* designed to train the "body as a machine" and to optimize "its capabilities, the extortion of its forces, the parallel increase of its usefulness and its docility, its integration into systems of efficient and economic controls."[17] Transposed into the sado-erotic imaginary, this new anatomo-politics offers limitless resources to the techniques of pleasure. And it casts some light upon the division between man and his body posited by Descartes. Despite his materialist doctrine and his pursuit of jouissance, the Sadean man seeks to master whatever might remind him of his body by maintaining his distance from it.

The apology for the machine, then, has the mechanical model as its corollary: "The whole living group in the orgy is conceived, constructed like a machine."[18] This phenomenon needs no further demonstration. Let us rather linger for a moment on the alliance between man and machine in Sade that constitutes an early, if more complex and copious, example of those sexual contraptions that Michel Carrouges, commenting on the compositions of Kafka and Duchamp, has called "bachelor machines": "a double anthropological ensemble, combining male and female, joined to a mechanical ensemble, also male and female."[19] In both cases there is an alliance between the machine, eroticism, and sterility, and Sade emerges again as the invisible forerunner of a current that passes through the decadent novel of the nineteenth century and Villiers de l'Isle Adam's *L'Eve future*, to then adopt new forms in the twentieth century.

There is one difference, however: in Sade the positivist utopia of sexual mechanics basks in a euphoric glow whereas the examples of bachelor machines cited by Carrouges link the utopian dream to nostalgia, melancholy, and even at times remorse and self-chastisement.[20] In Sade, the bachelor machine catalyzes energy just as it multiplies pleasure. It directs the ballet of the erotic drives and symbolically neutralizes any danger inherent in disorder. Designed to afford sexual pleasures and pain, it valorizes the functional at the expense of the individual and the subjective. Above all, the unvarying order the machine imposes on the sequence of sexual combinations and the alternation of positions conceal its original heterogeneity. A common accessory in erotic literature, the machine develops on a large scale the organization of organ pleasure around the erogenous zones. The latter function independently of one another even as each zone contributes to the multiplication of pleasure. The following much quoted example displays a euphoria outside of sadism that is rather rare:

> A new and much more singular mechanism was working beneath the woman's belly. When she lowered herself upon the portion of the seat assigned to her, the woman was thrust, as it were involuntarily, upon a soft and flexible dildo. . . . A very pretty girl, whose head alone was visible, her chin leaning against the dildo, licked the clitoris of the kneeling woman, and was replaced at her position by means of a trapdoor as soon as she became weary. At the head of the woman who had been placed in this way there could be seen upon round stools, which changed according to the woman's desires, there could be seen, I say, either cocks or cunts; in this manner, the woman had at the level of her mouth, and could suck at her ease, either a tool or a clitoris. The result of this whole mechanism was that the woman, placed on a sofa moved by specially contrived springs, was first gently laid down on her stomach, threaded upon a dildo, sucked by a girl, while frigging a cock with each hand, presenting an ass to the very real cock that would come to sodomize her, and sucking in turn, according to her tastes, sometimes a cock, sometimes a cunt, or even an ass. (9: 376–77, 973)

The mechanism operates through groups or "quadrilles" of young girls and boys who take turns four by four "in a voluptuous dance . . . , to the sound of enchanting music," and the polymorphous pleasure is accentuated by the aphrodisiac essence of jasmine. In other analogous scenes, the mechanical invention may serve men, but Juliette and her female friends are often in the starring role. The central position of the women also relates back to the pornographic genre: the sexual scene is famous for targeting the voyeurism of the male reader, hence the centrality of the female body and the primacy of polymorphous female pleasure, itself a testament to the prowess of the male organ. Nonetheless, Sade can be distinguished from the pornographic model in that the jouissance of some and the exploits of others are independent of their sex; for all the male libertines, the orgasmic woman is an active agent rather than a viewed object, and everyone is exclusively concerned with organ pleasure.

We have seen how phantasies of dismemberment erase the feminine by physically destroying it. The pleasure machines have the same goal, but follow a different strategy that minimizes sexual difference by substituting the male and female mixture of mechanical or mechanized parts for the whole body. The machine openly displays hybridness and the preponderance of organ pleasure. But it goes no further. A hierarchy has obviously been established between the function of the dildo and "the very real cock." The privilege given to phallic and anal jouissance is immediately obvious in the warning given to the women to "offer only their asses" to the machines (9: 375, 972). Sade may talk about the equal function of all partial objects but he never makes this the mainspring of the orgy. The machine serves to introduce some functionalization and order, not to challenge the hierarchy.

With the pleasure machine, the tendency toward indistinctness is soft-pedaled and there are no victims. The pain machine seeks indistinctness through violence. Usually applied to women, such machines destroy the whole body, not just the pleasure and reproductive organs. Thus the rotating machine thought up by the executioner Delcour inscribes in the mangled flesh of his victims the centripetal movement that breaks the body's limits and reduces it to indistinctness:

> The victim, bound around this wheel which was enclosed within another wheel furnished with steel teeth, was torn, as she turned over these fixed teeth, in detail and in every direction; a spring brought the fixed wheel down upon the individual bound to the turning wheel so that, as the teeth chewed through the mass of flesh, they might close further down and find something to bite upon. (8: 322–23, 334)

This double wheel seems to have haunted Sade from the time he wrote *Les Cent-vingt journées* (13: 427, 667) Rending the flesh "in detail and in every direction," the wheel inscribes an ultimate manifestation of the heterogeneous in the work of homogenization. At the extreme limit of reduction to the Same, grinding gets very close to the annihilation of matter.

A representation of the social, the wheel orchestrates and neutralizes the threat of unrest by opposing to it a body that has already been pulverized and has neither boundaries nor definitions. So in the orgy scene, participants who begin as executioners end up as victims, and Clairwil and Saint-Fond, though they are of the masters' class, will still be liquidated by their accomplices. This is no mere chance: the destructive potential of the desire for mastery may turn at any moment against the agent who, as he takes on the position of executioner, uses symbolic representation to check for a time the threat he has interiorized, before falling victim to it in his turn.

## Sexual Reductiveness in the Orgy

The bisexual game entails many heterogeneous effects, but these are always incomplete since bisexuality turns out to be merely a derivative of the masculine. It is true that, for both woman and man, bisexuality contributes to the representation of a polymorphous sexuality, but its discourse and its orgiastic figures develop the traits proper to the male much more strongly in both sexes. This ambivalence is true for both anatomy and behavior.

### BISEXUAL ANATOMY

In the first place, the female genitals are named in the orgy scene as well as the anus and the male genitals, and, in the context of a generalized sodomy, this small point should not be taken for granted. It emerges, however, more as a factor of heterogeneity than of heterosexuality,[21] a term that is meaningless in the Sadean context. As in all pornography past and present, the clitoris rather than the vagina holds pride of place and is presented as the indispensable key to female pleasure. "It is the true seat of pleasure in women," declares Delbène at the beginning of *Juliette* (8: 19, 7). Several scenes among women illustrate this point: "It was easy for me to see that this wench's passion, as indeed with almost all women who have a taste for their sex, was to have her clitoris sucked, while she did as much to another" (9: 233, 829). Nonetheless, what seems at first to be a recognition of female specificity is in reality the sign of a bisexual design that is in turn defined by comparison with the male.

In fact, even though the clitoris does share in the polymorphism of orgy practice, its valorization helps to blur the difference between female and male sexuality, and indeed to assimilate the one to the other, without suppressing the hierarchy of the sexes. A parallel is created between clitoral and phallic pleasure that proves to be characteristic of a medical discourse still quite common in Sade's time. Pierre Darmon summarizes thus: "The clitoris is in every respect similar to a penis, but a degenerate penis." And he cites Nicolas Venette, a French doctor who wrote in 1685, "In the act of love, the clitoris is filled with spirits, and then stiffens like the man's penis: indeed it has all parts like to the penis. One may see its tubes, its nerves, its muscles; it lacks neither glans nor prepuce; had it but a hole at the tip, one would say that it was quite similar to a virile member."[22] As Thomas Laqueur says, "Seventeenth-century writers seem to have welcomed the idea that male and female pleasure was located in essentially the same kind of organ."[23]

The statistical frequency of hermaphrodite characters in Sade, indeed their proliferation (another feature borrowed from pornography) serves to highlight this resemblance and symmetry.[24] The transgressive force of hermaphroditism is indisputable. Foucault writes that "for a long time, hermaphrodites were criminals, or crime's offspring, since their anatomical disposition, their very being, confounded the law that distinguished the sexes and prescribed their union." Isabelle Vissière notes that in the eighteenth century "a tight connection is still made between physical and moral and social abnormality," adding that "the Law joins forces with the Church to prevent this impure mixture of the two sexes from undermining the foundations of the monarchy!"[25] This is a particularly striking example of a political interpretation of the sexual.

In *Juliette* the hermaphrodite characters are named Volmar and Durand, and they are true hermaphrodites even though the term is not used and proportions are exaggerated. In both these women, the clitoris reaches monstrous proportions, reacts like a little penis, and can do the work of a male organ. Revealingly, this transformation moves the female closer to the male, that is, toward a higher degree of perfection. Thus it corresponds to the cases "history" has documented for us,[26] or rather to the way those cases were interpreted in conformity with the patristic tradition, which itself originates in the classical tradition. Saint Augustine recommends that the hermaphrodite be referred to as "he," assigned, that is, to the "nobler sex."[27]

The example of Volmar, a boarder at the convent where Juliette begins her education, foregrounds the goal of bisexuality and seems at first sight to be a factor of heterogeneity. Volmar has attributes of both sexes and, although referred to facetiously as a man, she is described as a hermaphrodite:

> —Don't you know," said Sainte-Elme, "that Volmar is a man? Her clitoris is three inches long, and since her fate is to outrage nature whatever sex she may adopt, the whore must be tribade or bugger; she knows no middle way. (8: 33, 23–24)

This formula perfectly sums up the way the hermaphrodite is constructed according to a male model and offers some insight into her transgressive role in pornography: to engage one person in the largest possible number of sexual combinations. Nonetheless the dialogue is satisfied to assign the man's role to Volmar, in relations with either sex. The case of Durand confirms this interpretation. Here the excessive development of the clitoris is reinforced with an additional malformation—the absence of a vagina. Durand is "barred" (9: 431, 1032).[28] Such a combination is exceptional outside of fiction,[29] but it serves to make Durand much more masculine than the other "tribades" in the *Histoire de Juliette*. Not only does Durand know penetration only in the form of sodomy, but, while she cannot be penetrated vaginally, she is capable of performing penetration.[30] Her special talents thus constitute a test case for one of the meanings of the clitoris in the Sadean orgy whereby female anatomy is made analogous to male.

Still to be examined is a second form of anatomical bisexuality, or one that Sade presents as such, that of the physically effeminate male. Rarely found in Sade's work, this anatomical condition suggests the passive homosexual position for which, as we know, the texts of Antiquity express a special scorn in cases when the subjects move out of childhood and adolescence. As John Boswell has remarked, the Romans seem to have derived this prejudice from their tendency to associate sexual passivity with political impotence. "Those who most commonly played the passive role in intercourse were boys, women, and slaves—all persons excluded from the power structure. . . . A male who voluntarily adopted the sexual role of the powerless partook of the inferior status they occupied. He did not actually forfeit his position, but he invited scorn in metaphorically abdicating the power and responsibility of citizenhood."[31] Here is yet another example of the homology between the social body and the sexual body. On rare occasions Sade does write a paean to the effeminate man's bisexual potential, and this may constitute a subversion of the prevailing model, to which he generally subscribes. Thus, even though Sade proves fairly innovative and audacious in frequently representing the passive position, this occurs as an alternation of active and passive, and most often in relation to virile homosexuals. Is this a trace of conformity within subversion? Be it as it may, a passage in *La Philosophie dans le boudoir* boasts that the advantage of being with a young man rather than a young woman is that one procures a double, not a single, pleasure, "that of being both lover and mistress" (3: 460, 277). The text is exceptional since it goes on to explain this taste in terms of the effeminate physique:

> Examine how he is made: you will observe absolute differences from men who have not received this taste as their share: his buttocks will be whiter, plumper; no hair will shadow the altar of pleasure, and the inner parts, covered with a more delicate, sensual, ticklish membrane, will be found to be like a woman's vagina; the character of this man, once again different from that of others, will have more softness, more flexibility; you will find in him almost all the vices and virtues of women; you will note even their weaknesses in him; all such men have women's little ways, and some of their features. Could it then be possible for nature, who has made them like women in this way, to be angry if they have women's tastes? (3: 460–61, 277)

The biological determinism invoked here seems questionable given all Sade's harangues on the relativity of social mores and on cultural determinism.[32] The bisexuality of a character such as this is not based on organic deformity, which lessens the heterogeneity effect on the symbolic level, but is solidly anchored in the physical, which disavows either any real libertine *choice* or any real androgyny. The spiritualist component of the myth is well known.[33] Furthermore, bisexuality is often encountered in male characters who carefully avoid all contact with female organs, or even with women. Once again, the hierarchy between the sexes is confirmed: no Sadean tribade would dream of escaping the embraces of a man. Thus we have the same gradation, from congenital inescapable bisexuality to the conscious choice of the masculine.

## BISEXUAL BEHAVIOR DURING THE ORGY

Even without the help of an ambivalent anatomy, and despite the predominance enjoyed by a physical bisexuality skewed toward the male, the orgiastic figures are meant to challenge the biological sex of the agents and to muddy definitions. This raises the issue of the psychological criteria of sexual difference. At first sight, all the actions performed by the Sadean agents seem to illustrate a distinction that Freud was also to make many years later: even if certain anatomical features define male and female, no psychological features can be attributed to the sexes in the same way,[34] and the attribution of a specific set of behavior to one sex rather than to the other is a cultural decision. On this issue, the Sadean discourse is less clear than the scene, and always refers to stereotypes, if only to indicate how to oppose them. Three areas of orgiastic behavior will allow us to complete our discussion of the symbolic meanings of Sadean bisexuality: the *sex of the victims* preferred by the women libertines; *transvestism*; male and female *homosexualities*.

We must first set aside one constant that does not contribute to the bisexual effect—quite the contrary—the overwhelming numerical superiority of female victims in the orgy, which is the corollary of both male homosexuality and male heterosexuality. Only the women libertines display sadistic behavior patterns that depend upon different forms of their bisexuality and correspond to their sexual preference. Once this general rule is established, some contradictions do occur in practice; sometimes members of the preferred sex are murdered, at other times members of the hated sex; but the reasons for the choice are always quite explicit. On the other hand, indifference to the sex of the victim is the mark of the most complete bisexuality, as we see in the case of Durand when she proclaims such indifference. What matters to her, is the excitement of crime and transgression:

> It is not the sex which arouses me, but the age, the bonds, the state of the person. When these properties are found in a man, I take as much pleasure in immolating him as I would a woman; should they be found in a woman, she is immediately given preference. (9: 438, 1039)[35]

Though she lacks Durand's anatomical justification, Juliette sometimes expresses the same bisexual proclivity: "I ordered as many persons to be killed of one sex as of the other," she declares (9: 412, 1012), and her anarchic eroticism certainly fits this option.

Clairwil, on the other hand, proclaims a cerebral bisexuality which replicates that of the great male sodomites. Their hatred for woman is matched by her hatred of man: "I use men because my temperament wills it, but I despise them and loathe them; I should like to immolate all those who have seen me abase myself" (8: 265, 276–77). This man-eater, endowed with "the stature of Minerva and the charms of Venus" (8: 262, 273), supplements her exclusive love of women with an accumulation of heterosexual encounters of a notably predatory kind. She wishes to immolate only men: "I enjoy plaguing women," she declares to Juliette, "but for the complete dissolution of matter, if you follow me . . . a man would be what I would need . . . I love to avenge my sex for all the horrors men inflict on us, when the ruffians have the upper hand" (8: 284, 294–95). It is Clairwil, drunk with a power inseparable from male emblems, who cries out:

> Cocks yes, God damn it, cocks! they are my gods, my parents, my friends, I breathe only for that sublime member, and when I have no cock in my cunt, or in my ass, I have one so well in my head, that when they dissect my body one day they will find it in my brain! (8: 472, 492–93)

She castrates and murders Brother Claude in order to make the monk's enormous penis into "the strangest and finest dildo ever seen" (8: 436, 454; 445, 464), and her cannibalism feeds on castration: "The hellish Clairwil drank his blood and swallowed one of his balls" (8: 430, 448). We shall discuss later how sex and power are inextricably linked to the male as an ideal of arbitrariness and despotism. The libertine women are pitiless opportunists who can only rise into the master caste by borrowing the masters' criminal and orgiastic practices. Their bisexuality is more real than that of the libertine men, but nonetheless it cannot break out of the male mold.

Similar conclusions are to be drawn when we compare the respective treatment of female and male transvestites, which in any case are more common in *Les Cent-vingt journées* than in the *Histoire de Juliette*. Acts of both male and female transvestism are plainly designed to add spice to the libertinism, because they not only blur the modes of sexual exchange but also make the girl more like a boy. In fact, young boys are the transvestites of choice. They are called Zephire, Adonis, or Antinous, and they are as pretty as girls. In inverted marriages, the beauty of such boys is always vaunted in preference to that of young girls.[36]

The occasions when Juliette crossdresses have a quite different value. The scene when she decides to give in to "the extreme need" she feels to "commit a crime by her own hand" parodically repeats the accepted signs for physical "courage" and "ferocity" (8: 288, 299). In contrast to the closed space of the orgy, she chooses to move outside into "a secluded street," and she puts on male dress. Armed with two pistols, she falls on "the most wretched of women," and she blows out the brains of this ideal victim after trying in vain to seduce her (8: 288, 300). It would be difficult to push the imitation of a stereotype of virility much further. It is only as secondary outcome that "her male crossdressing (perfects)" Saint-

Fond's rapture, when she boasts to him of her *"street* crime" (8: 290–91, 302), and when the virility of the crime and costume finally adds one more refinement to Saint-Fond's sodomic inversions. Later, once again dressed as men, Clairwil and Juliette get into a carriage and set out to steal forty millions from Duke Ferdinand of Naples (9: 419, 1019).

The relationship set up between female and male homosexuality reproduces what we have observed on the level of anatomy: the slippage from an artificial symmetry between the sexes to a no less artificial hierarchical resemblance. In all cases highly symbolic, the homosexuality that prevails among actors of either sex tends not only to declare a preference for the Same but to demonstrate that the Same is by definition single and male. All the Sadean sodomites alternate between active and passive roles. This serves not to feminize but, on the contrary, to virilize them by multiplying the number of their encounters with men. The libertine's alternation between active and passive is more frequent in Sade than in ordinary pornography, but to evaluate just how subversive it is, it would have to be compared with that in the sub-genre of homosexual pornography. Although it constitutes one of the principal ways of transgression and orgiastic confusion in Sade's work, active-passive alternation is still based on male schemata of identity.

As for lesbianism, a requirement in all pornography, the false symmetry of the two homosexualities makes the lesbian merely a replica of the male homosexual. Juliette on many occasions proclaims and displays her preference for women, if not as victims, at least as partners, and she attracts women even more than men (9: 41, 633; 503, 1107). Although she resorts to men on a vast scale, her bosom friends are always women—first Clairwil, then Durand. Yet despite her woman's body, she identifies with a man and regrets not possessing a male physiology: "I could not resist the sight of that divine ass. A man by taste as well as principle, how I should have wished to celebrate it with more real incense!" (9: 105, 699). Occasionally, her creator forgets, or pretends to forget, the female anatomy he has endowed her with:

> —But if we are taken, we shall perish.—What would that matter? The thing I fear least in the world is being hanged. Isn't it well known that one discharges when one dies thus?" (9: 413, 1014)

Sometimes Juliette waxes eloquent on the joys of lesbian intercourse, but other dialogues see this only as "compensation" for women who live in an environment dominated by male homosexuality (3: 512, 328). In most cases, lesbianism can barely be distinguished from the other figures in the orgy and shares with them two features which go beyond the pornographic norm: the constant use of dildoes, which allows women among themselves "to mimic the male sex whose qualities they lack" (9: 120, 715), and the ceaseless practice of sodomy between women, which is accompanied by rapturous praise that designates it as a fabrication of the Sadean imaginary.[37] This, added to the fact that sodomy is the prevailing practice between the two sexes, demonstrates just how far the suppression of sexual difference extends. This system of uniformity is the product of a double symbolism, anal and phallic, or *phallic-anal*.

There is very little exclusive homosexuality in Sade and, of all the figures of the orgy, bisexuality is probably the most difficult to assign either to heterogeneity or to the reduction to the same. More than the anatomical hybrid (ephebes and hermaphrodites), bisexuality prizes the erotic hybrid, by choosing an object of the same sex after the Greek model of homo-bisexuality. In other words, it represents the autonomy of the drive over the object, and the orgy is performed against this backdrop of disorder and freedom. Bisexuality also prizes the hybrid by being equally accepting of passive and active sodomy. But it neutralizes the hybrid by always in the end modeling itself after and positing the superiority of the male Same where it might have affirmed a fundamental difference between the two sexes. This would, admittedly, be another form of ordering. Thus bisexuality bestows male organs on the anatomy of a few libertine women, without touching the sexual organs of a few physically effeminate men. The great sodomites like Noirceuil and Saint-Fond are in no way effeminate, whereas the great libertine women who have become associates of the master caste carry upon their bodies or in their psyches the insignia of the male. Sade's procedure is double and contradictory; it endlessly dramatizes the ambivalence of every subject (activity/passivity), but it works equally tirelessly to reduce that ambivalence, not by means of a binary opposition such as we have today[38] but within a hierarchy entirely governed by degrees of maleness.

## THE MALE MONOPOLY ON GENERATION

Phantasy takes on the mask of science in the discursive exposition where Sade offers an irrepressible, though partial, disavowal of a physiological role of woman in procreation and thus completes the shrouding of female specificity. Jean Deprun is the critic who gives the most concise and best documented summary of Sade's statements on this issue.[39] A few of these are scattered through the *Histoire de Juliette*, but, in order to give the question as swift a treatment as possible, let me start from the much quoted dialogue in *La Philosophie dans le boudoir*, which claims that man alone, with no contribution from woman, has the power to transmit life. First we shall read the passage at the initial level and place it in its historical context. It begins with a *reductio ad absurdum* of the part granted to woman in conception:

> Eugénie. — And is it necessary for the formation of the fetus that the two seeds join?
> Mme de Saint-Ange. — Certainly, even though it has been proved that this fetus owes its existence to man's fuck alone; were the male semen to thrust forward alone, without being mixed with the female, it would indeed fail; but the seed we women furnish merely elaborates: it does not create, it helps in creation, without being the cause of creation. Certain modern naturalists go so far as to pretend that it has no useful function. (3: 390, 206)[40]

Passing from science to ethics, and basing the latter on these supposedly scientific data, the dialogue argues that nature has decreed that children should love their father and hate their mother, and the interlocutors hasten to confirm this from their personal experience:

> Therefore the moralists, always guided by scientific discoveries, have concluded, with some resemblance of truth, that, in that case, the child that has been formed from the blood of its father alone owes affection to him alone. This assertion is not unpersuasive, and though I am a woman, I should hesitate to combat it.
> Eugénie. — In my own heart I find evidence for what you say, my dear, for I am mad with love for my father and feel that I loathe my mother.
> Dolmancé. — That predilection is in no way astonishing. . . . I am still unconsoled for the loss of my father, and when I lost my mother, I lit a celebratory bonfire. . . . I cordially detested her. (3: 390–391, 206)

The violence of this disavowal of woman's generative function must not be minimized but it must also be set in its historical context. However aberrant Sade's dialogue may seem, it merely cites the most extreme — and also the least accepted — of the theories on generation current in the eighteenth century. What is more, all theories of generation, following Aristotle, tended to minimize the role of woman. Aristotle gave a phallocentric twist to the seminal theory of Hippocrates, who attributed the formation of the fetus to the mingling of male and female seed,[41] and

Aristotle's deformed model prevailed. Direct quotations from the historic account given in the entry on "Generation" in Diderot's *Encyclopedia* make this abundantly clear. Sade may well have read this account; it has the right period flavor and, despite its reasonable stance and occasional humour, it suggests a significant subtext.

Among all the implicit assumptions that underlie the scientific discourse on reproduction since Antiquity, the most insidious is the mind/matter dichotomy, with its homologue the male/female opposition, which establishes the double equivalence of man/mind, woman/matter. This equivalence is always supported by the female inability to give life. Patriarchal ideology has no better ally than spiritualism, a fact that is revealed nowhere more plainly than in theories of reproduction. One need only compare the way they describe, respectively, male and female "sperm."[42] No naturalist, whether or not he grants the female seed some part in the conception of the fetus, would dream of lowering man's "seminal liquid" to the level of vulgar matter: in those instances where woman is given some part to play, she provides inert matter which man animates by the "efficient principle" or "efficient cause," in sum *by the spirit, that is to say the sperm*. Man creates "life" and "movement," which in turn give *form* to the organs and ennoble them by moving them symbolically out of the category of female matter.

From Aristotle to the seventeenth century little change occurred, but it is interesting to see the ways in which seventeenth-century scientific discoveries—of the ovaries, on the one hand, and of spermatazoa, on the other—were affected by the traditional division. Both discoveries inspire two opposed, and equally fanciful theories—both of which, we may note, are equally ridiculed in the *Encyclopédie* entry on "Generation." The first, ovist, theory makes no bones about deciding that "women are entirely responsible for generation: fully formed fetuses are perhaps already contained in the eggs." Each female fetus itself contains another egg containing another fetus, and so on. All the same, this theory allows no way out of the mind/matter hierarchy. These little statues are "without life," and only man can animate them, thanks to the seminal liquor "that man spills with such pleasure in copulation; a liquor whose effects are like unto those of the fire which poets have feigned that Prometheus stole from heaven, to give a soul to men who had hitherto been mere automata." On the other hand, the discovery of spermatozoa at the same period is immediately used as evidence to support the phallocentrism of the hypotheses (theory of animalcules): "The fertility once attributed to the female of all the animal species in fact belonged to the male. . . . The spermatic worm is thus the true fetus, the substance of the egg merely nourishes. . . . No longer is it the first woman, but the first man who . . . contained within him all posterity. The preexisting germs . . . are little animals, little homunculi, really organized and actually alive."

This particularly bizarre and already discredited theory, whereby woman does not even provide matter, is the source of the last part of Mme de Saint-Ange's speech.[43] The *Encyclopédie* compares these two "opinions about generation" and states that "the system of eggs has been most widely accepted." Both theories have a common feature, both take away woman's ability to create movement, life, intelligence, and spirit. The true scientific minds probably did not subscribe to this position. Maupertuis in 1745, and Buffon in 1749, writes Deprun, "argue that a bilateral theory of generation is needed, since this alone would account for the complexity of the facts, and the bilateral resemblance of children to their parents" (p. 193). Pierre Roussel said the same thing in 1777.[44] Sade was certainly aware of this third hypothesis, the only one that respects common sense, however imprecise it may be. Does he actually believe in the thesis on animalcules preached by his characters? This is rather doubtful because of elements internal to the passage itself and to *La Philosophie dans le boudoir*, and because of the author's materialist philosophy.

Of the elements internal to the passage which contradict the animalculist views that have been advanced, let us note simply two. First, a provocative strategy—Sade entrusts a woman with a speech that is misogynist and destined ultimately to justify matricide. Second, he recalls, as if in passing, that morality is based upon the discoveries of science. This is to posit not only that morality is relative—and we know how strongly he believes this—but that it is absurd when dictated by absurd scientific theories. This implies, at the same time, that the idea of nature is variable since it depends on scientific concepts. And does this not also imply the incompatibility of morality and nature and suggest that morality must be founded upon something other than science or the idea of nature? In this way Sade throws discredit on all the naturist arguments with which he loves to season his most outlandish propositions. This habit of reshuffling the cards is characteristic of Sade, and it lends his discourse a never-failing corrosive charge.

Furthermore, this dialogue is at odds with other passages in *La Philosophie dans le boudoir*, for example the one in which Mme de Saint-Ange insists, albeit in order to justify infanticide, that the fetus belongs solely to the mother. Only one point remains coherent: since the child owes everything to the mother and nothing to the father who could confer an ontological status upon it, the child is reduced to a mere scrap of body waste:

> Do not fear infanticide: this crime is imaginary; we are always mistresses of what we carry in our wombs, and we do no more harm in destroying this kind of matter than in excreting the other, through purgatives, when we feel the need. . . . There is no right upon earth more certain than that of mothers over their children. (3: 432, 249) [45]

Elsewhere, it is again Mme de Saint-Ange who says that the children of adultery "have definite rights to the dowry of their mother," a particularly innovative idea.[46]

In the third place, Sade's materialism may lead us to doubt whether he believes in a theory that grafts the idea of the self-fertilization of the spermatozoa upon the Aristotelian tradition of man as distinct and unique promoter of spiritual life. This thesis is self-contradictory, as Sade was certainly aware, and it also runs counter to his materialist doctrine. Indeed, if the spirit is merely a product of matter, as he believes, and if matter is female (which he may or may not believe), it is hard to see how the father alone could be at the origin of spirit. Must we therefore conclude that, since Sade invokes an argument of very slender scientific merit even for his time, he is attacking morality and science more than he attacks the respect conventionally owed to the mother? Not in the least. Rather, he is leaving no stone unturned, and thus his matricidal attack is all the more clearly identifiable as a phantasy. To all this may be added his taste for mystification, which we may compare with this tall tale reported in the same entry on "Generation" in the *Encyclopédie*: "A certain Monsieur de Planade, secretary of the academy at Montpellier, claimed to have seen these animalcules (the sperm) grow and turn into men, all on their own. He confessed that he had just wanted to have fun."

The phantasy dimension can be discerned even better in the attack on procreation which concludes the matricidal speech. It is clearly more difficult to deny woman's role in gestation and parturition than in conception. Therefore it is necessary to make it physically impossible for her to accomplish either of these two functions. This is the meaning of the final scene of *La Philosophie dans le boudoir*, which completes Eugénie's education. The final torture inflicted on Eugénie's mother, after she has been raped by a "poxy" valet, consists in having her vagina sewn up by Eugénie herself who will thus never have any "brothers or sisters" (3: 546, 363). In this scene, as in the pseudo-scientific speech, the point is to reject an unaccept-able reality, woman's ability to give life. In this case it is accomplished by weaving a fiction that attacks the reproductive organs, obstructs the means to conception, and effectively deprives the female body of any possibility of giving birth. Lacan interprets this episode as proof of the taboo on the mother: "V . . . ed and sewn up, the mother remains silent and forbid-den. Our verdict upon the submission of Sade to the Law is confirmed."[47] No doubt the scene is polyvalent and reveals that the schemata for hetero-geneous fragmentation are connected to the reduction to the Same. The taboo on incest with the mother results in the choice of the male as well as in the destruction of the maternal body. Reproduction is "to be de-stroyed," not so much because man is evil and the earth overpopulated (the usual rationalizations of Sadean discourse), but because the ability to give birth makes woman dangerously incompatible with the model of oneness. As Dolmancé explains in *La Philosophie dans le boudoir*, sodomic sterility, far from being an offense to nature, is a sign of confidence in nature's omnipotence and ability to create, which human reproduction weakens.[48] The evocation of mother nature replaces the threatening proximity of the mother with a distant and disembodied image whose power is exerted over everyone indiscriminately rather than directed to one single male.

The sterility of sexual pleasure is the necessary condition for the re-duction to the Same. The torture of Eugénie's mother heralds the rites of dismembering which, in the second part of the *Histoire de Juliette*, target the female reproductive organs. Together with sodomy, all these examples form part of the same semantic network as abortion and infanticide—ste-rility. In the face of all these convergent elements, it would be idle to deny the strength of the attack being launched not only against woman but also against patriarchal ideology. Parricide in fact occupies a respectable posi-tion in the scale of criminal values, and it will later be examined. When he preaches in favor of the order of sterility, Sade attacks the very foundation of paternal law. It is hardly possible to decide whether he remains subject to that law or whether he mocks it when he exaggerates the principle of male superiority. Such ambivalence characterizes his whole symbolic sys-tem.

Whether in the case of the reproductive theory of animalcules or of the definition of the female as an inferior male as conveyed by the bisexual motifs of both scene and speech, Sade elects the most backward theories of his time. In fact, he was writing at the very time when a conception of the feminine as difference, and indeed as irreducible difference, was dislodging the thesis claiming a hierarchical likeness between the organs of the two sexes which had been quite accepted until the end of the seventeenth century and which survives in Sade.[49] For such a change to be possible (given the undeniable lack of any change in the sex organs themselves) the whole socio-political order had first to be put in question, then overturned. As Laqueur writes: "The cultural construction of the female in relation to the male, while expressed in terms of the body's concrete realities, was more deeply grounded in assumptions about the nature of politics and society. It was the abandonment of these assumptions in the Enlightenment that made the hierarchically ordered system of homologies hopelessly inappropriate. The new biology, with its search for fundamental differences between the sexes and between their desires, emerged at precisely the time when the foundations of the old social order were irremediably shaken" (p. 16). The theory of animalcules is a part of that ancient, hierarchical, or, in Laqueur's word, "vertical," notion of the sexes, which situates man in the chain of being as *pattern and father* of the human race. Laqueur probably does not put enough emphasis on the following two points: the progress of materialist thought and its role in this socio-political and scientific change, and the persistence of a hierarchy between male and female which is henceforth founded upon a *natural difference* between the sexes.[50] Nonetheless, an overall correlation exists between, on the one hand, a hierarchical social order in harmony with the order of the universe, more precisely, an absolute monarch by divine right, and, on the other, a sexual hierarchy in harmony with the male model only.

A heterogeneous erotic body corresponds to a social body in upheaval. The treatment of the bisexual body and the maternal body seems at first sight to be isomorphous with the menacing social currents, but it also represents their reduction by means of a mythic integration into a superior body. Sade's phantasy betrays its dream of omnipotence by tirelessly organizing the disorder of the body and the orgy scene according to the phallocentric goal of oneness, and this is so despite Sade's materialism, his atheism, and his transgressive designs. Sade turns his back on what he knows; he adopts the view of an antiquated metaphysics he does not believe in and of an outmoded political order he is the first to attack but which he feels no real urge to renounce.

## Closure: Thresholds Are Joined and Soldered
## (Schemata of Identity and Circularity)

Formalism, ritual, and magic are interdependent. All are to be found in the Sadean orgy, which can function only within small, protected and codified circles that repel any kind of interference.[51] Orgy transgresses the law only to set up its own code, an autonomous social system that reproduces the conditions of exclusivity once guaranteed by aristocratic privilege and whose magic efficacy rests on the group's realignment and cohesion.[52] Incest, the common ownership of women, sodomy, certain kinds of ingestion, are the main socio-erotic practices that produce the conditions of closure needed for the ceremonial of the orgy.

### INCEST

Until the end of the eighteenth century, different codes (canon law, Christian pastoral teaching, and civil law) "did not make a clear distinction between violations of the rules of marriage" (adultery, incest) and "deviations with respect to genitality" (sodomy, the mutual "caress").[53] Incest holds a remarkable place in the whole of Sade's work, and he considers it complete only when it is sodomic and thus unites the two kinds of violation.[54] All the same, we should not take literally the sentence from *La Nouvelle Justine* that compares the family of Gernande to that of Oedipus (7: 181, ****). The rarity of mother-son incest—*Juliette* offers only one isolated and insignificant case—while confirming the persistance of the maternal taboo in Sade, supports the findings of contemporary ethnography that, contrary to accepted wisdom, "a good number of patrilinear societies allow intercourse with the daughter and . . . are not troubled by intercourse with the sister,"[55] whereas mother-son incest is subject to frequent censure or even to general prohibition. Sade offers proof of a double anthropological intuition by tirelessly invoking cultural relativity in defense of incest, while reducing it to a limited number of combinations. His aversion to mother-son incest, whether it be cultural or instinctual, is obviously the corollary of his absolute phallocentrism.[56]

Thus it is examples of father-daughter and brother-sister incest which occur most frequently in Sade. This type of incest tightens patrilinear bonds. It completes the formation of the small group already constituted by the family where the father's authority holds sway, but, even as it shows this authority in its most despotic form, it achieves a transgression of lineage and thus, in one sense, of the law of the father. This is why Sadean incest, in its most exacerbated forms, can lead to parricide or serve as its unavoidable accompaniment.

Although Hénaff does not explore this particular contradiction, he paves the way by distinguishing three functions in the Sadean apology for incest, the first two of which are inspired by Lévi-Strauss's analysis of the ban on incest.[57] Sade advocates incest because he sees in its prohibition the passage from nature to culture, the entry into the order of the law through the deferment of sexual pleasure. Since "the concept of nature becomes for him the name for a suppression of bans," Sade relentlessly attacks the primary social interdiction. In this view, incest serves first of all to impede the social exchange effected by exogamy, itself based upon the incest taboo, and secondly to achieve immediate sexual pleasure. Conversely, for Sade exogamy represents, in Hénaff's words, "the abomination of mediated desire."[58]

The third function of incest acquires its final significance only in relation to the rarity of the mother-son combination, which it shows to be irrelevant: incest serves to tear girls away from mothers and introduce them into the world of men, into "the circle of the Same as the circle of the conspiracy."[59] Note that, once there, girls become either an exchange currency, or libertines, or both. Paradoxically, this third function confers on the apology for incest a trait shared with its prohibition in society: in both cases, it is a matter of putting women into circulation for the benefit of men. Despite its alleged function as immediate sexual pleasure, Sadean incest is a reasoned act that arises out of the cultural order rather than from nature. It serves the same purpose as exogamy even while refusing the relation of reciprocity and social responsibility which exogamy is meant to establish, or at least while limiting that relation to the small circle of the masters. The latter, indeed, exchange their wives and happily give their daughters, after seducing or raping them, in marriage to their friends.[60] Thus the contradiction between the refusal of paternal lineage and the maintenance of the law of the father is obfuscated through a form of patriarchy which operates despotically within the little group of agents. In this mode of relations, father-daughter incest and brother-sister incest in which the brother stands in for the father, constitute the starting point for a kind of "endogamy" in a caricature of the closed system of alliances of the old nobility.[61] One remark in *La Nouvelle Justine* indicates that Sade was aware of this analogy: "It was from a fear that families who allied in this way might become too powerful that our laws in France have made incest into a crime; but let us have no confusion here and never take as the laws of nature what is merely the fruit of politics" (7: 183, ****). This is to imply, despite the argument from "nature," that to marry within the family may also be a political act.

The autobiographical tale of Borchamps, Clairwil's incestuous brother, develops the first stage of this "endogamic" process: incest is committed within the family cell through an adelphic marriage which legally ratifies the transgression, confirms the closure of the family circle, and doubles the identity schemata.[62] With imperturbable gravity, Borchamps tells of his childhood and the bonds that united his family to another family which exactly replicated his own—a libertine father, a virtuous and devout mother, a son and a daughter on each side, all inseparable and soon incestuous playmates:

> By dint of being brought close to nature, we soon harkened to her voice, and the extraordinary thing was that she did not inspire us to mix. Each remained within his family . . . Thus incest does not run counter to nature's plans since her first movements inspire us to commit it. (9: 221, 817)[63]

"Nature's plans," here as elsewhere, are invoked against the taboo instituted by the law, but the most telling argument, because it clearly points to a contradiction, is that "each remained in his family." Beneath the apparent geniality, the humor is ambiguous and, as always, insolent. Sade valorizes one of the virtualities of family organization—the incestuous family insofar as it is the place of the Same and nature, a model which in his work acquires a social function replacing exogamy.

We can go further, and say that incest seals the paternity of blood, about which there is always some doubt, and guarantees it by taking possession of the body of the child, daughter or son. The Borchamps episode is particularly representative in this regard, for even the adelphic incests are performed under the ferule and in imitation of the fathers, and are described in terms of physical "junction": "Our marriage is celebrated; my father unites me to my sister; Bréval does the same for his children. They arouse us, prepare the paths, consolidate the junctions; and, while they serve us thus in front, they sound out our asses, each yielding his place to the other in turn" (9: 224, 820). The homosexual union of father and of son sheds even more light upon this function of lineage. It intensifies the schemata of identity, and its absolute sterility cements closure. This is what the multiple incests of the Borchamps family accomplish. Between the young Borchamps and his father, who feels only "coldness" for his daughter, will be instituted an incestuous relationship that takes on the idyllic connotations of a certain male homosexuality (9: 225, 821). Such decisive motivations are lacking in mother-daughter incest, where only murder can provide enough force for transgression.[64] If restricted to the search for immediate sexual pleasure and without the father and brother, the transgression of incest stimulates the Sadean imaginary extremely little.[65]

All the same, the incestuous scene does violently challenge the law of the father in a few remarkable episodes in which it is not the father, but his son or daughter as agent of the orgy, who takes the initiative in the father-child incest. Just like the particularly atrocious scene when Cloris is forced to commit incest with his daughter (8: 319–21, 330), these examples violently gainsay the desire for offspring instead of gratifying it. Such is the case with Juliette's memorable incest with her father, which accumulates inversion upon inversion, and in which Juliette takes command of "endogamic" exchange by seducing her father. She further outwits paternal power by crowning her incest with parricide, and then, pregnant by her father, by aborting the child.[66] Juliette replaces the world of fathers with a world of men, in which she then circulates at will. The contradiction between incest and filiation, based upon the destitution of the father, is here manifest. The same content can be found perhaps even more clearly in the brief scene where Saint-Fond strangles his father: Juliette completes her incest with parricide, and Saint-Fond, while slowly strangling his father, completes his parricide by forcing the old man "to bring him to orgasm" (8: 254; 265).

The counterpart of parricidal incest, infanticide after incest, feeds several sadistic inventions and reaches paroxysm in the episode of the Noirceuil marriages, itself the culmination of Juliette's tale, which comes to an end only two pages later. Without examining all the components of this overdetermined episode, I would merely note that it offers a savage rebuttal of the identity schemata of the two adelphic Borchamps marriages and suppresses the closure of the family circle. In fact, there is no way to take a rosy view of the double homosexual and incestuous marriage of Noirceuil and Juliette at the end of the novel, when the former weds his two sons and the latter her daughter and a young woman friend. The religious ceremony and crossdressing complete the ritualization of incest. For the first ceremony, Noirceuil, dressed as a woman, marries his elder son, and Juliette, dressed as a man, marries her own daughter, aged seven. The combinations are inverted for the second ceremony, in which Noirceuil, dressed as a man, marries his second son, who is dressed as a woman, and

Juliette, dressed as a woman, marries her young friend, who is dressed as a man. The marriages last less than twenty-four hours and the marital knot is cut when the child-spouses are tortured and murdered. Here homosexuality duplicates the incestuous closure and identity schemata, and paternal despotism is given free rein. Noirceuil arranges to be penetrated by his son while counterfeiting "the cries, laments, and affectations of the young bride being deflowered" (9: 574, 1180).[67] The two girls are given over to Noirceuil's inventions although Juliette is permitted to attack Noirceuil's sons only on his instructions. As Angela Carter says, the scene does not present a true "anarchy of the sexes." There is no question of Juliette, dressed as a man, marrying Noirceuil, dressed as a woman, "even in fantasy." That would be a "kind of class dominance over himself."[68] In his female clothing, Noirceuil marries a man, and when he wears his male garb, he marries a "bardache," that is to say a passive homosexual.[69]

Although this episode, like the previous ones, takes as its starting point the closure of the group and the junction of thresholds, it stages their fragility and collapse. The transsexual combinations partially blur definitions, and only a close analysis reveals that in fact the identity schemata and the phallocentric model survive the confusion. Above all, the scene illustrates the precarious nature of the orgiastic circle, which shrinks and all but disappears, as Juliette and Noirceuil remain the only surviving masters of the orgy. Saint-Fond and Clairwil have long since disappeared, killed off separately by their two accomplices, and two agents alone cannot ensure the continuity of the masters' group. In the end, the murder of the children strips all significance away from the closure of familial space and reduces the circle of the Same to nothing. The *Histoire de Juliette* ends a few pages after this scene of terror and disintegration.

FROM THE INCESTUOUS CIRCLE TO THE FRATERNAL CIRCLE:
COMMON OWNERSHIP OF WOMEN

Obviously it is no easy matter to disentangle the contradictory meanings of incest. However, let us retain from this symbolic presentation of the threatened and closed world of the aristocracy the fact that even its reassuring versions dramatize the breakdown of the line from God to King to Father. Once the filiation is broken, the family must also cease. Only as a first move and probably as pure provocation is incest presented as the firmest support of the family. One page of "Yet another effort, Frenchmen, if you would become republicans" (a section of *La Philosophie dans le boudoir*) associates incest with the utopia of holding women in common in a truly republican regime and thus highlights its real function, which is to replace the small family group with the circle of a voluntary fraternity:

> It extends the bonds of families. . . . I dare to assert, in a word, that *incest should be the law of any government based upon fraternity.* . . . Given that the community of women I am establishing necessarily entails incest, there is little to be said about a supposed misdemeanor so null and void that it is vain to spend any more time on it. (*La Philosophie dans le boudoir*, 3: 508; 324, my italics)

Two points about this speech. First, the logical skeleton I have just quoted is interspersed with statements I have omitted which insistently and yet contradictorily reiterate the naturist and familialist argument. If the community of women makes incest inevitable, it also makes it harder to discern. Why, in the absence of any transgression, would men (for it is as usual a question of father-daughter and brother-sister incest) have any particular liking for their blood daughters and sisters? Unless the voice of blood speaks even when kinship bonds are unknown? Sade does not go so far as to argue this. Second, once returned to the political context of "Yet another effort, Frenchmen," the fraternalist argument becomes heavily ironic and reads as a parody or even a reductio ad absurdum of the egalitarian ideal of the Revolution.

Such vacillation disappears in the *Histoire de Juliette*, in which one dissertation clearly espouses a link between the anti-paternal goal and the utopia of fraternity:

> Which in your view, seems most united, either a single family of kindred beings, as each government on the earth would then be, or else five or six million small families, whose interests are always personal and therefore necessarily divide the general interest and oppose it incessantly? (8: 73, 65)
> As far as the father is concerned, he becomes wholly detached from his progeny, if such there be. And how could he possibly be concerned about children, given the community that I am imagining? A little seed that he throws into the common womb . . . cannot saddle him with the obligation to care for the germed embryo. (8: 75, 68)

The disappearance of the paternal principle and of the family implies the erasure of the mother. Nowhere in fact does Sade envision a family that is not structured according to the law of the father:

> Therefore set up public schools, where children may be reared as soon as they are weaned; placed there as children of the State, let them forget the very name of the mother who nursed them, and, uniting vulgivaguously in their turn, let them act like their parents. (8: 76, 68)

At this stage, the transgressive value of incest disappears in favor of a leveling function which blurs all incestuous motives. These fade in a general sexual economy in which the phallic principle takes refuge in the abstraction of the State and merges with it.

The fraternity which is meant to result from the community of women achieved through incest and other means corresponds to the logic of the orgy, from which Sade borrows his social utopia based on the elimination of kinship bonds. (There is one notable difference, however: in the orgy circle, incest, while achieving the utopia of the brotherhood, must keep its transgressive value, or else it loses its main raison d'être. In the future society, the notion of transgression would necessarily disappear.) By placing women in common ownership, the orgy promotes the equality only of the agents in a caricature of the republican ideal, if not of its practice. From the dissertation to the orgy scene, we pass from the republican sophistry of social equality (which Sade does not believe in) to the ideal of the brotherhood, in which generalized incest leads only to a restricted fraternity.

## Brotherhood and Sodomy

The first statute of the Society of the Friends of Crime prescribes equality while distinguishing it carefully from republican egalitarianism:

> 1. There will be no distinction between the individuals who compose the Society. Not that the Society believes all men to be equal in the eyes of nature—indeed it rejects this popular prejudice, the fruit of weakness and false philosophy—but it is persuaded that any distinction would hamper the pleasures of the Society. (8: 401–2, 418)

In fact social and sexual difference remain operative and meaningful. The Friends of Crime are only talking about the caste of masters when they grant both sexes like privileges in erotic practice, and although the speech establishing this principle is tendentiously attributed to Clairwil, it takes the point of view of the male masters from the very first sentence:

Here, one hundred husbands, one hundred fathers, corporately with their wives and daughters, obtain everything they lack. When I give my husband to Climène [a theoretical gift since Clairwil is not married], I afford her all the charms her husband lacks, and I find in the spouse she gives over to me all the delights that my own was incapable of affording me. The exchanges multiply, and in one single evening, a woman enjoys one hundred men, a man enjoys one hundred women. (8: 285–86, 296)

As so often occurs, phantasy ends up with a utopia that is as little achieved within the fiction as without, the utopia of egalitarian sexual and economic exchange among the masters:

> The mere desire to extend sexual pleasures places all these riches in common. From this moment on, general interest sustains the pact, and private interest is bound up in the general interest, thereby making the bonds of society unbreakable; our own society has lasted now for fifteen years, and I have never seen a single disagreement, a single instance of ill temper. (7: 286, 297)

The perfection of this communality is in part belied by the organization of the orgy and the role of the master of ceremonies in programming the operations. Furthermore, the main function of the Society of the Friends of Crime is to codify the circle of the orgy and double its closure.

"The cosmic implications of God and the devil; inside and outside; purity within, corruption without; here is the complex of ideas that is associated with some groups with clearly marked membership and confusion of internal roles," Mary Douglas writes.[70] She goes on to evoke the Manichean dualism that characterizes small closed communities and their tendency to associate the "badness of some people with the cosmic powers of evil." These traits can be found in the Sadean dissertations as in the orgies, once it is understood that the confusion of sexual roles in the orgy takes the form of phallic-anal reduction. Sade may perhaps assign an unusual content to the "good" which he places within the orgy circle, and he may like to designate it as "evil," but he is still intent upon safeguarding the *purity* of that evil. He often endows this evil with supernatural powers, for example in the case of Durand. Orgiac heterogeneity and the confusion of sexual positions have as their corollary the expulsion of all foreign elements. And within the orgy itself, the rigidity of the hierarchy does not exclude reversals of alliances, betrayals, and turnabouts. Thus Saint-Fond, who had promised Juliette "the most complete impunity for her whole life" (8: 206,

214), will sentence her to death for briefly hesitating to commit a crime, and thus force her to fly into the provinces and then on to Italy.

Sade is truly fascinated by the social utopia of the brotherhood. This is a rosy version of his carceral universe, offering a positive counterpart, a phantasmatic refuge from the marginal status he suffered even during his years of freedom. The favorite haunts of the brotherhood, apart from the Society of the Friends of Crime, are convents and monasteries and, in Borchamps's embedded narrative, the secret society of Swedish senators conspiring against Gustavus III, king of Sweden. The presence of convents and monasteries does have some basis in reality. In some historical periods such places did favor sexual license, but they recur in pornographic fiction mainly because they provide one of the ingredients for transgression and thereby also feed into Sade's anticlericalism. Finally, and above all, convents and monasteries are closed spaces. As such, they evoke a separate, secret universe that merges easily into the orgy circle and has obvious affinities with the Sadean imaginary.

With the society of Swedish senators, Sade fictionalized an historic event, the 1772 coup d'état by Gustavus III, interpreting the arrest of the whole senate as the king's reply to a conspiracy concocted by a few of its members (9: 260–75, 852–73). If Roger Lacombe is right, this episode in Sade's novel was inspired by his readings about the order of the Templars and the "Templar legend of freemasonry."[71] Very probably, Sade is also recalling the theories which gave secret societies a decisive role in the French Revolution and went so far as to claim that the Revolution was an act of revenge by the Templars.[72] In fact, the formula used as an initiation oath resonates like revolutionary extremism: "I swear to exterminate all the kings on earth; to wage everlasting war upon the Catholic religion and the pope; to preach freedom to the people; and to found a universal Republic" (9: 267, 864).

The conspirators are the leaders of the North Lodge, which had been "instituted by Molay himself from the depths of his prison in the Bastille" (9: 267, 864). These elite "brothers" make no distinction between conspiracy and orgy, or between regicide and anti-religious struggle (267, 864). Human sacrifice forms a part of their initiation rites as it does in the rites of lechery and, despite the presence of women within the group, the members indulge exclusively in sodomy, both homo- and heterosexual. The Templars were reputed to have practiced the former. After "a fraternal accolade," Borchamps recalls, "I was ordered to expose my backside, and each member, of either sex, came to kiss it, lick it, and then thrust their tongues into my mouth" (9: 269–70, 866). Similarly Diderot's *Encyclopédie* claims that the Templars had to deny Christ, spit on the cross, and, in their admissions, "the novice kissed the profess who received him upon the mouth, the navel, and parts that are otherwise not destined for that usage, and at last he vowed to yield to his brothers."[73] The Swedish plotters in the *Histoire de Juliette* gather in "a pavillion situated at the bottom of the garden. . . . Tall trees surrounded this spot that might have been compared to a temple erected to the god of silence" (9: 264, 861). Such details clearly evidence the closure and confusion of roles (here a refusal of female genitality) that characterize the small group.

Brotherhood here implies sodomy. Sodomy cements the unity of the group. As we have seen, sodomy, more than any other practice, achieves the sexual reduction of the actors of the orgy. Its social symbolism is no less important. By becoming a general condition, it transforms deviation into norm. Rather than feeling excluded from the social community, the Sadean subject rejects it and claims his own alterity only in order to suppress it. He refuses the feminine—the other par excellence—in favor of a narcissistic and auto-reflexive circle.[74]

In Sade's work, sodomy, together with male homosexuality, constitutes the key example of Turner's compromise formation between the need for social control and the drive. Promoted to the status of norm, sodomy imposes its phallic order on the little group and transforms this mode of satisfying instinctual drives into an essential sign of social dominance. A central symbol, sodomy mobilizes several secondary symbols, which, like itself, mark distinctions and suppress differences. The care paid to the *choice of food* on the one hand and *cannibalism* on the other illustrates these antithetical functions.[75] The former corresponds to a quest that is not only sensual but ritualized. It translates the concern to protect the body's—and the group's—frontiers, to desist from polluting the inside by introducing impure elements. Olympe, Clairwil, and Juliette bring a cook along on all their excursions around Naples. Clairwil, in particular, combines insatiable hunger and a search—characteristic of the orgy—for the most elaborate of hybrid dishes with alimentary scruples and taboos:

> Clairwil would eat nothing but poultry and game that had been boned and prepared in the most varied and best disguised ways. She never touched any kind of popular foods. . . . Her usual drink, whatever the season, was iced sugar water, containing, per pint, twenty drops of lemon essence and two teaspoonsful of orange blossom water; she never drank wine, but a great deal of liqueur and coffee. (8: 284, 295)

Only social groups that fear external pressures on their borders (just like the individuals who retain a strong permeability between self and other) see a risk of defilement in certain forms of food preparation.[76] This is precisely the situation of the Sadean brotherhood, an (anti)social formation and phantasmatic haven against the legal reprisals Sade has experienced: the group either excludes or absorbs.

This complementary move helps to explain how cannibalism and coprophagia are often understood in Sade as processes of reduction to the Same and identity support for the self. The absorption or introduction of sperm, shit, and human flesh give rise to commentaries which echo one another. All three are equally invigorating and more or less interchangeable: as is well known, excrement and dead bodies are equivalent in the unconscious. And all three reinforce the physical integrity of the subject:

> (Minski). It is true that the vast quantity of human flesh I consume greatly contributes to the increase and thickness of the seminal matter. . . . You need only conquer your first revulsion, and, once the dikes are breached, you cannot get enough of it. (8: 559–60, 582)

> (Juliette). People mistake the nature of the exhalations arising from the *caput mortuum* of our digestive systems; they are in no way unhealthy, are indeed most agreable. . . . The same basic essence applies as with medicinal herbs. There is nothing one more readily becomes accustomed to than eating a turd. (8: 161, 163)

> A delicious supper awaited us, and twenty-five soldiers, chosen for the superiority of their members, were detailed to exhaust themselves into our behinds and thus give us the energy needed for the projected expedition. (9: 273, 869–70)

Chapter 1 included a discussion of the ingestion of sperm and excrement in relation to heterogeneity. Certain details of anthropophagy also stress the heterogeneous:

> And there, smeared with fuck and blood, drunk with lust, we carry ferociousness to the point of mingling with our food pieces of flesh which we tear from the bodies of the unfortunate women lying on the table. (9: 324; 922)

"Whether it is a symbol of evil or is actually practiced, ritual cannibalism makes a statement about the sources of life and death and suggests how these sources are to be controlled and dominated by humans in the perpetuation of social and biological life."[77] As far as the species is concerned, all the Sadean declarations contradict this last point. Nevertheless, Sadean cannibalism serves to ensure the survival of the subject and of the little group, which it sustains and strengthens, as well as to divide up and annex a hostile world whose alterity it helps to suppress; this brings it wholly into the category of closure.

And the main symbols of closure—incest and sodomy—sometimes are joined in the anthropophagic orgy. This triple relationship is inherent in cannibalism, which can properly be discussed in terms of "homosexual satisfactions," for if "consummation is a word that can be used for both food and marriage, consuming the Same takes the form of a homo-erotic relation."[78] Incest with the mother will also be compared with cannibalism, as "two modes of the fear-desire of *returning to the same*."[79] With respect to the *Histoire de Juliette*, we should also apply these remarks to father-children incest and to the figures for evisceration since all of these are screens for the Sadean taboo on incest with the mother. Hence the episode of anthropophagic incest I described earlier that a virtuous father and his children are forced to engage in after the father has been castrated (9: 296, 894). And the homo-erotic cannibalism of Borchamps with his daughter:

> With indescribable delight I suck the blood distilled by Philigone's body. It is my own, I thought; and that idea gave me the most extraordinary erection. (9: 309, 907)

This brings us finally to the incestuous anthropophagy of Noirceuil, who sodomizes the son whose heart he is eating while at the same time executing his other son:

> With these words, he throws himself upon his son Phaon, thrusts into his ass, has himself fucked, and orders me, while I am being frigged by Théodore, to tear the living heart out of the child he is fucking, and give it to him that he may devour it. The villain swallows it, while at the same moment plunging a dagger into the breast of his other son. (9: 579, 1185)[80]

When it fails to annihilate itself as here, the circle of the Same is closed only in order to confirm the power relations established within its sanctuary and to protect their arbitrariness. We must now go on to examine the articulation of this inner hierarchy with the social hierarchy.

# 3. The Hierarchy of the Orgy: The Power and the Law

A continual interaction between frenzied creativity and a sharp awareness of the real is the mark of the orgiastic universe, built upon a phantasy of the social as Sade distorts and corrects it. The notion of a male model as model of the Same—as single model—takes the form of phallic-anal symbolism. The corollary to this is the hierarchy of the sexes which coincides in large measure, but not to the point of fusion, with the hierarchy of master-slave and executioner-victim. We will look first at what distinguishes the sexual hierarchy from the master-slave hierarchy and then move on to consider the opposition Sade establishes between private and public despotism.

Traditionally, woman has a double social status. She is defined through her sex and through her class, inferior on the one hand yet, if she belongs to a privileged social class, superior on the other. This ambivalence makes woman the perfect model for any hierarchical system in contradiction with itself, and so, by and large, for any society in the process of change. Taken as the sign of something other than herself, but not as an empty sign, woman as metaphor for the social represents a potential menace. Thus we will need to clarify her representational function for the Sadean agents as both sex and group, and as symbol for other dangerous classes, and we shall see the phantasy solutions the text proposes as it develops an ideal hierarchy.

## A Representation of Dangers as Female

The parallel between class relations and sex relations shows that their respective contradictions block the existence of a clearly defined hierarchy. Sade's social portraiture primarily presents the traits of a class at war with itself—his own noble class—but at the time he was writing, the bourgeoisie had long constituted a dangerous rival class in the struggle for power.

After the Revolution, the bourgeoisie supplanted the nobility by profiting from the support of the masses even while consolidating the modern bases for exploiting them. Sade transposes this situation: the brotherhood of masters in the *Histoire de Juliette* is split by rivalry, and enmity soon arises among them. Noirceuil has Saint-Fond assassinated in the hope of succeeding him. This hope is first disappointed, then fulfilled, an additional twist to the plot that emphasizes the unpredictable nature of the system and even its inconsistencies.[1] Palace revolutions are more the norm than the exception in the Sadean universe. They reproduce and maximize the nobility's internecine feuds, the power cabals and class rivalries common both during and after the monarchical regime.

In eighteenth-century society, women of the privileged classes were able to enjoy considerable autonomy without the patriarchal principle ever being contested. Whereas the daughters of the nobility and the high bourgeoisie were indeed often condemned to live in convents or marry against their will to ensure the fortune of the eldest son or prevent the division of landed property, once they were married, these women could often live as they wished, taking advantage of the superiority conferred upon them by the birth, wealth, and rank of their husbands. As leaders of salon life or as mistresses consulted by powerful men, they could at times achieve considerable personal influence. But this was not the whole story. The assumption that social inequality and the power of one class over others was founded in nature had been increasingly questioned, and this could not fail to raise doubts about the traditional place of woman.[2] Thus a new kind of misogyny developed which attributed female inferiority not, as in the past, to the female's anatomical likeness to the male,[3] but to her difference from him. Metaphorically, this new definition gave general currency to the idea that groups and classes need to be separated by impassable barriers, an idea that served symbolically to calm social anxiety. With the Revolution, the collective risk of revolutionary action by women of all classes became a reality; women's clubs sprang up, women intervened in the assemblies, women marched on Versailles when they learned that soldiers had trampled the tricolor cockade into the dirt.

These social contradictions and upheavals—exacerbated, warped, and confused—structure Sade's novel. The male libertines' furious hostility to their female victims warns us that these women are symbolically representing something. It suggests a parallel with the violent class rivalries that run through the whole of society—as if relations between the sexes "had to bear the tensions of the strongly competitive social system," and as if it became all the more necessary to reaffirm the superiority of the male principle because of its "vulnerability to female influence."[4] Whether the victims of the orgy belong to the same class as the masters, or to a lower one, in so far as they are women they belong to a class of inferiors and therefore, in the eyes of the aristocrat agent, to a class of intruders and enemies. As a result, "relations between the sexes take on the character of a conflict between enemies in which the man sees himself as endangered."

When the power structure is seriously threatened in some way, the feminine as defilement invades the sexual representation of social relations.[5] Too little note has been taken of how omnipresent defilement is in Sade, in its dual association with the feminine and the social. It is true that the orgiastic discourse develops in large measure as a negation of disgust, and that many comments boast of the spice afforded to the jaded sensations of the libertine by some old, ugly, ignoble object. The point is, as François Peraldi has noted, that disgust vanishes thanks to "a contest of disgusting activities." Disgust "preferentially bans pleasure [from certain zones of the body] in the reaction formation of the period of latency and puberty: anus, mouth, and breast . . . the border areas where the inner membranes fold outward and become skin."[6] When moving beyond disgust, the masochistic or "perverse" subject "makes his libido win out over the prohibition" (p. 79). This analysis, which stresses crossing a frontier, helps us to understand defilement in Sade. In the symbolism of Sadean orgy, the negation of disgust acts as exorcism and ensures that frontiers (bodily and social) are controlled. While turning disgust back into desire, this negation nonetheless continues to actualize defilement.

One exceptional passage in the *Histoire de Juliette*, on the other hand, reaffirms the need for distancing and demarcations, by associating it with the very repulsive sketch of the female body Belmor, the new President of the Society of the Friends of Crime, complacently gives in his inaugural address:

> Is she girl? inevitably she gives off some unhealthy odor; if not at one time, then at another: what need is there to enthuse over a sewer? Is she woman? the relicts of another man may, I admit, temporarily arouse our desires, but our love? . . . And what is there to idolize anyway? The vast mold to cast a dozen children? . . . Picture your heart's delight when she is giving birth : watch the shapeless mass of flesh emerge, sticky and smelling, from the center where you aspire to find happiness; finally undress, even at some other time, this idol of your soul; can those two short and crooked thighs make your senses reel? or that foul and fetid chasm that they support? . . . Ah, perhaps

it will be that apron, falling in flapping waves over those same thighs, which will fire your imagination? or those two sagging globes, hanging down to the navel? Perhaps your hommage rises at the back of the coin? And it is those two pieces of flaccid yellow flesh, enclosing a pallid hole joining up with the other; oh, yes, doubtless, these are the charms your spirit feeds upon! and it is to enjoy these that you lower yourself beneath the condition of the stupidest beasts! But I am in error, it is none of these things that attracts you; much finer qualities enslave you. It is that false and double character, that perpetual state of lying and guile, that shrewish tone, that voice like a cat's, or that whorishness, or that prudery (for no woman is ever free of those two extremes), that calumny . . . that maliciousness . . . that contrariness . . . that inconsequentiality. (8: 488–89, 510–11)

Such a diatribe once more demonstrates the hatred for the maternal body, by attaching that hatred to the theme of defilement. At the same time, it is so clearly part of a collective discourse that a parodic dimension cannot be ruled out. The last section repeats all the old saws of medieval theological discourse (which themselves were echoed in Hébert's speech attacking Marie-Antoinette, probably an intermediary link), in which the moral condemnation of women is based on physical defilement at another period of great social instability.[7] All the same, the hate-filled energy of Sade's attack and its personal tone lend an intense reality to a threadbare discourse. Pursuing the parallel with the representation of the social, it could be argued that the distinction between desire and disgust that appears here and is rare in Sade replaces exorcism with a veritable counteroffensive against the hydra of the feminine and the outer and inner threat.

And it is also through the mediation of the sexual that Sade hints at some solutions. If in his works disgust constantly yields to desire while constantly feeding it, it is because woman is subjugated in the orgy scene and the threat thus tamed. Mary Douglas notes: "When male dominance is accepted as a central principle of social organization, and applied . . . with full rights of physical coercion, beliefs in sex pollution are not likely to be highly developed." On the other hand, when this principle, even though present, contradicts others, "such as that of female independence, . . . then sex pollution is likely to flourish."[8] Seen from this point of view, the absolute subjection of the victims in the orgy, which we are about to examine, might possibly suppress disgust together with the inherent risk of pollution and offer an imaginary solution to the contradictions. Nonetheless, the regular mention of pollution continues to alert us to the omnipresence of the threat.

## Sex Hierarchy and Executioner-Victim Hierarchy

In western tradition, there has long been a cultural current that places male homosexuality above heterosexuality. Though an organized female homosexuality may also have existed in antiquity in addition to the private practice of lesbianism, it seemingly occurred only in a religious and ritual form. Male homosexual brotherhoods, on the other hand, were secular as well as religious. Excluding women, they combined homosocial and homosexual intercourse. In Plato's *Symposium*, food and the love of women are scorned as vulgar and finite pleasures, inferior to that love of wine and of youths which accompanies the talk of the banquet—the *logos sympotikos*.[9] In Sadean orgies, the only alternative to the phallic-anal reduction is the male-female hierarchy. Far from being "all . . . indifferently hetero- or homosexual," as Hénaff states,[10] a large number of the male characters forcefully proclaim the "superiority" of sodomy among men:

> Do as she will, turn as she might
> A woman will always be a woman (Martial). (8: 473, 494)

In "Yet another effort, Frenchmen," Sade invokes the precedents of Greece and Rome: "We read finally in Plutarch that women must have no part in the love of men" (3: 511, 327). In his usual chaotic crescendo, Sade cites ancient Greece, the Gauls, the Turks, the Italians, the Spaniards, the Indians: "When America was discovered, its peoples were entirely of that persuasion" (3: 510; 327). Contrariwise, he vaunts female homosexuality as a good way of keeping women outside the structures of power:

> The Greeks similarly accepted that women should stray thus, for reasons of state. The result was that, being sufficient unto themselves, women had less frequent communications with men and in no way harmed the affairs of the republic. (3: 512, 328).

Sade is not the only writer in our modern era to introduce the praise of male homosexuality into doctrinaire discourse directed against woman. In his discussion of Proudhon, Jean Borie speaks of the "equation established between liberated sexuality and pederasty."[11]

In its social dimension, sexual symbolism, by claiming the superiority of man over woman, represents order over disorder. Saint-Fond, a highly symbolic character, is the incarnation of male despotism and of the primacy of the phallus. His astonishing beauty and the physical well-being that accompanies his virility (8: 210, 219) suggest the perfection of that aristocratic power of which he is both model and spokesman.[12] Noirceuil, Saint-Fond's moral double, expresses his will to power and controls the details of his own cult according to a phallic symbolism whose unitary character is quite remarkable. The sight of his own member plunges him into a frenzy of self-adoration which he summons Juliette to share:

> There is no object upon earth I would not sacrifice to it: it is a god for me, let it be as much for you, Juliette: worship this despotic rod, give praise to this proud god. I should wish to expose it to the homage of the whole world. (8: 180, 185)

Juliette then worships "enthusiastically the mover of so many actions," but must take care not to carry this ceremony too far without the help of other participants, for the "passions" of Noirceuil, concentrated in this single point, "are like unto the rays of the day star magnified by the burning glass; they at once set fire to the object they focus upon" (181, 185). Through a double inversion whose meaning is not simply parodic, the male subject's pornographic voyeurism turns into self-adoration and exhibitionism as soon as it has been transferred to the woman who, from being the one looked upon, becomes instead the one looking upon the phallic sun. This voyeurism, once assigned to the woman, endangers her and reaffirms the supremacy of the male.[13] Sade's humor distances itself from the libertine's position, but it does not wholly neutralize the vehemence of the speech.

This emblematic and sovereign male unity is further enhanced by the female amorphousness that is its necessary counterpart. Article 6 of the rules dedicated to the conduct of women in the Society of the Friends of Crime refuses to allow women any distinct identity.

> A woman must never have a personality of her own; she must artfully take on that of the people she has most interest in humoring, either for her lust, or for her avarice, though this suppleness must never deprive her of the energy she needs to plunge into all the kinds of crime which are designed to flatter her passions or serve them. (8: 416, 433)

She needs energy, for, by serving her own passions, a woman will serve those of men. This reasoning turns her unbridled sexuality—yet another stereotype—into a vice to be cultivated like other vices. Nonetheless, such reasoning only dictates a mode of conduct and by implication considers

the question of identity as irrelevant. The orgy relegates women to im-
manence and mirrors their social inferiority by forcing them to "have no
character." In *Margot la Ravaudeuse*, which Sade may possibly have in mind
here, we find exactly the same advice given to the professional prostitute:
"She should have no personality of her own, but should rather study her
lover's with care, and learn how to adopt it as if it were her own."[14] Sade's
novel strongly connects this cliché of pornographic fiction to phallic sovereignty and thus gives the cliché a quite different satiric significance.

To say this is neither to credit Sade with any really satiric project in this
area, nor to deny him one. It may, however, serve to make clearer the social
implications of the sex hierarchical model. The representation of a woman
"without personality," exclusively devoted to imitating the master and to
the service of sexual drives, is linked with the representation of the dangerous lower classes. Associated with the themes of defilement, it considers
both groups, as well as the fetus, as filth, as ill-determined beings, neither
fish, nor fowl, derived from several categories at once[15] and related to the
figures of Kristeva's "abjection." Such beings cannot attain the perfection
of the most gifted members of the species and must therefore be narrowly
confined if society is to function properly. Thus the Sadean woman is the
principal sub-structure for Sade's "sovereign man," who, as Bataille senses,
defines himself through the denial and exclusion of the female other.[16]

Without phallus, without personality, without power, the woman is
soft wax. Nonetheless, moved by instinctual violence, she is not to be
confused with the inert matter cited in the old theories of reproduction,
barely good enough to nourish the fetus into whom the creator man has
breathed a spirit. It is because he has endowed woman with such dangerous violence that the Sadean executioner is so moved against her. Readers
soon become familiar with the diegetic redundancies and raving, satirical,
or cynical rationalizations that bestow a male privilege on the notion of
identity:[17] woman is born "to be fucked" (passim), her weakness inspires
cruelty (9: 494, 1006), there is no difference between "a slave and a wife"
(9: 247, 844). In "Yet one more effort, Frenchmen" the thesis that men
should own all women in common (if necessary by force) is put forward
in a speech four times longer than its reciprocal, a very lukewarm statement that is in any case amply contradicted by the hierarchy of the orgy.[18]
That hierarchy depends upon the absolute submission of women, including Juliette, even though she associates with the masters.

It is no exaggeration to say that the executioner-victim, or master-
slave, hierarchy takes female submission as its prototype and presents a dis-

tinct and simplified version of it (pp. 220–21).[19] Here we see most clearly
how tightly the various signifieds of the category "woman" are bound
together—as sex, as social group, and as metaphor for other social groups.
One detail in the autobiography of Borchamps makes explicit the equivalence of woman-(victim)-slave in both its social and sexual dimensions.
As he journeys through Georgia, Borchamps buys "two fine girls." He explains that "the chief commerce of Tiflis is in women: they are sold there
publicly for the seraglios of Asia and Constantinople, just like oxen in a
market. . . . There is no country in the world where whoremongering is
so prominent" (9: 294, 891). No sooner has he juxtaposed and assimilated
slavery and forced prostitution[20] than he goes on to discuss the servitude
of the Georgian peasants which feeds the lubricious sadism of the nobility,
which, in its turn, prostitutes its own children of both sexes to the prince:

> But what a contradiction! these nobles who treat their vassals like slaves,
> become slaves of the prince, in order to secure offices and money; and, to
> promote this end, they prostitute to the prince, from the earliest age, their
> children of both sexes. (9: 294, 891–92)

It is not so much the "contradiction" as the logic of the chain of slavery
into prostitution which the text describes so clearly. And this vision is
rooted in a social reality whose contradictions it glosses over, and upon
which it imprints a more perfect but regressive coherence. Cruelty and
venality are indeed inevitable components of an autocratic government
and they are reflected at all levels of society. But, under the successive
regimes through which Sade lived, prostitution, corruption, and the excesses of power were not the unique norm, and contradictions did appear
in the functioning of society. Sometimes wrong was righted and merit
recognized, and in certain cases women managed to escape the arbitrariness and subjection of the paternal principle. Christian doctrine, the law,
and philosophy had long agreed that woman was possessed of a soul, certain rights, and a brain. The fundamental contradiction, at the end of the
Ancien Régime, therefore consisted in the fact that women represented a
commodity in the social circuit of exchange, but that they could not be
purely and simply reduced to slavery.[21] Sade, for his part, performs this
reduction in his work, thus eliminating the contradiction. He takes the
workings of power apart, and attributes to them an analogous function
for all the exploited groups. He develops the despotic principle in all its
purity and reveals that all social inequality is as necessary and as arbitrary as
female inferiority. This is what gives Borchamp's anecdote its paradigmatic

value. The hierarchy of the sexes, which infallibly entails female prostitution, and the executioner-victim relationship in the orgy are the figures par excellence of the master-slave relationship which structures Sadean society.

Leading to the physical extinction of bodies, this brutal hierarchy of extremes practices a feudal economy of waste whose full meaning becomes apparent in the sexual context. Sade's utopia comes closest to the worst violence of feudal despotism, for which he shows a real nostalgia.[22]

## Private Despotism, Public Despotism

A whole series of comments, both in the notes and the dialogue of the *Histoire de Juliette*, take up either directly or indirectly a theme already heralded in "Yet Another Effort, Frenchmen": the opposition between "absurd political despotism" and the "very lustful despotism of libertine passions" (3: 529, 344), and, as a result, between the crimes of the State and those of individuals, between the death penalty and other public sentences, and the murder and cruelty meted out in the orgy. The Sadean text as a whole does not succeed in sustaining this opposition, and in fact undermines it.[23]

The opposition is based on the assertion that all humanity has a natural and irresistible taste for murder and despotism, and that it is essential to find some outlet for that taste which does not harm the community. This reasoning leads to a eulogy of private despotism and its practices and to the condemnation of state despotism and its judicial system, on the one hand because the latter is cruel, unjust, and arbitrary, and on the other, because it prevents the safe, private indulgence in those same excesses of power, which when private are supposedly not arbitrary, but justified by the natural superiority of an individual.[24] This is a clear denial of any social contract and a regression to the excesses of feudal times. Thus Chigi, the chief of the civil police in Rome, sees in the despotism that prevails under the laws of any regime an obstacle to the exercise of private despotism, which he deems on the whole to be less oppressive (at least to himself and his friends): "I much prefer to be oppressed by my neighbor, whom I can oppress in my turn, than by the law, against which I am powerless. The passions of my neighbor are infinitely less to be feared than the injustice of the law, for the passions of that same neighbor are held in check by my own, whereas nothing halts, nothing constrains the injustices of the law" (9: 136, 731). Is it by chance that a chief of police is speaking here? The logical flaw is inscribed surreptitiously in the speech situation, for Chigi indeed has the power to extend private despotism beyond the orgy circle and into the public domain and, therefore, to suppress the opposition between the two by making the whole of society subject to the law of the strongest that prevails within the orgy. This is certainly the general practice of the libertines, since they violate all laws with impunity, including those their public office charges them to uphold. Conversely, all the libertines preach in favor of a kind of government based on the corruption of the citizenry by lust: "As long as the subject grows weak and gangrenous in the delights of debauchery, he does not feel the weight of his irons. . . . The true policy of a State is therefore to multiply a hundredfold all the possible means of corrupting the subject" (8: 308–9, 320). We are here quite far from the distinction between public and private that was proposed at the beginning of the argument.

Sade's entire opus gives the lie to this distinction. None of his political characters observes it, and many even preach the contrary. Quite apart from the nostalgia Sade felt for feudal times, the state of the monarchy in the eighteenth century, when the border between public and private was shifting, colors the picture he paints. Under Louis XV, as Sarah Maza has observed, there occurred a "feminization, eroticization, or privatization of the public sphere."[25] Conversely, the State had for a long time been intervening in family life through the lettre de cachet, which many preferred to the judicial system: "The family is the privileged place where private tranquillity produces a certain form of public order. Thus the king has the right to oversee the workings of the family and its periods of unrest."[26] Sade in his universe goes further and achieves the complete collusion of private and public, even as he denounces and exploits that collusion by turn. Some historians have argued that the French Revolution attacked private life to an extent hitherto unknown in the West,[27] but Sade's arguments have a more precise origin. They arise out of his mortifying experience with lettres de cachet and particularly with the legal justice meted out by the Parlement of Aix: his death sentence and execution in effigy. This autobiographic motivation is more apparent in the minor text *Le Président mystifié (The Mystified Magistrate)* than in his great works:

> Supposing you had yielded to some fantastic whim in the privacy of your own home, would you find it quite just if a herd of oafs, carrying flaming torches into the bosom of your family, and using the cunning of the inquisition, guile, and paid informers to uncover some minor trespasses forgivable in a man of thirty, should then exploit these atrocities to secure your ruin, banish you, sully your honor, dishonor your children, and pillage your estate,

tell me, friend, in your opinion, would you find these rascals just? . . . Such a
stigma, ten years in exile for one evening with whores, base connivance with
families, money received to ruin a nobleman.[28]

Sade's political discourse owes both its depth and its limitations to the
light he casts on the presence of instinctual drives in the working of institutions. The distinction he makes between public and private falls short of
the mark because it constitutes a self-defense and touches him too closely.
He objects to the State's interference in people's lives, but submits all
society and public life to the allegedly private despotism of powerful men.
Whether his characters indulge in their murderous lubricity or in affairs
of State, in fact their story enacts and their speeches advocate an ideal of
anarchy. It is easy to see how Pasolini in his film *Salo or the One Hundred
and Twenty Days of Sodom* was able to telescope the public and private domains: he thereby kept faith with a dominant element in Sade's universe.
Pasolini has said that he made his film as a "parable of what men in power
do to their fellow citizens." Everywhere in Sade he finds a link between
despotism and anarchy, and he makes this into a general statement: "The
people who govern us seem to represent order and legality and laws and
codes, but their rule is quite arbitrary and, as Marx has said, they practice
the exploitation of man by man."[29] Whether this generalization is true or
false—and Pasolini himself admits that there are different degrees of abuse,
which is nonetheless inherent in power—this comment is particularly relevant to Sade. It elucidates the tangled network of relations Sade describes
between the collectivity and individuals, between despotism, anarchy, and
arbitrariness, and the law which does not check them and may indeed favor
them. Thus he half facetiously proposes in a note to the *Histoire de Juliette* that "rich people should be allowed to do whatever they like in return
for their money and to use their wealth to gain absolution from all their
crimes" (8: 561, 583), as this system would have the advantage of enrich-
ing the State and exempting less wealthy citizens from paying taxes.[30] All
that would be needed is to turn the venality of political regimes into law,
instead of treating it as a crime (or tolerating it). This note in turn blurs
the distinction between public and private, since it plans to legislate, and
therefore to justify, the inequality of wealth in favor of the "very lustful
despotism of the passions of libertinage."

Using the example of Hitler's regime, a comparison which could not
fail to give rise to misunderstandings, Pasolini contrasts the ideological anarchy of that regime with its organization on the operational level: "The

more madness is organized, planned, studied, the madder it gets, right?"
(interview by Eugenia Wolfowicz, p. 10) There is no doubt that it was
his meditation on the Sadean ravings that led Pasolini to systematize this
point of view because, in Sade's work, it is the delirious numerical ar-
rangements, the arithmetic of despotism and, as here, the binarism of false
oppositions which organize the indistinctness and map out the disorder.[31]

The telescoping of the public and the private is supported by the
interweaving of the sexual and the political, the specious logic of the proof
through nature, and, as always, the will to power. Numerous scenes and
speeches conflate social and sexual despotism and justify the one by the
other, reducing social inequality to sexual and/or natural inequality, even
though the discourse may at times recognize the advantages accruing to
rank and riches. This double reduction also marks the orgy as the model
or replica of social relations and justifies their respective despotisms: if all
political systems encounter the tendency to despotism, it must be because
that tendency is not only innate, but unavoidable.[32] This is precisely what
Saint-Fond explains to Juliette: "All men lean toward despotism; it is the
first desire nature awakes in us" (8: 305, 316). If the word "man" in this
passage is first to be taken in its generic sense, it soon implies only the
male sex, which is stronger and more fit to rule. And it is the practice of
sexual despotism in the orgy that offers insight into social despotism:

> Any power that is shared is weakened; this is an accepted truth. Seek to give
> pleasure to the object which serves your pleasures; you will soon learn that it
> is at your own expense: there is no passion more self-centered than lust. (8:
> 257, 269)

If this sexual despotism is most often ascribed to men, Juliette's particular position suggests on the one hand that what is really at stake in the sex
hierarchy is power, and on the other hand that, according to Sade, this
power exceeds the social and is basically power over the other.

Let us continue to trace the sex hierarchy since it highlights the fact
that erotic satisfaction hangs on the politics of power as well as on the will
to power. This hierarchy is less clearcut when Clairwil, Juliette, or Durand
take a turn in organizing the orgy, but, left to themselves, the women
libertines attack only men who are their social inferiors and do so only
when Noirceuil and Saint-Fond, their class equals but sexual superiors,
are absent.[33] They have no hesitation, however, about sacrificing women
of a rank equal or superior to their own. We may note, among a score of

such examples, that Juliette and Clairwil end up by sacrificing the Queen of Naples, rather than her husband the king.[34] As agents and associates of the class of the masters (Clairwil is of noble birth and Juliette, the daughter of a rich banker who has gone bankrupt, marries into the aristocracy), they have the right to sexual pleasure in any form, yet they still do not escape the obligation to submit to their own masters. An important dialogue describes this articulation between sexual and social dependence:

> —"As a woman I know my place, and that dependency is my lot."—"No, not absolutely," "Noirceuil rejoined: "the affluence you enjoy, your brilliance and personality take you wholly out of that slavery. *Wives* and *whores* [italicized in the text] are the only ones I subject to this, and, in so doing, I just follow the laws of nature, which, as you see, allows such beings as they to do nothing but grovel. Intelligence, talents, riches, and good name *promote out of the class of the weak those whom nature destined for it* [my italics]; and from the moment when they enter into the class of the strong, they become heir to all the rights of that class, tyranny, oppression, impunity, and the entire exercise of all crimes. I want you to be a woman and a slave when with my friends and myself, a despot with any others . . . and from this moment, I swear to provide you with all the means to achieve this. (8: 201, 207)[35]

Sade understands the role of social conditioning and allows that the "natural" norm should have exceptions like "intelligence, talents," but he cannot give up the idea of a sexual inferiority almost always founded in nature, which justifies the roles of "slave," "wife," and "whore." This is why even the formidable Clairwil kills only on a modest scale, thus conforming to the relative value of the sexes, a proportion of one man to ten women: "Savage men! she cried out, massacre women as much as you want; I am content, provided I may merely avenge ten members of my sex with one of yours" (8: 499, 520–21). Noirceuil and Saint-Fond owe their immense political power not so much to their birth as to the strength of their nature. It is through unleashing that strength in the realm of evil that they can establish their social and sexual dominion so absolutely. Nevertheless, certain situations illustrating male despotism turn into a kind of satire on social vanity and servility that is worthy of Jarry's Père Ubu. In a scene of almost caricatural comedy—Juliette's first interview with Saint-Fond—the latter orders her to show him the greatest respect for "nature has placed the great ones on earth like stars in the firmament; they must lighten the world but never come down to its level." She must address him in the third person and never use the familiar "tu" form. Finally, he demands that she perform a sexual service for him which, as the conclusion to such a conversation, can be read only as a literal interpretation of the phrase "ass-kissing" (8: 210, 305). Other details also link farce to the satire on vanity, but without ever staging a true female supremacy. In the Society of the Friends of Crime, everyone must "kiss the ass" of each new president at his inauguration—a privilege not extended to women presidents (8: 480, 501). This Society—which Noirceuil, followed by Saint-Fond, claims to have left since "everything there passed into the hands of a sex whose authority he dislikes" (8: 287, 298)—proclaims the equality of the sexes within the class of the masters and may elect a woman president. Its bylaws, however, include a section called "Instructions to Women" which contradicts these principles by expressly enjoining woman to submit to the pleasures of man and "to turn those pleasures to the advantage of her purse and her lubricity" (8: 414, 431–32). Whereas men are obliged to lend themselves "freely" to all those who solicit them, women are encouraged to charge for their compliance. Prostitution remains the inevitable and justified corollary of inferiority, and, in the kingdom of inversions, sex hierarchy is not inverted.

We may wonder why this Juliette who, to the very end, has not the slightest will of her own in regard to Saint-Fond and Noirceuil and practices the much extolled treachery only on her equals of the female sex,[37] was regarded by Apollinaire as "the new woman . . . a being who is yet to be imagined, who leaves humanity behind, who will have wings and will renew the universe" unless Apollinaire was merely quipping and seeking to "shock the bourgeois."[38] His assessment, which is still often cited in an attempt to establish Juliette as the archetype of the free woman, is in fact nothing but a retread or inversion of the ideology of the woman-savior, which goes hand in hand with the ideology of the woman-slave.[38] In reality, Sade never describes a complete reciprocity between Juliette and her masters, any more than he does a wholly free and egalitarian utopian society, and the sexual hierarchy of the orgy remains the model for an ideal of despotism. Contract and desire "remain in total conflict," since reciprocity is attainable only under the constraint of the law, not only in the sexually communal existence of men and women in "Yet One More Effort, Frenchmen" but even among the masters of the Society of the Friends of Crime (to say nothing of the class of victims which that society cannot do without.)[39] In "Yet one more effort, Frenchmen" a contract is merely accepted whereas for the Friends of Crime it is a freely chosen contract, but in both cases the contract entails the obligation to lend oneself sexually to another even if one feels no desire. At the end of his anarchic revolt, the libertine finds himself compelled to reinstate the law—even if in a ludic mode. Thus the new president of the Society cannot refuse the sexagenarian whom he has inflamed with his eloquence (8: 495, 516). With wry humor, Sade puts his finger on the fault in the system. That said, the only contradictions he recognizes are limited to the order of phantasmatic desire—to the restrictions on sexual pleasure which are likely to persist even in the best of all possible worlds—and he never touches either the sex hierarchy or the caste hierarchy.

Two complementary ideas surface and become dominant in this system, that of the hierarchy of extremes and that of an inequality founded in nature. Jouissance is attained through the exercise of power. Sade, says Hénaff, exposes "the erotic repressed" of the thesis of just inequality, a thesis which he finds, for example, in the work of d'Holbach and Voltaire. Social inequality is founded on nature, and—Sade is alone in saying this— "the knowledge of this inequality produces jouissance."[40] In so far as one dissociates the desire for power from the desire for jouissance, the will to power comes first, since it is a factor that the social and the sexual have in common.

Inequality of beings, inequality of classes, inequality of sexes: "Ah, who can doubt that, among men, there is one class sufficiently superior to the weakest species to become what poets once called gods!" says Saint-Fond (8: 311, 322). "Cast your eyes upon the works of nature . . . , and judge for yourself the extreme difference nature's hand has put to the formation of men born into the first class, or born into the second. . . . Do they have the same voice, the same skin? . . . The man of the people is but the species that forms the first rung up from the monkey of the forest" (8: 311, 322). Similarly, there is as much difference "between a man and a woman as between a man and a monkey of the forest" (8: 489, 511 n). Respect for women "was never in nature. The inferiority of that sex to our own is too well established for there ever to arise any reason for us to respect it" (8: 484, 506). The despotism of the orgy makes this double inequality into law and carves it into the bodies of the victims.

In many pages of the *Histoire de Juliette*, Sade strongly criticizes naturalist philosophy. He pours scorn on Rousseau's notion of man's innate goodness or invokes nature to justify every deviation and its opposite, while he continues to address the relativity of cultures. Nonetheless, Sade still sticks firmly by two theses which form the elements of a true naturalism. First the notion that Nature as first cause of creation is now cut off from man and even hostile to him (see below, Chapter 4, "Simulacrum,

Repetition Compulsion, and Death Drive"). Second, as we have just seen, the notion that inequality is natural and therefore justified, as ceaselessly promoted by the despotic ideal of the orgy and its discourse. Sade barely distances himself from this second idea and then only in a few unusually comic episodes. I would go further: the most regressive and unsound part of his political philosophy is based upon that model of a necessary adequation between nature and society. Ernst Kantorowicz has shown that such a view (whose content is inverted in Sade) informed medieval legal science, defined as "the art of the good and the equal." Just like art, law was supposed to conform to Aristotle's maxim, and imitate nature.[41] During the same period, one of the goals of the Revolutionaries, following in the path of the Enlightenment, was to remedy social and/or natural inequalities— even though the situation of women rarely formed part of this program. The orgy and its despotic system do not constitute Sade's last word on the subject, but it would be an error to see an ideal of freedom in this utopia (as some have done), or even, on the other hand, to minimize its importance within the whole context of his political ideas and his worldview.

# PART 2

# Body, Text, Parody

*D**espite important differences*, both writing and perversion are creative activities.[1] As Sade grows more practiced, his writing grows richer, a richness that can be felt all through the two thousand pages of *La Nouvelle Justine* and the *Histoire de Juliette*, as compared with *Les Cent-vingt journées de Sodome*.[2] The later novels stress the polyvalence of repetition and its function in satisfying instinctual drives, and probe its textual possibilities more and more, including all the modes of parody. The orgy, which stages the repetition of the sexual performance, activates the link between textual body and erotic body and constitutes the narrative kernel of the novel. From scene to scene, repetition takes on parodic and self-parodic connotations, all of them reinforced by an ostentatious intertextuality and by the overcoded character of the pornographic text and its quotation effect. Parody is at the heart of the orgy scene and becomes rapidly apparent even in the most run-of-the-mill description.

A parallel has often been drawn between the fragmented body in the orgy and Sade's juxtaposition of interchangeable episodes or fragmentation of the narrative syntax. This is an attractive hypothesis, but one that loses force once one remembers that many works, and many genres, offer the same fragmentary organization without focusing upon the erotic body. More fruitful seems to be the parallel between Sade's preference for partial objects and the absence of any interiority in his characters, except in a few lyrical passages. The unity of the subject, without which interiority is impossible, can only be constructed around the whole person. Stripped of any coherent psychology, motivated only by sexual instinct, Sade's hero flouts the novelistic convention of the rounded character and reveals its artificiality. More, perhaps, than in the fragmentation of narrative syntax, it is in Sade's puppet-characters that an identification with the fragmented body emerges.[3]

Critics have also described the body of the text as exclusively female and maternal, on the basis of a sentence in *Idée sur les romans* (*Reflections on the Novel*, preface to the *Crimes de l'amour*) where Sade invokes incest with mother(-nature) as the source of fictional writing: "Oh you who wish to venture upon this difficult and thorny career, bear ever in mind that the novelist is the child of nature, that she has created him to be her painter; if he does not become his mother's lover the moment she gives birth to him, let him never write" (10: 16–17, 110).[4] Let us not be hasty, however, and turn a hackneyed metaphor into a declaration of general intent. Barthes influenced many other critics in the seventies when he reduced the play with the maternal body to a mere question of language. He cited Sade, Lautréamont, and Matisse as his examples and invoked what he calls *the mother tongue*.[5] None of this, however, is truly relevant to Sade's writing. Pulled in opposite directions by the maternal and the law, his text does say all there is to say about its origin in the sexual drives, but it strives to *say* everything only in order to control everything.

It is not Sade's writing but what it describes that illustrates, with some distortion, a conception of the text as a product of incest with the mother or as an appropriation of her creative powers. One has to take into account the figures and the speeches of the orgy, instead of ignoring the precise content of the Sadean phantasy. Quite apart from the total absence of mother-son incest in the fiction, the sentence from *Reflections on the Novel* where Sade speaks in his own name presents a very euphemistic view of the relation with the mother. The work itself, however, develops the dark side of this relation. The orgy scene moves the maternal body into anonymity and then eviscerates it. And even if one posits that the creative impulse arises out of the pre-verbal maternal stage, it must be recognized that it is usually Sadean scatology that manifests such a fact. The scenes in which maternal abjection is joined to phantasies of pregnancy recall those infantile theories of procreation whereby children come out of the mouth or the anus. Sade constantly confuses organic body and erogenous body: for him they are one and the same.

Thus if Sade identifies with the feminine, this is related to the prerogatives of the creative act, not to the erogenous body of the woman, which always appears in his work as an alterity to be inscribed with phantasies of destruction. We shall see that it is in the phallic figures which occult any overt female representation that the erotic bond with writing is marked.

# 4. Repetition and Writing, Imaginary and Simulacrum

## Fictionalization of Speech and Writing

Sade's repetitive writing gives rise to a textual interplay which in turn illustrates the crucial role in the text's production of the compulsion to repeat. The linguistic imaginary becomes the stuff of fiction, and Sade represents desire by the vast space he gives to speech. The libertine explains quite clearly that he is forced to begin the transition from desire to deed over and over again because the deeds are always unsatisfactory: "I was exhausted but in no way calm" (8: 301, 312).[1] This gap between desire and act may give rise to some quite rational-sounding syllogisms: "—'Sad to say, there is no such thing as crime,' said Delbène. 'So since these scoundrels are forever inferior to their desires, it is no longer they who fail to live up to the horrors, but the horrors that fail to live up to them'" (8: 94, 88). There is surplus of desire and excess of demand, both incommensurate with need.[2] It is speech that triggers sexual pleasure and nurtures the imaginary, before, during and after the action.[3] Speech organizes the preparations for the orgy. The Sadean agent acknowledges that speech serves as an actualizer, in terms that evoke linguistic exchange rather than sexual exchange, and the novelist's work rather than the character's:

> You must have noticed that the sweetest sexual pleasures I taste with you are those in which, giving full rein to our two minds, we create beings of such lubricity that their existence is sadly impossible. (8: 500, 521)[4]

As we move through the novel, the chief organizer becomes more and more confused with the writing subject, indeed with Sade himself. It is his own pleasure in imagination that the latter analyses and indirectly links to his work as a writer. The doubly specular function of orgiastic speech becomes apparent: it works first as fiction describing the relation of the characters to their phantasies and second as metafiction, designating the narrative act as a writing of the imaginary.

Even the passage into writing, which became more and more the essential term for the work of the Sadean imaginary, is fictionalized in the *Histoire de Juliette*. Writing declares desire and the mastery of desire in a more concrete way than speech does; it makes sexual pleasure more present. Juliette gives writing a determining role in her famous erotic recipe: "Is it not true, my sweet girl, that you have already found your desires far greater than your means?" she asks one of her pupils. She advocates taking up the pen in order to counter this drawback, but only at the conclusion of a mental discipline which is a true education in the imaginary, and in which Barthes recognizes the protocol for Saint Ignatius of Loyola's Spiritual Exercises.[5] First one must "remain a whole fortnight without giving way to lust," even in one's thoughts, and then do the opposite, allowing the imagination to roam as lustfully as possible:

> Go to bed alone, in silence and deepest darkness: then call to mind all that you have just been banishing. . . . Then allow your imagination the freedom gradually to present to you different kinds of aberration; . . . convince yourself that the world is yours for the taking . . . that you have the right to change, mutilate, destroy, overturn every being at your pleasure. . . . This idea, which has been acquired in the way I've indicated, will master you, enthral you; frenzy will take possession of your senses and believing that you are already at work, you will discharge like a Messalina.[6]

The following stage involves reading and writing and it comprises two parts:

> As soon as this is done, *light your candles again, and transcribe on your tablets the sort of aberration which has just set you on fire, forgetting none of the circumstances which may have aggravated the details of it*; go to sleep at this moment, reread your notes the next day, *and by beginning your operation again, add everything that your imagination, however wearied it may now be by an idea that has already cost you much fuck, might suggest to increase the irritation. Now shape a body out of that idea, and as you polish it add again all the episodes your head will commend to you.* Now perform, and you will find that this is the aberration which suits you best, and which you will enact with the most delight. (9: 47–48, 640–41, my italics)

These lines, which inscribe both the desire of the author and that of the reader,[7] constitute a prescription for reading and have an obvious metafictional dimension. Barthes points out the "augmentative" nature of the correction applied to the initial transcription of the phantasy, then to the final draft. Likewise, the distinctive feature of the structure of the scene, and of the novel, is that of *augmentative repetition*.

The autobiographical character of this "recipe" cannot be doubted, even if it were not accompanied by a footnote, attributed to the scriptor, or to Sade:

> All those with some leaning toward crime will read their own portraits in this paragraph . . . ; they may be sure that the hand which offers this advice is guided by experience. (9: 47, 639–40)

Unlike his characters, for a very long period Sade was able to "perform" only in the solitude of his prison—and, as far as crime went, more in the imagination than in actuality. Juliette's words of advice link writing and masturbation, and the "hand" the note refers to also makes this connection and stresses the physical, material side of the writing activity, the way it works as replacement and supplement, both as pleasure substitute and as representing an excess of sexual pleasure. By piling page on page, Sade gives a presence to his phantasy. He enlarges it by perpetually repeating the operation described above, but, since he is unable to proceed to performance, he resembles his paper creatures and submits his dream to fiction's leveling effect. It is the writing and masturbatory hand which "shapes a body" out of the idea, without identifying that body or rather by confusing it with the organ of pleasure and without providing the sex drive with any living object of any sex. This phenomenon, in a Lacanian perspective, definitely proves that it is satisfaction itself which is the object of the drive. And we shall see that in Sade it is never the female body but the phallus as simulacrum which can become a figure of writing.

Such lyrical flights on the part of a character are rare but revealing. They demonstrate how remarkably aware Sade was not only that the act of writing is at heart a satisfaction of phantasy but also that it is linked to the erotic body, perhaps precisely because that body, in and of itself, also constitutes the fictional stuff of his work. "Oh, Juliette," cries the aptly named Belmor (fair death):

> How delightful are the pleasures of the imagination, and how voluptuously one follows all the paths its brilliant course opens up to us! You must own, my love, that there can be no notion of what we invent, what we create, in those divine moments when our souls of flame exist only in the impure organ of lubricity: what delights are savored as we frig each other during the erection of these phantoms, how raptly we caress them! (8: 500, 521)

In this equating of fiction and metafiction, the erotic imaginary and the novelistic imaginary are one, as is the language of their inventions. The above passage, spoken on this occasion by a man, conjures up a phallus ("the erection of those phantoms") that has been *unveiled as simulacrum*. In fact Sade sometimes uses the word "illusion" for the erect male member.[8]

The phallic simulacrum is at the heart of Sadean representation. It constitutes the origin and the end of that will to power which is primary in Sade, and it ties the political into the textual. Sade's ultimate goal is to correct the living, to vanquish nature while singing her praises. For to assert phallic-anal primacy amounts to willing the suppression of sexual difference and the positing of a model of despotism. To think one can be self-sufficient thanks to masturbatory phantasy (and pleasure machines), to give life to the imaginary by means of writing, is to pursue a dream of ascendency whereby language may bridge the gap between signifier and signified, representor and represented. Similarly, the unremitting use of obscene language is an attempt against all odds to unveil the phallus, in the hope that it will be there.

One of Sade's originalities is that, even as he nurtures the illusion, he allows us to detect it so clearly. He not only exalts illusion ("What you offer me is fair, what I invent is sublime"),[9] he thematizes it by creating a universe of simulation, in which everything happens and (almost) nothing is impossible. He identifies illusion as the stuff of his fiction by representing it in the form of simulacra—either objects, or episodes—which he introduces as such. In this way he finds both pleasure and truth. Striving constantly to seize hold of signifier-signified as a unit, he is always brought up against the reality of their separateness. He then exhibits that reality in order to dominate it.

This truth he discovers over and over again is evident, first of all, in the omnipresent dildo, that tired old prop of eighteenth-century pornography. In Sade's work, the dildo acquires the value of a fetish object, from both a psychoanalytic and a semiotic viewpoint. The fetishist, it may be recalled, wavers between belief and knowledge. This oscillation is based on the child's (or rather the boy's) discovery of the mother's anatomy: if woman is "castrated," he is in danger of being so too; therefore he wishes to believe that she isn't castrated, even though he knows she is. The fetish represents the maternal phallus, and Freud notes that it may look like a phallic symbol.[10] On the one hand, the Sadean dildo proclaims the primacy of the phallus, since it is habitually used to sodomize women and thus to deny their difference. On the other hand, with savage humor, the dildo emphasizes the illusion function, as evidenced by the perennially monstrous size of the device, or by its four-stemmed version, with two stems curved upward in a half circle (IX 503, 1107), which one of Juliette's female partners pulls out of her pocket, or again by the one Clairwil has fashioned for herself out of the mummified penis of a monk she castrates. Thus, from a semiotic point of view, the dildo strongly tilts the balance between belief and knowledge onto the side of knowledge. In other words, Sade never forgets the sign status of the dildo and other illusion factors in the orgy. He eroticizes these various props, all of which connote the absent body. They restore its impossible plenitude, though they never fall into a fetishist abstraction of the sign that would confuse the mark, the signifier, the "standing for," with a real object. And he reduces the mark of the sexual to the phallic-anal axis, though he does not believe in this reduction.[11]

Recognized as petrified, the simulacrum nonetheless refers back to the virile model. Behind the organs erected in the orgy, themselves anything but real, looms that castration anxiety which pervades the Sadean symbolic network. Linked to the taboo on the mother and the law of the father—for the child tends to imagine his father as the author of his mother's "castration"[12]—castration anxiety has its counterpart in the *rigidity* of the orgy ritual. In fact, if one agrees that the male superego has its origin in the drives and is related to the incest taboo, and if obedience to excessively strict rules is the corollary of a demanding superego,[13] then Sade's extraordinary superego can no longer be separated from the ceremonial of the orgy. This is where boundless desire, castration anxiety, and fetishist oscillation come together.

From a metafictional viewpoint, the dildo represents the act of narration while remaining a narrative object. It brings together writing and phantasy by unveiling the common unreality of their fabulations. It shows the phantasy to be a "mechanism that produces simulacra"[14] and a substitute for an absence, and consequently it traces the phallus-(simulacrum)-machine-writing sequence.

Furthermore, entire scenes offer a true figuration, with metafictional value, of this function of phantasy and thus demonstrate the reflexivity of the text. The whole art consists in making the narrative fabric coincide with the scenario intended to ensure perverse satisfaction. The deployment of the orgy, which constitutes a spectacle in itself, often doubles as a performance designed to *deceive* certain of the participants while the rest are informed and complicit. The thief Dorval, for example, in order to complete the cycle of his sexual pleasure, needs first a "real" theft (which he forces Juliette and her woman friend to perform on one of their male clients, and which he observes as voyeur), then a simulated theft that the two women believe to be real. He then accuses them of the crime and directs the staging of their punishment:

> —At the back of this room a scaffold could be seen, on which were two gibbets and all the necessary paraphernalia for a hanging. "—Ladies," Dorval said to us abruptly, "you are about to receive the punishment for your crimes." (8: 128, 126)

He completes the illusion when he strips Juliette and her friend of their clothing, as well as of the money they had just earned, and subjects them to a (false) hanging.

The "pervert, like the artist, is also a master of *illusion*," writes Joyce McDougall, but the artist creates "the illusion of reality . . . *his* illusion while seeking to have it accepted as such," whereas "the perverse scenario . . . is *the illusion that has imposed itself on the creator*, but which he then, for the rest of his life, attempts to impose on others in the hope that they will accept this illusion *as a reality*."[15] The work of art is a real exchange object between author and public, whereas exchange is aborted for the spectator in the perverse scenario. As a whole, Sade's text wavers between these two solutions, which are illustrated successively by the two phases of the preceding scene in which Juliette is first an accomplice and then a dupe. In the second phase, Dorval needs to deceive even Juliette if he is to achieve orgasm, and communication breaks down. In the denouement of the episode, the artistic game prevails once again when the illusion is unveiled: back in their chamber, the two women find a bonus of ten louis, as well as a "complete déshabille, far exceeding in value" the garments they had lost (8: 131, 128). In this game of mirrors between watcher and watched, Dorval the voyeur takes the place of the novelist, and Juliette the place of the reader vis à vis the spectacle of fictional creations that gradually emerge from the blank space of non-event and instinctual desire.

Many other episodes overtly create a universe of simulation. In the final sequence of the Noirceuil marriages, simulacrum and simulation make use of transvestism and incestuous combinations. The memorable episode in the madhouse develops the parodic potential of repetitive imitation and gives rise to a disquieting game of mirrors. "Sade restores to madness all its violence," writes Michel Delon, noting the identification at work between mad victims and agent torturers.[16] Madness is a living out of the belief in the universe of illusion. It has no knowledge of the distance between phantasy and its realization. It is in order to exploit the beliefs of the madmen, but also to simulate and perhaps share them, that the actors in the orgy cross the cypress hedge that marks off the scene of the action:

> Here, the cages surrounded a great courtyard planted with cypresses, whose gloomy green lent a graveyard air to the enclosure. In the center was a cross studded with sharp nails on one side; this was where the victims of Vespoli's villainy were garrotted. (9: 384, 981)

Vespoli, "once the first chaplain at court," now governs the "lunatic asylum," which allows him, as actor and spectator, to mime the "antics" of the madman ("And I too am a madman," he says), to direct the performance of sacrilegious acts, and to exercise his lubricious cruelty. The madmen think they are respectively God, the Virgin Mary, and Christ. It does not take Clairwil long to size up the possibilities of this situation and to multiply the reflexive game. She suggests imitating these madmen even as they themselves mime the actions of the persons they believe themselves to be:

> "Here is an arousing sight," she tells us; "do as I do, my fair friends, and as for you, villain, have your gaolers strip us naked, and lock us up in the cages: pretend we too are mad women, we will imitate them; you will have us tied up on the cross *on the side that has no spikes*, the madmen will whip us and fuck our asses afterwards." (9: 385, 983, my italics) [17]

The humorous detail preserves a margin of parodic difference within the imitation,[18] a distance which proves that, even while putting a perverse part of his ego in the service of his invention, the writer does not confuse the two.

Hence the metafictional value of these episodes. Simulacrum and simulation here constitute narrative elaborations of the structure typifying the orgy, with its specular relationship between the spoken program, speech-preface to the scene, and the execution of that program by the agents, each marked by unreality. If the orgy scene always seems to be the imitation of a preexisting speech that amounts to a program, this program coincides with the memory of a phantasy. The program orders the phantasy, puts it into words, and projects it into the future. Committed to writing, and even sometimes borrowed from an earlier text, such as the Gospels, the program of the orgy plays a mediating role between phantasy and the text of the novel.

The despairing search for a real body is at the root of the repetitive gesture of writing. In order to lay hold on that nonexisting object, the agents strive relentlessly to penetrate below the surface of the body. Even the skin forms a barrier to possession. This is why there is only a difference in degree between the impassioned cry of Juliette to Clairwil— "Let us cast off these importunate veils: are not the coverings of nature already enough? Ah, when I arouse transports in you, I should wish to see your heart throb" (8: 264, 275)—and the scene in which they flay a young woman by tearing off seven successive layers of her skin,[19] a scene that isolates and exacerbates the sadistic components in any desire for possession:

> There is no way to represent the agony that poor girl felt, when the Italian applied the thorny whip to the new skin that had been exposed when she was skinned. But it was quite another thing when this second was torn off, and the third layer had to be whipped; the unfortunate girl ground her teeth and struggled so desperately, it was the greatest pleasure to watch. . . . All the skins of this creature were torn off, but her vital organs were still unaffected. This ceased to be true when they applied red hot iron spikes to her nerves: her screams were twice as loud; she was very exciting to watch. (9: 471, 1073)

The Sadean agent erases the object in order to take revenge for its absence, an original lack that the story transforms into active destruction. No final revelation occurs when all the skins are off, and the annihilation of the object puts only a temporary ending to the aggression of desire. Hence the suppression of any exchange relationship: "It is a whim with me to put no store in what is given me, I prize only what I take" (9: 403, 1003), and the monstrous growth of the self-consuming ego and its closure: "I should like the whole universe to cease to exist when I raise my prick" (9: 497, 1100). And the repetition without end.

## Repetition and Its Correctives: Narration and Reflexivity

The overall structure of the *Histoire de Juliette* reproduces on the scale of its thousand pages the structure of the individual orgy scene. Let us take the most characteristic feature of the scene for granted, that is, its progressive intensification. It is too easy to interpret this as a reflection of the curve of orgasm, when in fact it merely maximizes a general phenomenon: any action, when narrated, obeys this same structure of rising to crescendo, reaching crisis, and then returning to calm. In Sade's work, moments of balance, in which the movement is regulated so as to avoid any paroxysm, often interrupt the scene and allow for renewed activity: "All was activity, all was arousal, all was accommodation" (9: 520, 1124). Very rapidly, the balance is broken and the action speeds up again.

## THE PROGRAM-SCENE SEQUENCE

In a narratological perspective, the program-scene sequence demonstrates Sade's mastery as a storyteller. Just as, for an actor playing the same play a hundred times, each performance assumes a unique quality, so differences occur in the narration of the program and the scene so that the specular relationship that continues to unite them turns out to be an effect of reading rather than a reality. In general, the length of the one is inversely proportional to that of the other, and formulas such as "everything is arranged, everything is executed" take the place of actual repetition. Very occasionally, there will even be a program without a scene or a scene without a program. Sometimes a piece of dialogue blurs the mirror effect, or else the scene does not repeat the details of the program and adds others instead.[20]

Thus we uncover the paradox of a double narrative unit which by its form postulates repetition while in fact *avoiding* it, and which, moreover, creates a repetitive impression either because, despite the care Sade takes as a writer, he fails to camouflage his erotic obsession, or because, from scene to scene, he works aggressively to impose it on the reader.[21]

## OVERALL STRUCTURE

The parallel habitually drawn between the fragmented body and the fragmentary and repetitive structure of the Sadean novel is only partly valid for the *Histoire de Juliette* and offers a far from adequate account of its overall structure. Now at the height of his novelistic powers, Sade uses suppler and more varied, if not more subtle, strategies, and a polymorphous narration.

Joan De Jean has shown that the arithmetical construction of *Les Cent-vingt journées de Sodome* is antithetical to the organic model of the novel (that was to be perfected in the nineteenth century), and in its rigor and rigidity constitutes the extreme case of the classical novelistic aesthetic, which tended to juxtapose episodes.[22] Thus repetition in *Les Cent-vingt journées* is strictly subordinated to numerical organization and gives the work its "paratactic" or metonymic structure, using juxtaposed sequences. The *Histoire de Juliette* corresponds to this model only in some places, and repetition is not controlled as rigorously. Indeed repetition takes such multiple forms that it retrospectively confers on *Les Cent-vingt journées* the value of a veritable *liquidation* of the classic heritage, thus allowing the author of the *Histoire de Juliette* full latitude to let his narrative breathe a little. Tirelessly exploiting all the modes of repetition, Juliette as narrator scatters juxtapositions within sequences and between them, instead of using them, as in *Les Cent-vingt journées*, to "discipline the body of the novel" (De Jean, *Literary Fortifications*, p. 292). Béatrice Didier refers to these juxtapositions as "buddings" and "multiple grafts."[23] At this point in his life, Sade makes use of techniques that are more varied, if not newer.

This practice in *Juliette* does not amount to a regression, in part because of its parodic potential. Sade seems both to be applying corrective measures to the problems of repetition and achieving a parodic gesture. By stressing the old tried and true strategies for motivating the reader, he implicitly refers to generic models of narration and gives a semblance of organic structure to disconnected and monotonous episodes. Such models would include the fairy tale of going off to seek adventure and returning in glory; the picaresque novel in the Italian section; an initiation-like structure for the episode of Minski's castle; the Bildungsroman,[24] for even though Juliette is dedicated to evil from the beginning, she nonetheless *makes progress* in her quest for evil under the aegis of a series of pedagogues of both sexes. Other strategies mark an attempt to free *Juliette* from the narrative impasse of *Les Cent-vingt journées*. First, it uses a first person narrative, focused exclusively on Juliette (or upon the narrators of tales within her tale). This economically corrects the dispersion of viewpoint of *Les Cent-vingt journées*. Secondly, this narrative is not only linear, but also presents a paridigmatic dimension, where the episodes create a *mise en abyme* effect between the main story and the secondary tales of Minski and of Brisa Testa-Borchamps. This last story, in particular, offers the model for an intensification of tortures which will then be continued in Juliette's own narrative. Finally, some metanarrative remarks underline the short cuts taken in the narration: "You are weary of lubricious descriptions, and I shall enter into detail only for things I think merit it, because of their singular or criminal character" (8: 539, 561); "His passion is singular enough for me to enter into details for you" (9: 35, 626); "To avoid the monotony of the details, I shall pass lightly over those of the new orgies" (9: 209, 805).[25] The overall effect may still be repetitive and such remarks may seem somewhat disingenuous, but they underline the distance traveled from *Les Cent-vingt journées* in terms of esthetic ideal.

The two narrative modes in *Juliette*—the scene and the narration—correspond to two types of temporality which in turn entail a difference in the intensity of the violence effects. The oneiric present of the orgy and its regular return refer to a cyclical or iterative time, whereas the unfolding of the plot refers to the linear time of events. The first, which is at heart the time of myth, ordinarily functions as a regulator and tends to reduce "the world of excesses and anomalies surrounding man to norm and system," whereas the time of chance is that of anomalies, of "crimes, calamities—anything considered the violation of a certain primordial order" established by the laws of myth."[26] The narration in *Juliette* does not follow this model. In the first place, neither plot nor scene abandons anomaly. And it is the narration that normalizes the violence, not the scene. Virtually all the tortures in *La Nouvelle Justine* and in *Juliette* are already written into the plans for *Les Cent-vingt journées*, but one need only compare these narrative outlines with the fully executed paintings in *Justine* and *Juliette* to be convinced that the orgy scene—in which the plans are, in Sade's term, "detailed" and in which the atemporal present seems to immobilize the succession of acts—achieves levels of violence far superior to those in the plans (even if the reader's sensitivity may get blunted as scene follows scene). On the other hand, the linear narrative, which relates the same type of acts, tends to neutralize the scenes' violence by inserting them into a time sequence.[27]

Having said that, one should add that the temporality, more highly developed in the plot of *Juliette* than in *Justine*, is inseparable from the link between orgy and parody. To keep the reader involved and willing to accept tortures and dissertations, Sade exploits established narrative models, but since he is really only interested in unveiling their arbitrariness, he overuses them and inevitably moves into parody. Thus, for example, he reintroduces a schema of causality that ties in with the interest aroused by Juliette's "story," but he usually does so without entering into motivation—a caricature of narrative logic which amounts to a disavowal. Another example: the tension raised between the focus on Juliette as first person narrator and the peculiar nature of her exploits constantly undermines the reader's readiness to identify with her view. The "repetition" of familiar schemata makes the text more readable but there is always some dissonance.

A concern for narrativity joins forces with parodic subversion in the mirror construction of scene and novel which propels the crescendo into excess. Far from being interchangeable, the episodes frequently succeed one another according to the principle of augmentation. The moments of equilibrium which, in the scene, prepare for the resumption of activity, are echoed for the novel as a whole by moments of narrative pause. This happens, for example, when Juliette sums up the two brilliant years that followed her adoption by Saint-Fond. In the French text she uses the imperfect tense of continuous, uncompleted action.

> Two years passed in this way without anything particular happening to me. My luxuriousness, my debauchery increased to such a degree that I no longer had a taste for the simple pleasures of nature, and if there were not something extraordinary and criminal in the fantasies proposed to me, I remained absolutely insensible to them. (8: 526, 548) [28]

The "pauses" still obey the urge to up the ante, but they substitute summary for the narration of action. They set the crescendo going (narrative function) and underline the progress achieved by the earlier crescendos (metanarrative function).

Beneath the veneer of genre models, the only organic principle is clearly that of intensification, even if, for the naive reader, a paroxysm seems already to have been reached when the game began. The very first episode in the *Histoire de Juliette* already includes torture, murder, rape, and the preference for sodomy. But it still lacks, from the qualitative viewpoint, theft, massacre, pedophilia, bestiality, all the variations of incest and family murder, coprophagia, cannibalism, the few examples of castration, and the frequent assaults on the vagina. These are to be supplemented by perforated ear drums and gouged-out eyes, the indispensable tearing of flesh at the moment of penetration, fetuses ripped out of wombs, and limbs and tongues cut or torn off. A few pages before the end of *Juliette*'s interminable chronicle, yet another original torture is explored: the harrying of a naked young woman with firecrackers on a frozen pond (9: 576, 1182).

The sado-erotic inventiveness, the very stuff of Sade's fictional inventiveness, is so exceptional that it gives rise to an at least relative effect of renewal in which it is difficult to distinguish the qualitative from the quantitative. Nonetheless, quantity is more important. In the first place, the appearance of new characters who introduce Juliette to new horrors ensures that more excess will occur at different points. Second, it is the most atrocious crimes that return most frequently, with an increasing frenzy of violence. Third, there are times when mere numbers or numerical increase directly generate the story (but only occasionally, as opposed to *Les Cent-vingt journées*). The obsession with numbers (whether an arithmetical series or the model of speculation) reveals the desire to control chance and the "uncanny."[29] It could be argued that the model of speculation indirectly governs the whole production of the narrative. Its most exemplary illustration is Clairwil's precious plan for "a crime with perpetual effects," or "moral crime." Such a crime would continue to be effective even after the act and would develop its effects according to a reasoned geometric progression:

> A libertine determined to engage in this kind of activity can easily corrupt three hundred children in the course of a year; after thirty years he will have corrupted nine thousand; and if each child he has corrupted imitates him only by twenty-five per cent, which is more than likely, and if each generation continues to act in the same way, then at the end of his thirty years, the libertine will have witnessed two generations of corruption born under him, and there will already be nine million beings who have been corrupted by him or by the principles he has laid down. (8: 504, 525–26)[30]

From the metafictional perspective, these examples theorize the narrative modes, since the operations of intensifying, accelerating, and accumulating all obey forms of arithmetic or geometric progression. Sade exploits a third procedure: instead of describing the crescendo, he merely names it, in dialogues with a metanarrative function in which assertion must take the place of proof. Thus Juliette, in her capacity as organizer of the pleasures, is kept on her toes by Saint-Fond's demands: "I shall not conceal from you, Noirceuil said to me, that you seem to have been losing your grip for a while now; Saint-Fond has noticed; there were not even fifty dishes at the last supper" (8: 246, 257). This hardly resembles, however, the long descriptions of the *Satiricon*, and we never get much detail about the fifty dishes. Similarly, when Clairwil and Juliette run into each other again, Juliette declares: "I am very far today from the pusillanimity which once seemed likely to be my ruin, and you may be sure that your bosom friend today blushes only at virtue" (9: 215–16, 811). She has already made many similar assurances to Minski and the pope,[31] and she will later confess to Durand (her new passion), "Clairwil was a mere child compared with you" (9: 439, 1041). If one crime does not exceed the one before, it must at least appear to raise the ante. The sheer impertinence of Sade's technique is striking here as he caricatures the hero's progress in the Bildungsroman. In the end, Juliette has not changed, she has at most hardened a little, and these moments of dialogue praise her for a progress in evil which concerns only the gradation of actions. Not only does this procedure deliberately confuse actions and "character," it underlines the contradiction constantly raised in the text between the assessment made by the characters and that of the reader, another discordance with a parodic effect. Juliette, who has set fire to a house and burned a family with eight children, is sharply chided by Clairwil for her pusillanimity: "Indeed! Can you believe, dear friends, that when I told this story to Clairwil she assured me that I had merely trifled with crime, and I had behaved like a coward!" (8: 399, 415–16).

While unable to write without repetition, Sade nonetheless tried to diversify his narrative, in *Juliette* more than in *La Nouvelle Justine*. The repetition and numbering which in *Les Cent-vingt journées* had been a concerted system and a general principle of organization, persist in a pure state only in a few episodes in *Juliette*. In most cases repetition contributes to reflexivity and quantitative acceleration.

## CLOSURE

The specular structure persists to the end. Orgasmic death, an economic death that brings the scene to an end, is echoed by the "real" death of the heroine, which brings the novel to an end, after a paroxysm of crime and sexual pleasure. In the meantime, we have also witnessed the definitive disappearance of several of the principal agents who become their partners' victims. These liquidations move the story forward to its conclusion. Juliette's death at the end of the book obeys the most classic narrative model, but Sade makes no attempt to hide how arbitrary it is. It is no more explained than the heroine's death in *La Princesse de Clèves*—a novel familiar to Sade. This death, which in *La Princesse de Clèves* seems like the harmonious, ineluctable, and almost expected consequence of the novel's spirit, in *Juliette* clashes with the heroine's cynicism and vitality. It could just as well happen earlier, or later.

The death of the storyteller closes the narrative on itself and opens up the scene of writing, referring the reader back to the beginning of the novel and to the oral telling. *L'Histoire de Juliette* concludes with this gesture of infinite repetition. The schemata of closure and repetition which govern the figures of the orgy are also characteristic of the reflexive structure of *Juliette*, which strips, exploits, and mimics the whole heritage of novelistic strategies Sade had at his disposal.

## The Book, the Referent, the Phantasy:
## Sade and *Don Quixote*

In this collective heritage, *Don Quixote* has a place apart, serving as a canonic model. Sade's essay *Reflections on the Novel* shows how much he admired the work. At each misadventure, Don Quixote believes he is encountering an exact replica of chivalric romances: an inn is a castle, a shaving bowl a golden helmet, and so on. The secondary tales borrow from stereotyped plots, and are again centered upon a confusion between real and imaginary. The whole of the novel with its embedded stories inevitably acquires a metafictional dimension. The narration never lets the reader forget that this is a book. Cervantes inscribed parody—reflexivity and heterogeneity—into his text by explicitly linking it to the notion of the literary simulacrum. The heterogeneous effect is often born of the brutal shock between the sublime dream of the hero and "thorny reality." The reader may recall the hymn Don Quixote intones in honor of his own hand and addresses to a servant, as he proffers it to her in the dark: "Take this hand, lady . . . take this hand, I say, . . . I do not give it to you to kiss, but that you may gaze on the structure of its sinews, the interlacement of its muscles, the width and capacity of its veins; from all of which you may judge what strength must be in the arm to which such a hand belongs."[32] This passage finds an echo when Noirceuil celebrates his own "rod" for Juliette's benefit (8: 180). The servant girl promptly ties the sublime hand to a hayloft door, and Don Quixote is left hanging for more than two hours. Juliette, on the other hand, encourages Noirceuil's phallic cult.

There are many similarities between the overall structure of *Don Quixote* and of the *Histoire de Juliette*—the journey by road, the meeting place that serves as a pretext for all kinds of unlikely scenes of recognition—but Cervantes skillfully holds the threads of the main story and the side stories together, a procedure Sade uses more crudely in the Borchamps episode. All the games of mirrors we find in *Juliette* had already been used for equally parodic purposes in Cervantes, sometimes with a subtlety Sade does not seem to care about. In the first part of *Don Quixote*, "The Tale of Foolish Curiosity" is *read* aloud from a handwritten manuscript—a moment of reflexivity that prefaces writing. The reading is interrupted in the middle of a tale of adultery, at a sequence that tells of a feigned wound, a simulated fight, and the announcement of a duel that will not take place. This motif of pretense is immediately taken up in the main story, with the farcical fight against the wineskins that Don Quixote in his sleep takes to be giants fit for the slaughter. Certain passages feature an alternation between action and speech (long dialogues between Don Quixote and Sancho Panza), a model of narrative heterogeneity Sade systematizes into the alternation of orgy and dissertation. The scene of the meal at the host's table, when Don Quixote makes a speech on the relative merits of the scholar and the warrior while the others eat, represents an early version of the Sadean dissertation.

Another parodic technique common to both authors addresses the arbitrariness of narrative logic. The episode of Don Quixote's "madness" deliberately eliminates motivation and underlines the crude psychology of the novels of chivalry. In the first stage, Don Quixote decides to go mad like Roland, but for no reason ("A knight errant who turns mad for a reason deserves neither merit nor thanks" [pt. 1, chap. 25: 203]). He therefore imitates, or rather (to bridge the uncrossable gap between fictional and real) performs all the actions of raving madness and gives himself some substantial clouts in so doing. At a second stage, he takes the opposite point of view and imitates the melancholy madness of Amadis de Gaule, this time claiming that his state is motivated by his distance from Dulcinea (chap. 25). This double strategy is of interest to Sade because it weakens the hold on reality and simultaneously does away with two alternative forms of causality.

Obviously, Sade could have found these same narrative structures in a hundred other novels, but not a reflexivity as developed as in Cervantes, and it is in this respect that I shall now analyze the profound affinities of the two authors. In the tale of Borchamps, a major story within the main story, the flippancy of the comments alerts us to the play of parody in which Borchamps will appear as a figure for the scriptor. As absolute master of the narrative, Borchamps gives his listeners prescriptions (for reading?) that lay bare the workings of the tale—the emphasis placed on the characters' functions and actions, the arbitrariness of their characterization. In a metanarrative declaration, he announces that Clotilde—who has plotted the murder of her whole family—must be fragile and virtuous if she is to play her part as erotic object, and Borchamps establishes these qualifications by a simple decree:

> So, in the eyes of those with whom I speak of her, Clotilde must lose nothing of the primitive character of candor, modesty, and mildness which I give her in this story. Whatever I may have said to her, she never stopped feeling remorse. . . . But let me say this once and for all, so that you may keep it in

mind, regard her only as repentant for as long as the remainder of the facts will oblige me to speak of her. (9: 244, 841)

This metalanguage is more aggressive than anything we find in *Don Quixote*, and brings Sade's text closer to parody.

As for the basic structure of the orgy—the relationship of program and scene—this has an obvious kinship with that of *Don Quixote*. In both cases, the character's actions must mimic a preexisting discourse. Cervantes has his hero express directly the whole issue of the book model that opens the novel's great debate on representation: "When any painter wishes to win fame in his art, he endeavours to copy the pictures of the most excellent painters he knows; and the same rule obtains for all professions" (pt. 1, chap. 25: 202). The critical point in this speech occurs when Don Quixote shifts from his comparison of one painting's imitation of another (and we might say of one book's of another) to the acting out of the work of art, whereby someone would in real life imitate the hero of a novel. This blurring of the distinction between real and representation is not innocent. It both reveals and conceals the speaker's status as literature:

> So what any man who wants a reputation for prudence and patience must do, and does, is to imitate Ulysses, in whose person and labours Homer paints for us a lively picture of prudence and patience. . . . In the same way Amadis was the pole-star, the morning star, the sun of all valiant knights and lovers, and all of us who ride beneath the banner of love and chivalry should imitate him. . . . the knight errant who best copies him will attain most nearly to the perfection of chivalry. (pt. 1, chap. 25: 202).

Unlike the script of *Don Quixote*, that for the Sadean scene is present from the beginning within the book itself, and the scene in its turn will be able to serve the reader as an erotic inspiration. However, Cervantes has done better. Between the first and second part of *Don Quixote*, he transports his book into the real world, only to reintroduce it at the beginning of the second part where it will come to supplant Amadis de Gaule as a model for his hero to imitate.[33] The final pages of *Juliette* are only a pale replica of this *mise en abyme* that foregrounds the reality-fiction relationship by means of two literary models that are equally fictional for the reader.

Finally, we find in Cervantes the example of a speech that turns into reality at the hero's will and thus constitutes, as in Sade, an actualization of desire. The reappearing shaving bowl, which Don Quixote deciphers as the gold helmet of Mambrini, illustrates this power of the word. When its owner, a barber, appears and proclaims its identity as a shaving dish (pt. 1, chaps. 44–46), Don Quixote expresses pity for such an error of interpretation, and, as a game, the other characters echo his words. The effect immediately doubles when an ass's harness is claimed to be a horse's saddle: "Whether it is a pack-saddle or a harness . . . Don Quixote has only to say" (pt. 1, chap. 45: 404). Merely by virtue of being named, the object is what it is willed to be, and, just as Cervantes introduced the external mediation of the book between his hero's desire and his acting it out in pseudo-chivalrous adventures, so Sade introduced the programmatic discourse of the orgy between the phantasy and its execution in the scene.[34] Both assimilate the question of the gap between desire and its realization to the question of the simulacrum of fictional representation. It is true that the attitude of the Sadean scriptor in relation to desire is more ambiguous. He nurses his own phantasy, in which his characters believe scarcely any more than he does, whereas the narrative voice of *Don Quixote*, wholeheartedly taking the side of knowledge, underlines the illusion and condemns it. (Certain interactions between the respective speeches of Don Quixote and of the other characters may weaken this explicit point of view, especially in the second part.) To develop the illusion, the two works both rely on repetition. What the orgy model adds to the chivalry model is precisely its erotic quality. This inscribes the order of desire which is the source of writing. And it problematizes in a different way the real-fiction relationship, since pornographic writing incites the reader to act in the order of the real, that is to say to imitate a literary model, as Don Quixote does. But what reader would wish in his turn to imitate Don Quixote? Apart from this, in both cases we are faced with exploits that are phantasies and, to a considerable degree, impossible.

Yet Barthes is not wrong to argue that, even if Sade did not exactly live his own writings, there is, due allowance being made, a parallel development between his life and his work.[35] Such a hypothesis is inherent not only in the pornographic genre, but in the program-scene relationship and in the introduction of the literary model into the "real world" of fiction.

This raises the issue of the relationship of the referent to the real. It is pertinent to introduce the issue with an allusion to Barthes, since his is the authority most commonly cited when it comes to refusing the Sadean scene any value as representation, or at least minimizing this as far as possible, insisting on its purely linguistic nature.[36] For Philippe Roger, Sade "does harm only to language" and "the Sade effect perhaps is all here: that at first sight, the scandal refers to the referent—monstrousness, cruelty, feelings outside of nature; then one realizes that the real victim is language."[37] No doubt language structures our symbolic universe, but to destabilize language (or, more precisely in Sade, story and discourse) is to destabilize this universe. Sometimes one senses almost a kind of blindness on the part of the critics; for example, Marcel Hénaff considers that "we learn nothing of the victims, of their grimaces, their trembling, their laments, the bursting apart of their flesh, the gradation of their sufferings, the flow of their blood." Several passages in the *Histoire de Juliette* contradict this statement. Hénaff does recognize, however, that "if written blood does not flow, it flows even less when it is not written." This is a way of accepting a certain referential basis for the descriptions of torture, while all the while adopting implicitly the limited point of view of the agents in order to affirm "the symbolic exclusion of horror" in Sade's work.[38]

Although a great part of the orgy scene cannot be put into practice, dismissing its relationship to the real world is a way of neutralizing it. In fact Barthes's position is more moderate than that of his followers. It is even contradictory. Thus, when he writes that "the impossibilities of the referent are turned into the possibilities of the discourse, constraints are lifted . . . it is on the level of the meaning, not of the referent, that we should read him" (pp. 36–37), one might argue in response that meaning itself depends upon the universe of the novel. That is to say, meaning depends upon the world of reference created by Sade and the mental images he conjures up. Hence one cannot take quite literally the way in which Barthes, somewhat playfully it is true, reduces the sites of the erotic body to a grammatical sentence, the orgiastic struggle to figures of rhetoric or to a "pornogrammar" with its "erotemes" and its rules of combination, and their representation to a metalanguage, "language about language."[39] His determination to smooth things over seems more serious, and hence more disputable, when he writes that the tortures form "a monotonous, scarcely terrifying list, since it is most often based on butchery, i.e. on abstraction" (p. 168), for what the abstract term "butchery" stands for, or its referent, is anything but abstract.

What is more, Barthes moves out of the semantic frame he has set up when he goes on: "Among the tortures Sade imagines . . . only one is disturbing: that which consists in sewing the victim's anus or vagina." Even though he goes on to recuperate this torture for meaning,[40] he finds it "disturbing" at first, or at least finds in it a "disturbing" meaning. And, while continuing to espouse a rhetorical position ("Metonymy is the sure path of horror"), he completely abandons this attempt at intellectual detachment when in the next page he writes: "For sewing the victim, a 'large needle with thick red waxed thread' will be used. The more extended the synecdoche, the more the instrument is broken down into its tenuous elements (color, wax), the more the horror grows and communicates itself" (p. 169) without pointing out that this red thread, as a reality effect, gives a referent to the torture. "Sadism," he concludes, "is only the coarse (vulgar) *contents* of the Sadian text." He must be read " '*according to a principle of tact*' " ("un principe de délicatesse" [p. 170], an expression which Sade uses in a letter to his wife to describe perverse phantasies). In fact, the metonymic horror of the red thread breaks down the opposition between "coarse contents" and "principle of tact," and the acuity of Barthes's reading does not free him from a few theoretical contradictions and a certain speciousness. Linguistic reductionism and semantic abstraction do not account for all the effects Barthes discusses, or the many registers of heterogeneity in Sade's work.

We all want to read Sade on the level of meaning, especially because he affects us first of all on the instinctual level. From arousal to nausea, the instinctual shock may vary, but this is no reason for denying its primacy or omitting it in a semantic reading. A kind of self-censorship and defense is perhaps at work in this zeal to de-fuse Sade's text and eliminate its referential implications—a fear of too close an identification with what Barthes calls Sade's "coarse (vulgar) contents," in other words his phantasies of violence, particularly in regard to the maternal body. In the last analysis, Barthes gives us a sanitized, bowdlerized Sade, and the novel has nothing to gain thereby.[41]

If one is willing to give up ascribing the same semantic value to representing the maternal body's dismemberment as to the dismembering of the mother tongue (and in fact this latter hardly ever happens in Sade, who subverts language much less than discourse), then one will have to admit that this universe is a rather good illustration of certain remarks Sade makes in his *Reflections on the Novel*. In this preface, Sade advises authors, on the one hand, not to "move away from verisimilitude" which he conceives of, moreover, in a rather personal way,[42] but on the other to "yield" to the imagination and "embellish," and not be constrained: "We want outbursts from you, flights of fancy rather than rules" (p. 111). "The profound study of the human heart, that veritable maze of nature," he also writes, "alone can inspire the novelist, whose work must show us man, not only as he is, or as he purports to be—that is the task of the historian—

but *as he is capable of being when subjected to the modifying influences of vice and all the jolts of passion"* (p. 106, my italics).[43]

In *Juliette*, Sade returned to the link between imitation and imagination and the path an artist takes in his creation: from reality to artistic imitation to the gaze of the receiver (spectator or reader) to the imagination—memory of real events or projection of a phantasy into the future (9: 23, 613). Without proposing fine distinctions between mimesis and verisimilitude, these remarks associate imitation with the work of the imaginary, and the writing of phantasy with the exploration of the human potential for turpitude, thus conforming to Sade's practice. The proposed path erases as irrelevant the distinction between the imitation—we would say the representation—of the real and that of a memory (or a model), and this brings Sade close to modernity, since it puts phantasy, as represented object, on the same level as the literary model. All his strategies of parodic reflexivity draw attention to the fictional status of representation, but the latter remains inseparable from the experimental function entrusted to the text.

## Simulacrum, Repetition Compulsion, and Death Drive

The incommensurability between doing and saying, and that contradictory demand—to represent the unrepresentable—force the libertine, and the novelist, to repeat (himself). Certain speculations in the *Histoire de Juliette* hint at a theorization of the link among *repetition, simulacrum,* and *death drive.* Sade describes the cycle of life and death in terms that Freud will come astonishingly close to echoing, though he will give such views an apparently scientific cast, reflecting the progress made in genetics. According to the hypothesis of *Beyond the Pleasure Principle,* the individual's tendency to repeat is part of a much more vast movement which would make it one of the manifestations of the death drive.[44] "Everything living dies for *internal* reasons. . . . *The aim of life is death* and, looking backwards . . . *inanimate things existed before living ones.*"[45] The example of the *fort-da* transposes onto the level of the psyche the instinctual tendency which, in the above definition, Freud attributes to a tendency of organic life as a whole:[46] to anticipate the painful and dangerous event in order to control it, to repeat it symbolically in order to take revenge on the person (the mother) who caused it. The recurrence of phantasies of destruction in Sade illustrates the *fort-da* in anticipation of Freud's theory.

According to Sade, who *in his selective manner reproduces* the materialist theories of his century, the return into inorganic matter forms part of a huge cycle of repetition which links a "mutabilist" point of view to the idea that at the origin of life we find the electrical fluid which explains "the soul," and a balance of elements:[47]

> The principle of life, in all beings, is nothing but that of *death*: we receive both principles and nourish them in our bosoms at the same time. At that moment which we call death, everything seems to dissolve. . . . Matter, deprived of the other subtle portion of matter from which it received movement, is, however, not destroyed; it merely changes its form. (9: 174–75, 769–70) Nothing is born, nothing perishes essentially, everything is but action and reaction of matter; . . . it is a perpetual movement that has been and will always be. (9: 177, 772–73)[48]

Jean Deprun stresses the distinction between this notion of mutation and the truly transformist point of view, which is quite foreign to Sade. Nature may indeed "change form" and create new forms, but this "perpetual movement" does not transform the material element itself. Thus it is not surprising that the notion of entropy does not occur in Sade, whose system would obey the formula: nothing is lost, nothing is created.[49] One detail of documentary interest: we can see that Freud is part of that atheist materialist thinking about the cycle of matter which goes back to the eighteenth century and already balances propagation—the Freudian Eros or life instinct—against the return to the inorganic or the death instinct.[50] According to Freud, this double tendency explains the twists and turns an individual life takes before it reverts to inorganic matter. And we recall that, according to Sade, "the principle of life, in all beings, is nothing but that of *death*, we receive both principles and nourish them in our bosoms at the same time."

This materialist profession of faith is all the more striking since Sade, in a parodic gesture of inversion, takes care to put it into the mouth of the pope. The most significant moment comes when an additional connection is made between repetition and simulacrum. Here man is described as a simple "resultative vapour," a creature independent of the laws of nature once the species has come into being, and obeying his own laws:

> This vapour is not created, it is resultative, it is heterogeneous, it draws its existence from a foreign element, and has in itself no price; it can be and can not be, without the element from which it emanates suffering any dimi-

nution; it owes nothing to that element and that element owes nothing to it. . . . The relations of man to nature, or of nature to man, are thus nil. . . . Once he has been launched, man is no longer attached to nature. (9: 171–72, 767–68; see 325, 923)

This passage encapsulates one aspect of Sade's "isolism"—man's independence, in this case from nature once the species has been created, elsewhere from other men, and the denial of any principle of communication.

The passage goes on to link the idea of perpetual movement to that of the return to inorganic matter:

> As soon as he springs forth, man receives direct laws which he cannot flout; these are the laws of his personal conservation . . . of his multiplication, laws which affect but him . . . if he destroys himself, he is wrong, from his own point of view. But in the eyes of nature, all of this changes. If man multiplies, he is wrong, for he takes away from nature the honor of a new phenomenon. . . . If the creatures which have been launched did not propagate, nature would create new beings, and rejoice in a faculty that she has lost. (9: 171–72, 767)

Crime, by accelerating the rhythm of the return to the inorganic state, favors the views of nature, since it can give her back the initiative of a creative gesture.[51]

Sade was profoundly aware of the perverse part of his personality, and this should be put in context with the connection he makes among three very common but not inseparable ideas: the cycle of matter (compulsion to repeat), identity of the principles of life and death (death instinct), and independence of the human species once it has been created. Condemned to repeat his script if he is to master his anxiety and find satisfaction, the pervert acknowledges the death-bearing quality of his repetition—" a perpetual movement, that has been, and will always be." Sade's insistence on repetition and death is no less remarkable than his assertion of independence vis à vis nature, an assertion that links the *hybris* of the pervert to the relativism of the philosopher. This thesis, which Juliette finds so seductive, was not developed in any earlier part of Sade's work, and it occurs only in the second part of the *Histoire de Juliette*. In expounding this thesis, Sade gives an intellectual justification to "anti-nature" inventions and a philosophical expression to the desire for mastery that lies beneath the compulsion to repeat. The latter presides over the incessant return of the orgy, the repetitive structure of the novel, and its cyclical composition. Finally, by making the human being into a "resultative vapor," a "foam," terms that deprive humanity of any substance, Sade brings it close to the fictive space where the orgy unfolds. This aspect of his materialist theory, which is the most personal, is also the one in which phantasy is most tightly entwined with his metaphysical speculation, which he inserts into the universe of simulacrum and repetition.

# 5. Themes and Motifs: Inverting and Diverting Models

Sade repeats himself tirelessly, imitates his models closely, and copies whole pages from other authors without attribution. He is not alone in this, for the notion of literary property was less clearly defined in his time than in ours. Even so he is, as usual, pushing a common practice to extremes.[1] The compulsion to repeat is again at work in his gesture of appropriation. Obviously, intertextuality in his work amounts to more than reminiscence, or collage, or imitation. Sade the novelist takes up the same distanced position as Cervantes the author of *Don Quixote*. Over and again, he mixes repetition with a transgressive inversion of the signifieds. This contrast between conventional forms and subversive content is one of the most constant effects of his text. Furthermore, his use of pastiche is essentially parodic, usually manifesting itself on the level of signifiers by a slight warping, an exaggeration, a dissonance, or some other heterogenous effect which marks his text off from his models while still ostentatiously pointing to them.

Does this mean that I am about to propose a parodic *reading*, or does the parody correspond to Sade's project? In fact such an alternative is false since there is no parody without uncoding. It is true that the many metanarrative processes discussed in chapter four self-consciously inscribe parody into the text, but now we need to come to grips with the fact that the parodic effect is part of a far more ambitious challenge. This in turn must be tied in with the subversive project Sade pursued in the wake of the liquidation operated by *Les Cent-vingt journées*.

From time to time I shall be making use of the terminology proposed by Gérard Genette in *Palimpsestes*. Even though this terminology must sometimes be forced to accommodate Sade's practice, it does facilitate a more refined analysis. Genette makes the distinction between *structural relation*, in the form of either textual transformation, or stylistic imitation (though obviously the transformation of a text may entail the imitation of a style, as in mock-heroic parody), and *regime* (or *function*) which may be ludic, satiric, or serious.[2] One point needs to be made at once: Sade's text offers examples of all these techniques, and this fact might serve as counterpoise to a remark by Genette: "The word *parody* currently gives rise to a very costly confusion, since it has come to mean variously: ludic distortion; or the burlesque transposition of a text; or the satiric imitation of a style" (p. 33).[3] In my opinion it would be even more costly, in the case of Sade, to systematically dissociate these different techniques, since Sade owes his mode of writing to the intertwining of many techniques. These also include collage, the zero degree of imitation that can arise out of the three functional categories Genette distinguishes, as well as generic parody—stylistic imitation, whether as pastiche or caricature—two forms it is difficult to differentiate, as Genette himself remarks (pp. 94–96). In the perspective I am adopting, which is more semantic than formalist, it is irrelevant to separate this technical skein into discrete elements. I shall be guided by the signposts offered by the various discourses that are "parodied" or, more precisely, by Sade's different *hypotexts* (with the *hypertext* being the final, or parodying, text).

Sade's many hypotexts have already been the subject of much remarkable analysis, particularly in the areas of philosophy and politics. Do they deserve another study that, in its turn, cannot be exhaustive? Sometimes readers are unaware of these references, and Sade's modernity is seen as a radical break with the past; at other times, on the contrary, readers interpret them as a sign of Sade's literary conformism and poverty of invention. Without seeking to name all the hypotexts, and without going into detail on how parody functions, I want to give a clear idea of the form of Sade's borrowings, their extent, and their significance for Sade's questioning of the whole social, political, and cultural tradition. I shall now focus on the discourses and themes that are parodied, both generically and individually.

## Fictional Models

In the infinite play of reminiscences, a wealth of filiations can be traced for each motif or situation in the Sadean novel. Let us first consider the main genres or sub-genres that give rise most directly to the *Histoire de Juliette*, and look next at some of the individual models to which motifs, situations, or techniques may refer. Sade's reading was vast; a recent valuable German study gives the most complete list of his readings available to date.[4] The literary judgments contained in *Juliette* and "Reflections on the Novel" offer some intertextual signals that serve to illuminate Sade's practice. In his theoretical remarks, Sade always places the novel in its socio-historical setting. *Reflections on the Novel* offer some intertextual signals that serve to illuminate Sade's practice. In his theoretical remarks, Sade always places the novel in its socio-historical setting. "Reflections on the Novel" attributes the growth in the libertine novel to the atmosphere prevailing in France under the regency of Louis XV, and traces the appearance of the English gothic novel to the "revolutionary shocks all of Europe has suffered" and which fiction could rival only by calling upon "the aid of hell itself."[5] Sade seeks indirectly to situate his own novels, and perhaps justify them, in relation to the French Revolution, but it would be naive to accept his argument and assume so direct a correlation between the English gothic novel and the "revolutionary tremors." This filiation would explain even less Sade's own debt toward the French tradition of the gothic novel, whose importance has been stressed by Jean Fabre.[6] Nonetheless, the social upheaval by which Sade was peculiarly victimized necessarily gave him a new burst of energy to exploit the gothic genre in his own way, as evidenced in the first part of this book.

## GENERIC MODELS

The pornographic novel, the "roman noir" (gothic novel) and the "roman rose" (romance) are the three sub-genres closest to the *Histoire de Juliette* in chronology, themes, and style.[7] Among themselves they maintain relationships of inversion which, as they find their way into the text of *Juliette*, reinforce the inversion techniques of Sadean parody.

Sade's explicit references to the erotic and pornographic novel[8] give some idea of what he sees as his own superiority vis à vis the genre he himself terms "obscene" (8: 442, 461). It all has to do with energy: "Lust, that daughter of opulence and superiority, can only be treated by persons of a certain calibre" (8: 443, 462), he has Juliette remark. He cites four works by name in this passage—*Le Portier des Chartreux*, *l'Académie des dames*, *Le Rideau levé ou l'éducation de Laure*, and *Thérèse philosophe*. The last is the best known of the four,[9] and the only one Juliette sees any merit in: "the charming work by the marquis d'Argens, the only one that shows what we should be aiming for, even though it falls short, the only one pleasurably to link lust to impiety" (8: 443, 462). *Thérèse philosophe* does indeed base its praise of libertine living on the same materialist naturalism as Sade, but it condemns all antisocial conduct and limits the use of violence to a few scenes of flagellation. As for the other works quoted, Sade finds them lacking. The *Portier des Chartreux* falls short of libertinage, in the erotico-philosophic meaning of the term; the *Académie des dames* is technically clumsy; and Mirabeau's *Le Rideau levé ou l'éducation de Laure* is too timid.[10] Juliette comments:

> If the author had come out with the word uxoricide, instead of hinting at it, and incest, which he pussyfoots around but never admits, if he had multiplied the scenes of lust . . . , shown in action the cruel tastes he only suggests in his preface, the work, which is full of imagination, would have become delightful; but such tremblers fill me with despair, and I had a hundred times rather they wrote nothing than give us mere half ideas. (8: 442–43, 462)[11]

This amounts to a justification of the quantitative aesthetic, parodic exaggeration, and libertine moral project in *Juliette*. Sade in fact makes use of all the resources of pornography, with its succession of orgy scenes. He adopts the situations, the psychological vacuousness and cliches of the genre, the sensual delights—always prodigious and almost non-stop—the "bacchantes" and "Messalinas," the "altars" or "temples" of love juxtaposed with obscenities. He is not alone in presenting erotic machines—they abound in Nerciat and had more than a few real life models.[12] In writers before Sade, one can find women who submit to male violence without protest and even with pleasure, as well as a tally of hermaphrodites and "barred" vaginas that bears no relation to statistics. All the same, Sade can be distinguished even from the best practitioners of the genre in that he, more than any other, exaggerates and thus draws attention to the often disavowed link between philosophy and eroticism in the eighteenth century. "The repressed historic connotations of the word (libertine)," writes Jean-Pierre Seguin, "still allow three levels of meaning to emerge in the dictionaries of the years 1680–1750: libertine is that which departs from the moral rule, notably in the order of sexuality; libertine is that which gives evidence of refusing the rules of thought and belief which pertain to the order of religion; finally, libertine is that which betrays a political, social, and behavioral independence; something like a libertarian attitude."[13] Certainly, among the novels that Sade recommends to the reader, *Thérèse philosophe* and the *Education de Laure* illustrate and bring together these three levels of meaning and alternate between scene and dissertation.[14] At the very least, satire of the clergy is to be found in the *Portier des Chartreux*. Yet, even though the Sadean dissertations are so frequent and lengthy that they delay the pornographic effect, they have done more than any other text to ensure the preponderance of this model which survives at times in our own day even in the most vulgar literature.[15]

In Sade's work, the trace of the "roman noir" (gothic novel) is inseparable from that of the "roman rose" (romance) since the one is only the flip side of the other. Similarly the pornographic novel acquires its full significance only in relation to the "roman rose": Nancy Huston has given a good analysis of this phenomenon and the motifs common to both sub-genres.[16] By constructing his novels as reverse images of the moral novel, Sade borrows the strategy of the novel of terror or the pornographic novel, and practices a double imitation, sometimes reversed, sometimes straight, always exaggerated, of the three sub-genres that inspire him. The gothic novel holds a central position in this three-fold lineage because it tends to absorb features characteristic of the other two: the terror, violence, and danger associated with eroticism; innocent, persecuted orphan girls; hidden places, convents, monasteries, and caves; rudimentary or nonexistant psychology; rather lax plots, stereotyped situations, extraordinary happenings. In the gothic novel, the erotic is veiled, the macabre is heightened, and the lack of realism is given a supernatural explanation. The French form of this sub-genre tended early on to feature familial murder, incest, and necrophilia.[17] From this tradition, the only eighteenth-century authors Sade quotes in *Reflections on the Novel* are Prévost and Baculard d'Arnaud — "Both dipped their brushes into the Styx," writes Sade (p. 108) — but he had certainly read many others.

Sade's main structural innovation vis à vis the gothic novel model anticipates the point of view of contemporary horror movies. Sade overturns the traditional focus of the narrative, and uses the point of view of the persecutor not the victim, by means of direct appeals to the reader, such as rhetorical questions. We read from the viewpoint of Juliette and her companions, but the atrocity of their exploits checks the movement of identification that this focus is meant to produce. Such a phenomenon entails a particularly "perverse" form of fetishist, split reading which Barthes commented on ("*I know these are only words, but all the same.*")[18] It is combined with all the degrees of parodic imitation and pastiche, the latter always brief and warped by breaks in the tone which twist it toward parody.[19] Generally, the exaggeration techniques are fairly obvious and the caricature is all the more unmistakable. Let us take as an example Minski's banquet, in which women's backs become tables and their vaginas candle-holders (8: 562, 584), or the macabre dinner organized by Juliette, whose decor juxtaposes noble and vulgar instruments of torture, such as daggers and whips, and in which the exacerbation of the fragmented body serves as a basis for black humor:

> The whole room was hung in black; bones, skulls, silver tears, bundles of rods, daggers, and whips were the trappings on this mournful tapestry; in each niche one of the virgins was being frigged by a tribade, both women naked, lying upon black cushions, with the attributes of death perpendicular to their brows. In the back of each niche could be seen one of the recently severed heads, and near the niches, to the right, was an open coffin, on the left a little round table bearing a pistol, a cup of poison, and a dagger. In a refinement of incredible barbarity. . . . I had ordered that the torsos of the three victims who had just been sacrificed should be sawn up; the only parts of the body that had been retained were the rumps from waist to knees, and the hunks of flesh were hanging from black ribbons at mouth height in each space between the columns in the niches: these were the first things to attract Saint-Fond's attention.—Ah, ah," he said, coming to kiss them, "How pleased I am to see again the asses which have just given me such delight." (8: 322, 333)

The semantic and stylistic unity is constantly broken under the flood of disparate references. Thus supernatural elements contribute to the rhetoric of excess while alluding to the intertext of the gothic novel: for example, Durand's prophecies (which will come true) are uttered in the course of a less than terrifying scenario of magic and lust, with the appearances and disappearances of a sodomite "sylph"[20]; or the fearful proportions of the giant Minski, which allow the tale to outdo itself in crimes and orgies.[21] The pornographic detail per se also entails a certain renewal of the Gothic model: this could be illustrated by a detailed comparison of the examples of sacrilege in Sade and in Lewis's *The Monk*. As for the "drawbacks" of the "roman noir" which Sade refers to in *Reflections on the Novel*, these he sees merely in the return in force of the supernatural in the English gothic novel. He himself had similar problems in *Juliette*: "Either one must explain the wizardry," he notes in "Reflections on the Novel,—"in which case the reader's interest soon flags—or one maintains a veil of secrecy, which leads to a frightful lack of verisimilitude" (p. 109). Obviously, in *Juliette* he opted for the second course, with a casualness which becomes one ingredient in the parodic effect.

The inversion of themes and motifs Sade favors is the most striking aspect of his text. It plays a central role in the parodic organization. No stereotype escapes inversion, nor do any of the beliefs which usually structure the fictional universe.[22] Sade slips multiple dissonances into stereotypic situations. Thus there is the scene in which the orphan Juliette finds her long-lost father—a cliché of the "romance" in particular—but this father is an adulterer, he is reduced to penury, and Juliette has no intention of helping him out. *The Novel of an Orphan Girl* could be the ironic subtitle of the *Histoire de Juliette*. The character of Juliette challenges the stereotype of the young, poor, virtuous, and defenseless orphan girl. Plotting her marriage to a rich and devout gentleman, Juliette expresses scruples quite foreign to her, and invokes her weakness as an orphan to justify the self-interested goal she is pursuing (8: 534, 556).[23] This lays bare the social reality behind "providential" marriages and the pious homilies of the "roman rose," as well as the hypocritical calculations that lurk behind the timidity and modesty of the conventional heroine. Not only characters but also actions are overturned in this way. Juliette is no passive victim, but rather an active heroine. As Nancy Miller remarks, she chooses to "widow and orphan herself" by executing both her natural father and her aristocratic husband.[24]

The whole episode devoted to the seduction and assassination of the long-lost father is handled in the mode of parodic inversion. It satirizes the Rousseauian contrast between town and country, corruption and purity, from the moment Juliette sends a letter to her father inviting him to join her: "The pure country air softens, I feel, that ferocity with which the air in Paris sullies our hearts. . . . Come and visit me in the bosom of nature and you will soon discover all that it inspires in me for you" (8: 450, 470). The anticipation of the rendezvous that will see the parricide consummated gives rise to a lyric effusion that exploits the code of nature only to defy it. ("Nature, that I was to outrage so gravely, had never seemed so beautiful to me; never had I found myself so fair, so fresh, so well.") The style, even the flow, evoke love expectancy, despite a few sinister dissonances:

> It came, that happy day when I was at last to taste the unspeakable charms of a crime which I desperately longed to accomplish. . . . As soon as I arose, I felt in me such lust . . . such malice . . . I was choleric, sulky, capricious, teasing throughout the morning. I whipped two of my women in anger; I spitefully dropped from a window a child that had been entrusted to one of the women, it was killed and I was enchanted. (8: 453, 472–73) [25]

It is Sade's custom to invert completely the stereotype that assimilates nature with the divine. He invokes nature to justify his challenge to the Christian God, for it is "in the eternal laws of nature that crime should triumph and virtue should be humiliated" (9: 213).[26] Annexed in this way to the narrative, this justification for the passions prolongs rather tritely the rationalist naturalism that Sade invokes on most occasions and thus contradicts the far bolder metaphysical speculations the pope engages in later in the novel.

## STEREOTYPED MOTIFS

*Juliette* tirelessly reworks certain motifs, like incest, in such common usage that they cannot be easily attributed to any particular genre. Mario Praz, who carefully studied the forebears and especially the filiation of the Sadean themes, is mistaken when he finds only two prototypes for the motif of the *persecuted beauty* that inspired Sade so much—Richardson's *Clarissa* and the English Gothic novel. The theme is heavy with ideology and belongs both to drama and to fiction—to the novels of chivalry and the classical theater. Another example is the *recognition scene* which Praz sees as one of the "pillars of the novel of terror," and which he relates to Greek romances[27] whereas such scenes are a staple of both novel and theater. Sade has fun piling up four such scenes of recognition in the autobiographical narrative of Borchamps, itself a story within a story. In the fourth of these scenes, the brigand Carle-Son, on finding his long-lost wife, two daughters, and son (all of whom will soon be ferociously liquidated), exclaims: "Captain, this is a day for recognitions: this family is my own" (9: 313, 910). In another example, Durand, whom Juliette "thought she had seen hanging from the ceiling of the room" of the inquisitors in Venice, rises from the dead, and returns at the very end of the novel, in a hilarious scene. As proof of her extreme affection for Juliette, she brings back all the fortune Juliette had been forced to abandon when fleeing Venice. It is easy to see in the tenderness the two infamous women now lavish upon one another a final parodic inversion, moving even further into caricature than the earlier scene when Juliette and Clairwil meet again in the house of Borchamps. The effusiveness expressed on that occasion, if somewhat shorter and less motivated, does not prevent Juliette from subsequently getting rid of Clairwil, in favor of none other than Durand: this might offer a clue to Durand's fate if Juliette were to continue the cycle of her *Histoire*.

It will come as no surprise that Sade takes up the old motif of the *devoured heart* and breathes into it some kinship with the myth of the House of Atreus. In medieval legends, the deceived husband takes revenge on his adulterous wife and her lover by killing him and making her eat his heart.[28] Michelet speaks of "anthropophagic love" in relation to "Coucy's heart devoured by his lady and which she 'found so good, she never ate again in her life.'"[29] Whereas the medieval tradition introduces two characters, the husband who orders the eating and the unwitting wife who does the eating, in the *Histoire de Juliette* Sade combines the two into one. It is no longer a question of adulterous love or revenge, and the drama is played out between father and son. This transformation may represent something unsaid or introduce a hidden kinship between the motif of the eaten heart and the myth of Kronos or Saturn devouring his children. A "young boy of fourteen" has his heart torn out and eaten by the ejaculating Braschi, pope and father of Christendom (9: 207, 803). In the final episode of the novel, when Noirceuil in the same way devours the heart of his youngest son, homosexual incest tightens the patrilinear filiation. In the end, by substituting anthropophagic jouissance for revenge as his characters' motivation, Sade lays bare the archaic origins of the desire for appropriation, the only form of love-hate in his work, while still cleaving to his favorite model, the assimilation of family bonds to sexual bonds.[30]

## INDIVIDUAL MODELS

From the allusions he makes, we can see that Sade looked far and wide to glean details and anecdotes for his gothic plots. Let us now move on from the concept of the generic or anonymous model to that of the individual model, to be set in the general context I have just established. Certain fictional motifs proper to a specific genre can in fact be found in works that transcend generic classifications and which Sade recalled on many occasions.

As we saw in the previous chapter, the underground, but decisive, presence of *Don Quixote* makes it a kind of *Ur*-text for the *Histoire de Juliette*. Equally, critics have already shown how frequently, if not constantly, Sade has *La Nouvelle Héloïse* in mind. He praises the novel warmly in *Reflections on the Novel*, admiring Rousseau's "sublime book" for its "vigor" and "energy," its "fiery soul," and "philosophical mind."[31] No doubt he wished to compete, in his own peculiar way, with such a literary monument, even though he was far from sharing its Christian idealism. Philippe Sollers has commented upon the echo of the names Julie/Juliette, Claire/Clairwil, and to these must be added the mockery of Wolmar/Volmar: Volmar is one of the most seasoned boarders in Delbène's convent, and one of the two hermaphrodites in the *Histoire de Juliette*.[32] Other examples of inversion go much further and rest on the fundamental incompatibility between the systems of Sade and Rousseau.[33] Hénaff notes that the attack on modesty takes the opposite tack, point for point, to Rousseau's thesis in *Emile* in that the origin of modesty is attributed to "a refinement of lust," a "pursuit of debauch" (8: 70–71, 62–63), not to spontaneous nature.[34] The negative intertextuality between Rousseau and Sade often centers on the aristocratic ideology which governs a large part of the Sadean novel, in contrast with the bourgeois ideology of *La Nouvelle Héloïse*: as Joan De Jean says, "the libertines' ostentatious opulence is the opposite of Julie's opulent frugality."[35] Like Rousseau, Sade takes issue with dueling, which is the subject of letter 57 in *La Nouvelle Héloïse*. This condemnation is a topos of the eighteenth-century novel, which perhaps in turn echoes Pascal's seventh *Provinciale*.[36] Sade criticizes the duel not for its inhuman or immoral character, but for its absurdity, arguing that it is less dangerous and more efficient to have one's aggressor murdered. Here Sade merely exaggerates the first argument Julie employs in her attack on the point of honor: "I shall not ask," she writes, "whether you are versed in the art of fencing, or if you feel able to hold your own with a man who is known throughout Europe for his superior swordsmanship," a sign of "bourgeois" concern Sade stretches to the point of caricature in the three successive speeches which form one of the most brilliant sections of the *Histoire de Juliette* (9: 348–52, 945–50). Foucault has already characterized Sade's novel as a "gigantic pastiche of Rousseau." The pastiche is based in the first instance on the "demonstration-by-absurdity," and then on the inversion of a theme beloved both to Rousseau and to contemporary philosophy, the theme of the "links between man and his natural being." We now return to Sade's most fundamental theme: man's independence with respect to nature, and hence "the inanity" of "man's ties to his natural self."[37] Sade develops this point of view largely through parody.

Sade also admired Richardson and Fielding for their vigor and what we would now call their realism. He praises them for their success in pushing their analyses far enough to show man "as he is capable of being when subjected to the modifying influences of vice and the full impact of passion" (p. 106)—exactly the form of verisimilitude which he espouses himself. He also praises the two English novelists for not inevitably making virtue triumph, and posits as an aesthetic rule that the triumph of vice in a novel, by rending our souls, "must inevitably arouse the interest which alone can assure the writer of his laurels" (p. 106). He read *Clarissa* (published in 1748, and translated into French in 1751) in Prévost's translation, as well as *Pamela* and *Sir Charles Grandison*. *Les Prospérités du vice* is an inversion of *Virtue Rewarded*, the subtitle to *Pamela*.[38] The black and calculating character of Lovelace, the hardheartedness and incomprehension of Clarissa's family, the soft-pedaled sado-masochism of the relationship between the two protagonists, were all well designed to stimulate Sade's imagination. The story of Borchamps, in an episode that in fact occurs in London, also contains a direct, if tacit, homage to *Clarissa*, in the form of a transposition of the most famous episode in the novel. To celebrate his marriage, Borchamps decides to "spend his first night nowhere but in a brothel, and there to prostitute his wife's charms to the first comer" (9: 245, 841), a plan he puts into operation after the wedding breakfast. In Richardson, Lovelace installs Clarissa in a place of ill repute for several weeks and finally drugs her in order to rape her, assisted by the brothel-keeper and her acolytes who had hoped to make Clarissa one of their own.[39] Neither Borchamps's wife, nor, at least at the beginning, Clarissa understands where she is. The resemblance stops there. Clarissa is the very model of active and resistant virtue. Borchamps's wife is merely a passive victim. Furthermore, Sade suppresses all motivation and reduces to two paragraphs and to the actions of a single night the power struggle and psychological debate which in Richardson's text is as deep as it is minute, extending over several volumes. We may be sure that Sade's procedure here is quite deliberate,[40] and this new caricature throws a spotlight on Richardson's erotic and sado-masochistic subtext.

The above survey, though far from complete, would be even less so if it did not include the *Pornographe* by Rétif de la Bretonne (1769). This work proposes that prostitution be regulated as a sanitary and philanthropic measure. It may be considered as an anti-model, because of its work ethic, its utilitarianism, its paternalism, its civic spirit, its egalitarianism, and its concern with population growth. Rétif's utopian vision, his taste for organization, the convent-like atmosphere of the brothel he envisions are, indeed, all to be found in Sade too, but in a diametrically opposite spirit.

## Discursive Models

### Christianity and the Scriptures: Ideology, Theology, and Ritual

The treatment meted out to the great commonplaces of Christian morality works as the background for Juliette's entire narrative. The morality of evil rests upon firm "principles" and a fervent "proselytism" (8: 27, 16; 61,

52; 570, 592). The text proceeds to systematically invert the virtues and vices (8: 28, 17; 29, 18). It reverses Christian discourse and rewrites biblical history: the Virgin Mary is a "whore"; her son a "ruffian" (8: 361, 373; 355, 368). It is true that the same insults can be found in the press during the Revolution[41] and in other pornographic works, such as Rétif's *Anti-Justine* (1798)[42] but, in Sade, Catholic rhetoric informs the whole text. Inseparable from semantic deviation,[43] this rhetoric inverts or displaces the themes. Atheism, anticlericalism, and hatred of Catholicism and its ravages, offer a choice stimulant to satiric invention. In fact, we need to distinguish among *several* Christian discourses.

In her remarkable essay "Sade as Theologian," Béatrice Didier has proved how extensive and solid Sade's grounding was in theology.[44] An omnivorous reader who for four years was a pupil of the Jesuit high school, Louis-le-Grand, Sade acquired a deep familiarity with the Scriptures, the texts of the Church Fathers, and the mechanisms of scholastic logic, for example, the *refutatio* (Didier, p. 221), as well as with Tradition, "the other pillar of theology" (p. 224). Last, the *Encyclopédie* is a "rich source of theological learning" (p. 228, n. 2). "The novelistic signifiers in the broadest sense, (vocabulary, argumentation, episodes, narrative schemata)" writes Béatrice Didier, "are largely derived from theological tradition" (p. 236), and she shows how Sade uses theological signifiers but inverts the signifieds; this is indeed the most common technique of parody.[45]

Certain constant elements in Sade's thought, however, even though in a perverted mode, still carry the direct if warped mark of patristic tradition. These references, which are already mutually contradictory, and Sade's treatment of them, produce a curious amalgam. Thus his virulent condemnation of passionate love[46] echoes the strictest prohibitions of medieval Catholicism, which he diverts to egotistic and libertine goals, while preaching the curbing of the passions like the sternest Fathers of the Church. Extending over some fifteen pages, the misogynist diatribe by Belmor,[47] the president of the Society of the Friends of Crime, borrows its flow and rhetoric from the sermon and its themes from medieval theological discourse against women. Georges Duby and others have described this misogyny as an early and uninterrupted current in Catholic thought: the Fathers of the Latin Church inherited the scorn and disgust for the flesh professed by the first century Church, and the latter was influenced by the "strong current that led urban intellectuals in the East to see the universe as a battlefield for the struggle between spirit and matter, and all that was physical as belonging to the kingdom of evil." The masculine perspective to which this tradition belongs, and of which Saint Augustine is only the most famous spokesman, regularly identified the flesh with woman.[48] When we come to the twelfth century, "clerical ideology is at its weightiest in the sermon," which embroiders on the themes of woman's lust and wickedness.[49] In *Juliette* Belmor inveighs against love (but advocates sexual pleasure), using as the basis of his argument, in the best patristic tradition, a degrading picture of the female body and character.

We are closer to real inversion when Sade condemns procreation in the name of an ideal that is both anti-populationist and libertine—"True libertinism abhors progeniture" (8: 406, 423)—whereas in the Middle Ages Catholic doctrine authorized intercourse even in marriage only with a view to perpetuate the species.[50] Saint Augustine, furthermore, does not share Christ's belief in the innocence of little children. He sees in the child, conceived in iniquity, a monster of egoism and wickedness—a point of view that recurs as late as La Bruyère—and posits the notion, shared by Sade, of a humanity born in original sin. It is no exaggeration to speak of a Jansenist vein in Sade, and even to find echoes of Pascal that convey "the erosion of bodies and desire" and that "finitude so often analyzed in theological discourse."[51]

The scenes of bestiality and those, conversely, in which the agents disguise themselves as animals, may, among other allusions, constitute a challenge to the taboos of medieval patristic tradition. The (apocryphal) Epistle of Barnabas, "the writings of many prominent Church Fathers (Clement, Origen, Eusebius, etc.)," the *Physiologus*, and the Bestiaries, which enjoyed immense popularity, all repeated and spread the idea throughout the Middle Ages that for a man to identify with animals is equivalent to his becoming female.[52] This tradition, which was probably known to Sade, perhaps may contribute to overdetermine the scenes of bestiality and animal disguise in *Juliette*, even if the choice of animals is first and foremost an allusion to Nero or Tiberius (9: 499–502, 1102–5). And it enriches the bestiality of the agents with an anti-Christian significance.

There is an even surer and more precise similarity between the Sadean orgy and the tradition of orgy rites in the gnostic sects of the first centuries after Christ, orgies which patristic writing painted in scandalous colors.[53] Mystic practices and perverse practices have a common goal which may explain a commonality of forms—the rupture of limits, which, for mystics, has the meaning of eradicating the barriers between man and God.[54] In the Sadean context, this kinship can turn into mockery of religious ritual. The gnostic sect of the Carpocratians, for example, did not believe in the divinity of Christ (see the article on the Carpocratians in the *Encyclopédie*) and all the gnostic sects supposedly ruled that women be held in common. The gnostics believed in the empire of Evil over the world and advocated opposition to social institutions, including the family, even to the extent of refusing to procreate. Salvation for them ultimately was won by passing through the stages of lust.[55] As Klossowski has noted, there are certain similarities here to Sadean doctrines, even though this does not mean that one can, like Klossowski, attribute to Sade the metaphysical beliefs of the gnostics.[56] On the contrary, in so far as he was aware of the gnostic tradition, Sade twists it just as he does all the others, in both scenes and dissertations. As an adolescent at Louis-le-Grand, or at some other stage in his life, he could not fail to have been interested in the erotic details contained in the patristic accounts and summaries.[57] In the entry on gnostics in the *Encyclopédie*, following the summary of gnostic doctrines, we find the following description:

> Women were held in common among them. . . . They also called their meetings *agapes* at which times, it is said, after eating excesses, they extinguished the lights, and all followed their desires without distinction: nonetheless they strove to limit reproduction as far as possible; they were even accused of aborting women, of grinding up newborn children in mortars, and eating their bloody limbs; of offering an unholy eucharist, and committing various sacrilegious abominations which are described in detail by Saint Epiphanus, who had seen the remains of the sect in Egypt.[58]

It is difficult not to compare this passage with scenes in Sade's novels. We may recall the episodes in *Juliette* when pregnant women are crushed to pieces and ground up, or in *Les Cent-vingt journées de Sodome* when fetuses are eaten (13: 150, 347). Some of these rituals, such as spermaphagia and, of course, cannibalism, can be found in other so-called primitive societies Sade learned about through his readings. Sade introduces these into the orgy ritual, but strips them of any religious, initiatory significance when he states matter-of-factly that sperm and human flesh are consumed to fortify and strengthen the individual.

In most cases however, it is the rites and practices of orthodox Catholicism Sade exploits to develop a formal resemblance whose meaning he then subverts. Many critics have already discussed the monastic organization of the Sadean way of life—division of time, closure, separation, classifications, and nomenclatures[59]—so I need not labor the point. Let me emphasize, however, that it structures the greater part of the narrative and serves as a parodic basis for many episodes. Juliette's admittance to the Society of the Friends of Crime clearly inverts the details of an ordination and also shows traces of baptismal and confirmation rites. Juliette is called up onto a dais, two serving brothers disrobe her, and she answers a series of questions:

> —Do you promise to live eternally in the greatest excesses of debauchery? —I swear it.—Do all lustful actions, even the most execrable, seem to you simple and in nature?—They are all as one in my eyes. . . .—*Is your godmother furnished with the sum you must pay in order to be admitted? Yes.—Are you rich?— Immensely*. . . . Clairwil then immediately placed the agreed sum in the hands of the secretary. (8: 411–13, 429–31, my italics)[60]

Sade does not hold a monopoly on this type of imitation, even if his own has the extra spice of a satire against the mercenary practices of the Church. The ceremonial of secret societies—both political and libertine—was historically modeled on those of the Catholic Church. Sade had probably read the issues or volumes of the *Espion anglais* (*English Spy*), Pidansat de Mairobert's journalistic and anecdotal chronicle. One episode in this work, a little erotic novel, is called "Confession of a young girl and Apology of the anandryne sect, or exhortation to a young tribade by Mlle de Raucourt, pronounced on March 28, 1778."[61] The initiation scenes in the two texts have many details in common: there is a description of the robing of both Sapho, the novice, and her godmother (whom Pidansat calls the "mother"), the postulant is undressed and examined from every angle—Juliette has a charming reaction of modesty at first (8: 411, 429). The content of the vows pronounced is what chiefly differentiates the texts, since in Pidansat the novice promises to "renounce intercourse with men." However, a more significant transformation can also be observed in the form. In *L'Espion anglais* the vows are reported in two lines of indirect speech, whereas in Sade the caricature, in direct speech, is as satirical as it is precise, and the questions and responses, modeled on Catholic liturgy, continue for three pages. Further on, Belmor's vitriolic speech against love and women (8:480–94, 502–16) can be read as a reply to the speech of the woman president of the anandryne sect, which is a lyrical apology for love among women.

Already in this initiation ceremony, the actions as well as the speeches undertake a reversal of meaning. This is also the role played by sacrilege in the scene of debauchery. It both inverts and twists ritual. We need think only of the scenes when the host is profaned, which always happens during a mass. The best known of these scenes occurs on the altar of Saint Peter's, and fulfills the wish Juliette conceived on her arrival in Rome: "Sodomized by the Pope, with the body of Jesus Christ up my ass, oh my friends, what joys!" (9: 206, 802).[62] The sacrilegious orgy organized by Clairwil on Easter Day is just as impious, blasphemous, and depraved (8: 468–69, 489–90), but from the point of view of parody, the most interesting and discordant form of staging involves introducing into the orgy scene the Gospels and, on several occasions, the crucifixion. The parodied model may in fact become an agent in the orgy and present itself in the concrete shape of a New Testament, placed on the back of one of the female auxiliaries. In every case, the Gospel text being parodied dictates the program of the orgy and its enactment functions as the parodying text. Thus the relation typically found in the orgy scene still pertains, that between the spoken script, which here is read by Juliette, and its execution:

> The history of the passion of Mary's bastard is placed upon the naked back of one of the old women: I am charged with reading from it, and directing. The young man who comes in has already been greatly abused; . . . He is nailed to the cross, and he suffers exactly what the wise Romans inflicted upon that base ruffian from Galilee; they pierce his side; they crown him with thorns, give him to drink from a sponge. Seeing that he is still not dead, they decide to improve on the punishment given to the witless mountebank from Judaea: the patient is turned over, and every kind of horror imaginable is executed upon his buttocks. (8: 355–56, 368)

This example brings out the structural kinship of parody and the Sadean orgy. Both take as their starting point a textual model, whether it be the transgressive program of the orgy or the text to be transgressed by parody. And whereas originally this model is external (hypotext) for parody and internal (the program) for the orgy, the narration tends to transform the thing parodied into an internal model through implicit quotation. By making the hypotext the script for the orgy, the parodic procedure blends with the very purpose of the orgy.

In the case of a known and respected text, the programming speech is telescoped together with the scene merely by some allusions: the model of the crucifixion reappears in the episode of the madhouse, which offers a peculiarly original variation on repetition and theatrical play. The three madmen think they are God, the Virgin Mary, and Christ, and, as Vespoli remarks in an enthusiastic oxymoron, a true paradigm of parodic inversion: "The whole of paradise is in this hell!" The Christ character reveals his illusion in his words, which the situation serves only to deride:

—Courage, brave Romans," cried the victim, "have I not always told you that I came to earth only to suffer; do not spare me, I beg you; I know that I must die on the cross; but I shall have saved the human race. (9: 386, 984)

No commentary intervenes to underline how bitterly the agents' actions give the lie to these words. The last suffering of Christ and of the two other victims, God and the Virgin, tied to his right and his left, peculiarly distorts the crucifixion of Christ between the two thieves. It substitutes for the Catholic Trinity another closer to the human family, as the two thieves are replaced by God and the Virgin Mary.[63]

The parody of the New Testament scenes is part of an ancient tradition of turning the world upside down which was certainly familiar to Sade. One version of the *Coena Cypriani*, in particular, probably circulated in the Jesuit schools and contributed to the amusement of the students. A new version of it has recently been given by Umberto Eco in some brilliant pages of *The Name of the Rose*.[64] Bakhtin retraced the main features of the tradition in one chapter of his *Rabelais*.[65] Like Sade, it relies on the inversion or subversion of New Testament episodes to create violence and disrespect, in scenes that might appear scandalous were it not for the spirit that inspires them—a spirit diametrically opposed to that of Sade; joy in living, carnivalesque freedom, and, finally, acceptance of the world as it is and of death as one stage in the cycle of life. Like the initiation ceremonies, these literary references introduce one more intertextual link so that Sade distorts both the Scriptures and the already parodic texts of the medieval tradition.

Béatrice Didier has made a careful study of Sade's metaphysics.[66] Let me simply add here that the metaphysical angst of Saint-Fond, who clings to the idea of a God of evil, sets off two types of parodic techniques, the first of which directly affects Saint-Fond's speech, the second his actions, as these are described in the course of his own long dissertation. In an inflamed prosopopeia, a remarkable pastiche of pulpit oratory, Saint-Fond lends his God of evil, whom he alone among the characters believes in, the rhetoric and clichés of the sermon or moral address:

Once you realized that everything on earth is vicious and criminal, the Being Supreme in wickedness will say to them, why did you wander into the paths of righteousness? . . . Did I not serve as an example of destruction to you every day? Why did you destroy nothing? Those plagues with which I crushed the world, while proving to you that *evil* was all my joy, were they not designed to enroll you in serving my plans for *evil*? . . . Imbecile! why did you not imitate me? Why did you resist those passions which I had placed in you only to prove to you how much *evil* was *necessary*? Your duty was to follow their organ, ruthlessly despoil the widow and orphan as I do, deprive the poor man of his inheritance, and, in a word, make men serve all your needs. (8: 386, 399, Sade's italics)

Saint-Fond is in despair at the idea that his victims, "goodified" by the tortures he inflicts upon them, will be happy in the next world; he solves this problem by means of a weird extravaganza which at the same time constitutes a wholly novel way of appropriating the other. "A great alchemist" has told him that, to prolong the victim's sufferings "beyond the immensity of the centuries," he needed,

> with blood drawn from his heart, to have the victim sign a note stating that he gave his soul to the devil, then to thrust this note up his ass with his cock, and at the very same moment to make the victim suffer the worst pain it is in our power to inflict. Never, with these measures, . . . will the individual you destroy enter into heaven. (8: 356–57, 369–70)

This infallible recipe would allow the agent to achieve that ultimate degree of crime in perpetuity which he dreams of, for the victim's sufferings,

> of the same nature as those you make him endure while thrusting the note inside him, will be everlasting; and you will savor the delectable pleasure of having prolonged them even beyond the limits of eternity, if eternity could have any limits. (8: 356–57, 369–70)

This hypothesis of a God of evil is not on the same level as the system developed by the pope much later in *Juliette*. It is based on only one mode of reasoning—the absurd: if God exists, it must be a God of evil. This inverts Rousseau's conception of a nature and a God of goodness. It makes mockery of the Christian dogma of eternal punishment, by laying bare the perverse component of that dogma. Even without the lengthy refutations of Juliette and Clairwil (8: 357–82, 370–94), even without the mass of professions of atheist materialism in which the writer expresses himself directly, the Rabelaisian comedy of Saint-Fond's recipe, which is close to farce, casts considerable doubt upon Sade's protestations of deism and should have prevented his more zealous readers from giving them too much weight.[67]

## GRECO-ROMAN ANTIQUITY

The examples Juliette cites from Antiquity do not always need to be subverted. Thus Mario Praz is perhaps right when he states that the thesis whereby nature devotes itself to perpetual destruction in order to be able to create is "the extreme extension of Empedocles's teachings, according to which struggle is not only a principle of destruction but also the origin of everything, except the Unique."[68] The same is true of the old belief in the superiority of woman's violence when associated with her homosexuality, an idea that goes back to the myth of Dionysus in which "women are the ones who . . . set the ritual violence in motion."[69] Sade himself refers to the models of horror contained in the archives of the convents of Syracuse (9: 411, 1011) (or to Bluebeard, 8: 335, 347). The episode engineered by Ferdinand of Naples, when a platform collapses crushing more than four hundred persons, reappears in *Isabelle de Bavière* under the aegis of Nero.[70] Sade possessed a copy of Suetonius's *The Twelve Caesars*[71] and he may have found there some of his orgy situations, such as the legend of Nero dissecting his mother's body, which is also found in medieval texts; Clairwil makes do with an enthusiastic paean of Nero's matricide (9: 357, 954). Again according to Suetonius, Tiberius "popularized" chains of human beings joined together sexually in front and behind,[72] and Nero, "dressed in the skin of a wild beast . . . leaped out of a cage, hurled himself on the natural parts of men and women tied up to posts, then having assuaged his lust, ended by giving himself to his freeman servant Doryphorus."[73] We need only think of the chains of people in Sade, of the passages in which the characters invoke the example of Nero, or the scene in which an episodic character, dressed in a tiger skin "whose four paws were armed with huge talons and whose muzzle was so arranged as to permit him to bite anything within reach" (9: 501, 1104), performs acts of cannibalism, while imitating with his mistress the howling of a mastiff. Feeding the crescendo of the second half of *Juliette* are scenes of bestiality,[74] and others in which victims are thrown to hungry beasts.

Sade uses similar distortion techniques for Plato. It is difficult to know whether Sade ever read Plato, and quite likely he did not, but he clearly had some second hand knowledge of him.[75] The *Encyclopédie* (in the person of Diderot) devotes entries to "the *Republic*," "Plato, the Platonics and the Aristotelians," and "Platonism or the philosophy of Plato." However, these entries probably did not inspire Sade to create his utopia in which all women and children are held in common, since they make no mention of this aspect of the *Republic*. Nonetheless, the similarities between Sade and Plato in this regard are fairly precise. In one passage, Sade takes up a double argument already advanced by Plato, to the effect that a wider sense of solidarity and a total fraternity would be achieved if all the women and children were shared.[76] At first sight, this passage seems in no way parodic, Sade does not overturn Plato's argument, and indeed makes the same additional point that such a situation would have the advantage of eliminating wars and rivalries. But this passage is part of a much longer dissertation which subverts the Platonic thesis. Plato recommends that all material goods be held in common, uses eugenic, moral, and civic considerations to organize his collective unions and births, and proposes certain rules aimed to eliminate or avoid the risks of incest. Sade, in the remainder of the speech, denounces the belief in love, praises adultery and sexual chaos, boasts of the lack of responsibility that accompanies paternal anonymity, and advocates the generalized incest that must result from the anarchic sharing of women and children.[77]

In the *Symposium*, the superiority that Plato grants to homosexuality is based upon the moral and spiritual progress which male love alone permits, and which is equal to a gain in "masculinity," whereas the love of women can only feminize men. In Sade, this concept, which in essence is based on sexual elitism,[78] is transformed into social elitism and becomes indistinguishable from aristocratic prejudice. The great characters barely distinguish between their social superiority and the homosexual superiority they take pride in. On the other hand, Sade's dissertations take up and invert the role played by speech in the *Symposium*, which is itself the origin of the tradition of table talk. This kind of speaking, writes Florence Dupont, "rescues the drinker . . . from despair when a voluntary limit is placed on his desire, by offering his body a sort of extension into the infinite of language."[79] This is indeed one of the roles of the Sadean dissertation, which surely reminds us of certain expository passages in the Platonic dialogue. Nonetheless, the Sadean character assigns speech an erogenous function so that, in the end, it serves him only as a *means* of returning to the body and sends the body back to the finitude of libertine pleasures.

Instead of hunting though the Greco-Roman tradition for models of virtue, as was traditional in pedagogic works right into the twentieth century, Sade searches for models of vice:

> Take your authority from the ancients, Juliette; yours is a cultivated spirit: call your readings to mind. Remember the Emperor Licinius who, on pain of the severest punishment, forbade any compassion for the poor and any kind of assistance to the indigent. (8: 271, 283)

This is a mocking echo of revolutionary discourse in which the evocation of classical heroism was a commonplace. Moreover, on the one hand Sade locks step with Voltaire and Gibbon in making Christianity responsible for the decline of Rome while,[80] on the other, Juliette advocates Roman decadence and its crimes and finds herself at home in the decadence of Italy where she sees an "opportunity for power and freedom."[81] Classic resoluteness becomes a ferocity devoted to Evil.

Sade denatured the original sense of the stoics' theory of *apatheia* to such an extent that it is now usual to give it the qualification of "Sadean" in his work.[82] Apathy occupies a central place in his libertine system, and the customary techniques of semantic subversion and reversal are applied. For the stoics, apathy is a final stage of detachment from the passions, whereas for Sade's agents it is an ascesis into crime and lust whose purpose is to increase sexual pleasure by "blunting" "sensitivity," that is, sensation and sentiment. Delbène, Clairwil, and Juliette harp insistently on the need for this physical and mental discipline and on the means to achieve it.[83] The masturbatory stage in Juliette's "recipe," during which the hand must be "at the orders of the head and not the temperament" offers one example (9: 48, 640). In the final analysis, Sadean apathy is a technique of the body intended to produce a positive reinforcement of sexual pleasure, and it implies mental mastery, stiffening of the will, refusal of sentiment, in a word, an ascesis:

> I was so strengthened in my views, my mind was so much in control of my body . . . that I was able, without feeling any arousal, to hold her naked in my bed for ten hours, and frig her . . . without my head becoming in the slightest degree heated. And that, permit me to say, is one of the happiest fruits of *stoicism*. By *steeling our souls* against anything that might move it, by familiarizing it with crime through libertinism, by allowing it only the pleasure of the physical, and stubbornly refusing it any delicacy, we enervate it; and from that state in which the soul's natural activity does not allow it long to remain, it passes into a kind of *apathy* which soon is metamorphosed into pleasures a thousand times more divine than those supplied it by weakness; for the fuck I lost with Alexandrine, although it was owed entirely to *this resoluteness* which I am describing to you, procured me far more lively pleasures than those which would have resulted from the enthusiasm or sad ardor of love. (8: 463–64, 484, my italics)

This *stoicism* and this *apathy* are in no way passive and describe a concentration of the will which, although mastering the physical, must in the end lead to physical satisfaction, while disciplining "natural" movement. Such passages (and there are many of them) may remind us—by antiphrasis—of the Descartes of the *Treatise on the Passions of the Soul*. The rule of Sade's apathy, which merely maximizes the rule of libertinage, seems to offer a verbal permutation of article 2 of the *Treatise*—"That to know the passions of the soul, one must distinguish its functions from those of the body," which in Sade becomes: "That to know the passions of the body, one must distinguish its functions from those of the soul." To serve the body, one must first tame it. As always, the head is committed to the service of the body.[84]

## THE REVOLUTION: DISCOURSE AND SYMBOLISM

We have already placed the *Histoire de Juliette* in the context of the violence and uncertainty of the revolutionary years, not that these are causes but rather an everpresent backdrop. Sade's imaginary was not transformed during this period, but it was affected by the revolutionary imaginary. His experience during the Revolution provided him with a new text to imitate/parody, and it is no exaggeration to say that this experience informed not only his political thinking but also certain aspects of his novels' plots, as well as their modes and themes of representation and discourse. One might even say that, of all the models which intersect in Sade's work, the revolutionary model acts as a catalyst because it has such complex origins.

If Sade parodied this model, it was probably not just because of his ambivalence toward the new regime. It was also because he was one of the first to have seized on the fact that, alongside its deliberate parody of Catholicism, revolutionary discourse is shot through with a vein of unconscious parody, notably of classic models. This makes it a choice target for burlesque imitation. In the nineteenth century, Quinet, de Tocqueville, and Marx—all of whom, like Sade, despise the polloi and the bourgeoisie—will reveal "a rising consciousness of politics as parody" and will point to this involuntary tendency in the revolutionary spectacle.[85] Seeking new models of representation, the Revolution necessarily wavered between invention and imitation. Even when serious, its imitations still contained a hidden potential for parody. The Sadean novel, in the 1790s, shares with revolutionary discourse such traits as Ciceronian eloquence, heartfelt cliches, tableaux vivants, *hybris* in confronting dangers from inside and outside, an inordinate development of dissertations/harangues after *La Nouvelle Justine* (or even after *La Philosophie dans le boudoir* if one classifies the extraordinarily long "Yet another effort, Frenchmen" as a Sadean dissertation).[86] Some new dramatic canvases are also connected with the

Revolutionary moment: the deployment of the parricide motif in *Juliette* and, both in that novel and in "Yet Another Effort, Frenchmen," the thesis that the state owns children.[87] Hardly if any of these elements appear in *Les Cent-vingt journées de Sodome*. Once developed, they amplify the dimension of parody without necessarily exaggerating the features of the model. When distanced from the fever, anguish, and conviction that sustained it during the Revolution, revolutionary discourse may strike us as naively bathetic and full of trite techniques. Like Sade's own discourse, it risks being read as a caricature. This continuity between the two texts, added to the ambiguity of Sade's republican convictions, is no doubt largely to blame for the many diverse interpretations to which his political musings have given rise.[88]

Thus in *Juliette* we find a hypertext with a dual or even triple foundation, a parody of an involuntary parody, something that indistinguishably mixes serious imitation, mockery, and automatism. There is no doubt at all that Sade was soaked in revolutionary rhetoric. As an active member of the Section of the Pikes and even above and beyond his official duties, Sade composed so many orthodox speeches, laden with the pieties of the moment, that he may have been in part sincere. Was he already at this point working as a parodist? How are we to decide between belief and mimicry?

In Sade's work, the number of acts of treachery and false denunciations increases, starting with *La Nouvelle Justine* and even more in the *Histoire de Juliette*. It is possible that these novels are alluding to historic and autobiographic events which seem right out of the tradition of the gothic novel. Among such historic referents we may count the republican obsession with plots (by the aristocracy) and conspiracies, and the resulting denunciations and executions. François Furet sees this obsession as a "central and polymorphous notion" in revolutionary ideology.[89] He attributes it not only to the threat of counterrevolution but to an ancient popular mentality, linked to oral transmission of information, hence to imprecision, and to the long experience of famine and hence to the belief in treasures, and, especially, hidden grain supplies.[90] Lynn Hunt for her part offers a very interesting theoretical explanation for this obsession with plots: the fact that, for the French revolutionaries, there was no real transition between "the political constraints of the Ancien Régime" and "the limitless opportunities to participate" in political life afforded by the new regime, whence the inability of the Conventionals to envision the function and value of the party system and their deep mistrust for anything resembling one. As Hunt explains, what was at first a reaction to the fear of the traffic in prices and the maneuvres of the nobility soon became an obsession which affected every aspect of political life, so that the practice of denunciation came to be considered "the infallible sign of vigilance at work."[91]

The autobiographical referents of this obsession with plotting in *Juliette* are perhaps even more decisive, since Sade went through extraordinary personal vicissitudes during the Revolution. After thirteen years of uninterrupted imprisonment (to say nothing of the short periods in prison before that) and faced with the constant threat posed to the life of any citizen by the daily denunciations, Sade must have been a prey to ceaseless anxiety throughout his years of newfound freedom. He was an aristocrat, and his two sons had emigrated. He himself kept reiterating his republican professions of faith. He was named secretary for his Section just before the massacres of 1792, which, as his correspondence attests, filled him with horror. After these massacres, his castle at La Coste was overrun, pillaged, and destroyed by the village people. Louis XVI was condemned to death at the end of December, and executed a month later. The Terror took hold. In July 1793, thanks to his republican zeal and his very real civic activity, Sade became the president of his Section. The Terror grew worse and after the month of August, in order to keep from a voice vote some unspecified proposal—"a horror, an inhumanity," he writes in a private letter[92]—he resigned and became vice-president. Suddenly, in December 1793, Sade was arrested following a denunciation,[93] accused of having volunteered two years earlier to serve in the king's *constitutional guard*. He appealed to his section, which, far from giving him support, left him high and dry and issued a report that criticized him for a lack of revolutionary fervor and sham patriotism. Seven months later a requisition was drawn up by Fouquier-Tinville against Sade and twenty-seven other prisoners— the equivalent of a death sentence. Sade, meanwhile, had no knowledge of this. He escaped the guillotine by twenty-four hours, thanks to the chaos of the lists and the overpopulation of the prisons.[94] The tribunal official who came to find him was unaware that Sade had been transferred four months earlier to the Picpus prison. That was on the ninth of Thermidor, the day of Robespierre's downfall. Another three months passed before Sade could obtain his freedom. The malicious denunciations of *Les Cent-vingt journées* are as nothing in comparison to such twists and turns of fate, which find a fitting counterpart only in the serial acts of treachery in the *Histoire de Juliette*.

Similarly, beheadings are extremely rare in *Les Cent-vingt journées*, probably because this manner of execution is too swift to offer any satisfaction.[95] However, toward the end of *La Nouvelle Justine*, a punitive beheading does occur, strangely mixing real memories with very Sadean embellishments. In June 1794 the guillotine had been moved to the Trône toll-gate, a few hundred yards from the Picpus prison (where Sade was at the time), a former convent in whose garden an open pit had been dug out.[96] Lely tells us that, in order to collect the victims' blood, "a lead-lined coffer [had been placed] under the scaffold, on top of a two-wheeled barrow" (p. 418). The coffer was then taken and emptied into the pit. This very coffer reappears in *La Nouvelle Justine* in the shape of a "round basin" designed to catch the victims' blood and out of which "reared a small scaffold upon which was placed a machine sufficiently remarkable to merit a description" (7: 353, 360, \*\*\*\*). Needless to say, this machine bears more than a fleeting resemblance to a guillotine.

Plots, betrayals, denunciations, beheadings: these fictional motifs and Sadean phantasies are linked with the reality and the imaginary of the Revolution. There is a no less certain convergence between the symbolic modes, and even the themes, of representation in Sade's works and those of the festivals of the Revolution. The revolutionaries either parodied Catholic ritual (as in the cult of the goddess Reason) or else they imitated it seriously (as in the festival of the Supreme Being). Such imitation becomes very common in *Juliette*, without ever ceasing to be burlesque or grotesque. The revolutionaries parody the form of the Catholic catechism, in the first place with anticlerical satire in mind (as, for example, the *Catechism of Liberty* by *Père Duchesne*) and then use it seriously for pedagogic purposes to spread the revolutionary ideal, publishing a *Catechism of the Democrats* with questions and answers.[97] This complicates even further the play of references in the scene of Juliette's admittance to the Society of the Friends of Crime, with its sequence of questions and answers. Let us pause for a moment to consider another comparison, which will lead directly to the satire of judiciary practices: the performances of tableaux vivants and sketches. In this genre rooted in oral tradition we can clearly see at this period a hatred for the institutions of the past, as well as the violence and crudity of the symbol. The theatrical structuring of *Les Cent-vingt journées* is not related to this type of sketch, but at the end of *La Nouvelle Justine* and in *Juliette* Sade does extensive parodies of summary justice, followed by execution. After 1791, revolutionary sketches were performed in which the pope,[98] and later Louis XVI, were burned in effigy. (This is the very pope Pius VI—Braschi—who is glorified in *Juliette* for his atheism and cruelty.) In Grenoble, at the time of the festival of January 21, 1794, the first anniversary of Louis XVI's execution, "on a platform sat a mannikin representing Louis Capet (with a crown and the horns of a cuckold). On his right sat the 'so-called' pope and on his left a figure representing the nobility. When the crowd gathered in the square cried out for vengeance, two 'French Hercules' appeared from behind the dummies to finish them off with clubs" while the crowd first screamed insults and then trampled the dummies to the ground and dragged them through the mud.[99] One is reminded of the insults the Sadean agents direct at their wholly helpless victims. And although in *Les Cent-vingt journées* there are many scenes of punitive correction, yet to find the equivalent of the revolutionary sketch we have to wait until *La Nouvelle Justine* and *Juliette*—the trial and condemnation of Justine 7: 403–4, ****), the Dorval episode (8: 128, 126), the interrogation and expulsion of Juliette by the Venetian inquisitors, with no other form of trial (9: 545–46, 1151–52).

When this type of tableau is a prelude to orgy, it offers a variation on the program-scene relation. And it always contributes to the oral pluralism of the novel, especially when accompanied by the ritual exchange of insults.[100] Marie-Hélène Huet has stressed the priority given to the spoken word in revolutionary justice, which claimed to be the justice of the people: the transcript of the proceedings came only after the interrogation and public proclamation of the verdict. This open way of doing justice, she writes, was conceived as an "anti-lettre de cachet" in that the lettre de cachet was a written order executed in the "muffled silence of absolutism."[101] Sade had experience of both forms of justice, and seems to dismiss each of them with a few strokes of the pen.[102]

Revolutionary speechmaking used two forms of rhetoric, both, according to Quinet, equally alienated from the people: the judicial eloquence of Robespierre and Saint-Just who imitated classical rhetoric (Sade was trained in the same, "the pomp of Cicero and the majesty of Tacitus"), and, in a certain kind of press, the eloquence of the obscene, a parody of plebeian language, "tatters from the theatre, sewn together with the rags of the sans-culottes!"[103] If one takes *Le Père Duchesne* as an example of the second form, one sees that this contrast is too stark: in certain pages of *Le Père Duchesne*, Hébert and his collaborators perfected a mixture of the obscene with the noble style, as Béatrice Didier has demonstrated in detail in a recent essay[104]—a mixture which, with its off-key comic effects, is one of the distinctive marks of Sadean discourse. Furthermore, the obscene language and the parody of Catholic ritual find a counterpart not only in the political press of the left, but also and early on in that of the right (for example, in *Acts of the Apostles*, and in the *Private Life of Blondy Lafayette, General of the Cornflowers*, or *Jacobite Sabbaths*).[105] The attacks on Marie-Antoinette mounted by *Père Duchesne* and other pamphleteers bring together two misogynist traditions, one clerical and one popular. "The Austrian tigress was regarded in all the courts of Europe as the most wretched *prostitute* in France. She was openly accused of *wallowing* in the *mud* with menservants, and no one was quite sure which scurvy fellow had produced the crippled, hunchbacked, gangrenous *freaks* that issued from her *wrinkled, three-story womb*" (written by *le Père Duchesne*, with the original italics).[106] This has both the style and spirit of Belmor's diatribe. Anti-monarchist patriotism gave new life to the ancient discourse of misogyny, whose phantasies had already been crystallizing for ten or more years around the real or supposed sexuality of Marie-Antoinette.[107]

Besides this source of models which was available to all,[108] Sade makes some specific borrowings from the titles and phrases of the Revolution. The name of the Society of the Friends of Crime is modeled upon that of "Societies of the Friends of the Constitution, better known as the Jacobins."[109] Or, better, the title of "Yet Another Effort, Frenchmen, If You Would Become Republicans" curiously echoes a text of the *Commission temporaire de la surveillance républicaine établie à ville affranchie (Lyon)* (*Temporary Commission for Republican Supervision established at Lyon, Freed City*) which dates from November 1793: "To be truly Republican, each citizen must experience and bring about in himself a revolution equal to the one which has changed the face of France."[110] No doubt Sade's title was parodying a very common kind of rhetoric, and his pamphlet caricatures republican morality, from which he draws a scandalous subtext and where he underlines several contradictions.[111] As Lefort has noted, "Sade exploits philosophico-revolutionary discourse in order to draw certain conclusions which destroy the principles upon which that discourse is based."[112]

This revolutionary model of discourse, and its rhetoric, can be found particularly in the dissertation or the harangue. In the harangue, we have more a plethora than a dearth of generic influences but nonetheless its bombast and insistent pedagogical intent, to say nothing of its prodigious length, are exactly those of the discourse of the Revolution. Pedagogical concerns are apparent in the "catechisms," in *Le Père Duchesne*, and in the oratory eloquence of the period, and they also seep into the theater—it would be interesting to compare Sade's dramatic works before and after the Revolution from this angle. Even for his fiction, the comparison is revealing. Judith Schlanger has emphasized the link which revolutionary drama makes between "an aesthetic of amplification and explicitness" and the "pedagogy of the imprint or the direct transitive mark. The pedagogy as well as the aesthetic share a belief in the effectiveness of expressing 'good sentiments' in the person of a spokesman." [113] If we substitute "evil sentiments" for "good sentiments," we can see that Sade shares the same assumptions, which he derives straight from classical didacticism and which he puts into practice most vigorously after 1789: belief in the value of the exemplum, direct exhortation, the quantitative aesthetic of bombast and repetition. On one point, however, the Sadean novel wholly departs from this rhetorical model. In revolutionary drama "the spectator finds himself placed, vis à vis the spectacle, in a state of 'abject contiguity' (Blanchot)" and is not allowed to experience "the possibility of an interval, of a return for reflexion, of a reinterpretation." [114] In Sade's novel, on the contrary, the constant provocation of what is said and done, unthinkable to the same degree on a public stage, and the self-consciousness of the narrative invite the reader to take his distance in a way quite alien to the drama of the Revolutionary era. [115]

All the various analyses in this chapter have showed that the Sadean hypertext extends in all directions beyond the notion of parody taken in its narrow sense but that, on the other hand, the text is never wholly lacking in a parodic dimension; and that, furthermore, whatever its hypotext or hypotexts may be, the hypertext always effects the same kind of distortion by twisting the signifieds toward a goal quite other than that of the model. Hence the inimitable tone of Sade's work.

Talking about Sade, Lacan refers to a "technique oriented toward a sexual jouissance that is not sublimated," and notes that "the things involved are commonly found in the works of Suetonius, Dion Cassius, and others. Read the *Mémoires sur les Grands Jours d'Auvergne* [*Memoirs on the Great Days of Auvergne*] by Esprit Fléchier, if you want to learn what a great lord at the beginning of the seventeenth century could get away with with his peasants." [116] Sadean cruelty imitates or invokes ancient chronicles, literary models, and the dominant discourse, all of which raises the issue of invention, and of the relation between phantasy and intertext. Sade does not wholly invent the form of the tortures, nor the alternation between scene and dissertation, much less the other narrative structures of *Juliette*. And yet he is unique. His inventiveness, per se, resides in the different strategies for subverting and distancing: notably parody, in the detail of the story, and, even more, of the perverse script, the staging of the phantasy. Phantasy is in no way incompatible with the literary allusions which

Sade absorbs, assimilates, and makes his own. This can be seen in a passage that comes close to dream narrative. After various tortures, the agents decide to throw the wife and daughters of Carle-Son to the wild beasts. They cut the women's tongues and tear out their eyes, in a situation which is not lacking in literary antecedents:

> This is all proceeding nicely," I said to him, "but won't those bitches be able to bite the tawny owls that are coming to devour them?"—Very likely."—We shall have to break their teeth." A stone serves us for this, and since we have no wish to spoil them any more, so that they can better feel the torments that the vicious beasts of this island will inflict as they devour them, we move away. A hundred paces further on, we climbed a little hillock from which we could get a better view of them. The owls, the bats, all the vicious animals of that island had already taken hold of them: all that there was to be seen now was a *dark mass*. (9: 311, 908, italics mine) [117]

Other scenes mix the burlesque with the horrible. The one just quoted conjures up the archaic phantasies of the fairy tale. Images of the phallic and devouring mother, owls and bats seem to rise out of the nightmares of childhood and meet up in the "dark mass" of the maternal abject. Such scenes are (relatively) impossible, yet such passages differ from the traditional annals of cruelty in their oneiric quality and the incongruous mixing of species, which obeys not the rules of zoology but the homophony of the signifiers.

Whether it is a matter of his imaginary or his intellectual strategy, Sade's gesture, dictated by the hypertrophy of the ego, always consists in swallowing, twisting, appropriating whatever comes to hand. All is grist to his mill. If in *Justine* and *Juliette* his ludic and grating *bricolage* with texts [118] remains, and must remain, very obvious, and thus of a parodic nature, this is because Sade has chosen parody as his favorite weapon against the whole cultural legacy—and, if the blade is to strike home, the target has to be exposed. On an even deeper level, this bricolage fits his way of thinking— thinking against. Pauvert quotes several times this sentence from one of Sade's letters: "It is not the way I think that has been my misfortune, but the way others think," a sentence that implies the writing subject's need for endless slippages in reasoning and continual evasions as a way of parrying the many different attacks upon him. It is these fluctuations in the positioning of the subject that we shall study in the last two chapters.

# 6. Voicing the Hybrid

It is no easy task to find one's way among the irreducible dissonances that resonate all along Sade's narration. The modes of the heterogeneous and of repetition together infiltrate different levels of the text, but enunciation is the most fundamental of these since it is here one recognizes the voices of the speaker or scriptor. Although his characters lack interiority, Sade creates many different voices, many different linguistic registers and forms of discourse and many contradictions of meaning. All of these are intricately intertwined; we need to disentangle them one by one if we are to understand their principal articulations. At times they appear to derive from, and at other times to be homologous with, a structure of doubling that from the outset lays out the problem of the Sadean subjectivity.

## The Division of the Subject

The use of a first person narrator in the *Histoire de Juliette* raises a twofold question: that of narrative voices, and that of the subject and subjectivity. I shall address the second of these first. As a general rule, a first person narrative can have two opposite effects. It can either create the fiction of an "I" that links the self of the past to the self of the present without any logical or temporal rupture, or it can highlight the distinction between the I of the story being told (the "I-self" of the past) and the I of the enunciation (the "I-self" who is speaking or writing), and through this distinction reveal the discontinuity, the transformations or the bad faith of one "I-self" or the other. Sade's novel illustrates both possibilities at the same time. The atemporal present of the orgies and the reiteration of the harangues give rise to a narrative space more reminiscent of the continuous present of a dream than of development through time, thus endowing the heroine with her immutable quality. However, this oneiric element coexists with the representation of an "I-self" that is lucid and capable of judging its former self. The division of the writing subject within a universe that is the product of both control and phantasy reverberates, on the level of the enunciation, in the voice of Juliette as narrator, as well as directly in the writing, where it reveals itself most remarkably in humor and obscenity.

## SPLIT SUBJECT OR SUBJECT IN PROCESS? STRUCTURES OF SADO-MASOCHISM AND FETISHISM

From a psychoanalytic standpoint, every subject is always divided—between unconscious and conscious, drives and reason, primary processes and secondary processes, imaginary and symbolic, id-ego-superego (without these last two groups corresponding term for term with the preceding ones)—but these divisions are not necessarily recognized. The notion of the unitary subject corresponds to the traditional conception of the subject as a conscious and coherent self. The unitary subject splits off and thus represses in the unconscious everything that relates to the drives while nourishing on the conscious level an illusion of unity and plenitude. Thus the unitary subject is also a split subject. On the other hand, the subject in process (as theorized by Julia Kristeva) is always in movement, pulled apart by the demands of the drives and of reason. This self experiences its own contradictions, questions the dominance of the rational consciousness, and may have access to the preverbal. In his discussion of Sade, Bataille remarks that eroticism is "the sexual activity of a conscious person" but nonetheless "eludes our consciousness."[1] Seen in the light of this remark, eroticism aims to carry the representation of the drive into the realm of the conscious in order to assert control over it.[2] Never resolved, this tension sets up the most pervasive contradiction to be found in the Sadean text, a contradiction played out between the wild unfolding of orgy and dissertation on the one hand, and the actualization of a subject which is master of itself, its sexual pleasure and its reasoning on the other.

The opposing structures which map out Sade's text are most specifically linked to structures of fetishism on the one hand and of sadism and its masochist reversals on the other. Fetishism and sadism govern the division of the subject, giving it its meaning, and they are echoed in the multiform dissonances of parodic heterogeneity. It is fetishism's characteristic oscillation between rational and irrational—between phantasied desire (believing in the reality of the mother's phallus) and reality principle (knowing that the phallus does not exist)—that is relevant here. As for Sadean sadism-masochism, it is anchored in a fundamental opposition between active and passive positions—an "indissociable structural unit"[3] rather than a description of the implicit author's own, fundamentally sadistic personality. In fact it is almost a misuse of language to designate as masochistic those rare episodes where the agents seek to experience physical pain. Unlike the masochist, who delegates the role of subject to "an external person," the libertine never gives up control over anything and in no way shares the masochist's desire to atone and yield to punishment. Gilles Deleuze, whose unique reference is Sade, rightly speaks of a masochism that is "proper to the sadist" (as well as a sadism proper to the masochist) and which should be distinguished from the masochism of the masochist.[4] I shall therefore be talking in terms of reversal—one of the basic structures of Sade's writing—rather than of complementarity, a notion that would suggest a sado-masochistic unity within the same subject. In all events, the sadistic position predominates in the Sadean orgy, for sadism is the inevitable result of the "need to do away with the (genital) universe of difference,"[5] or, to adopt Deleuze's formulation, sadism implies the suppression of the mother.

Deleuze's analysis is highly illuminating, but it fails to account for a few points in Sade's text. "A true sadist will never put up with a masochist victim," Deleuze writes (p. 41), and indeed the anonymous mass of eternally reluctant Sadean victims supports this statement. Nevertheless, it could easily be argued that Justine is a masochist—as some critics have already done, admittedly at the price of some extrapolation. Deleuze also refuses the association of masochism with passivity and sadism with activity, claiming that it "presupposes" the sàdo-masochistic unity (p. 67). This same association is, however, asserted by Sade himself,[6] it corresponds to a change from one position to the other, and, when limited to the choice of a physical posture, as in Sade's case, does not necessarily imply psychic sado-masochistic unity. Furthermore, Deleuze only sees in Sade negation and a form of fetishism which has broken with disavowal in order to bind uniquely with negation (p. 32). Similarly, he overlooks Sade's humor since he assigns humor to the masochist and irony to the sadist. Such divisions need to be refined. In fact, the Sadean libertine does flirt with disavowal when he cultivates illusion and simulacrum without believing in them, and humor is everywhere in Sade. Finally, referring to Freud, Deleuze notes that on the level of the body a properly masochistic erogeneity must exist which likes to use pain to procure pleasure (pp. 104–5). This is a well established fact, it seems, but it should perhaps not be limited to the "true" masochist, unless we are to conclude that Sade, who, just like his characters, loved being beaten (even with a barbed whip) was a masochist after all, since he was endowed with this particular form of erogeneity.

"The libertine's 'masochism' makes its appearance at the outcome of his sadistic exercises; it is their climax, the crowning sanction of their glorious infamy" confirming that the libertine has "inalienable power" (Deleuze, p. 39). This description is borne out by almost all the "masochistic" episodes in the *Histoire de Juliette*. For example, when Juliette has finished her preparations for the fire that will destroy a whole family, she immediately experiences extraordinary pleasure, but this is not enough to calm her arousal. Prey to insatiable sexual appetite, she desires and then engineers her own humiliation. In other words, she never for a moment gives up her role as subject, and the "masochistic" reversal is wholly conditioned by the sadistic excitement that preceded it:

> I ordered them to throw me naked upon a sofa in one of my boudoirs, and I told Elvire to bring in all my men, advising them that they might do what they willed with me, provided that they heaped insults upon me and treated me like a whore. . . . One of those libertines (I had given them leave to do anything) takes it into his head that he does not want to fuck me on a sofa but in the mud. . . . I allow him to drag me out onto a heap of manure and prostituting myself there like a sow, I urge him to humiliate me yet more. The scoundrel obliges, and goes off only after shitting in my face. . . . And I was happy; the more I wallowed in infamy and dung, the more my head was on fire with lust, the more my frenzy increased . . . and nothing, no nothing, calmed the cruel state I was plunged in at the very thought of the crime I had just committed. (8: 397–98, 413–14)

This description clearly exhibits the division of the subject, first by way of a partial identification with the victim ("the more I wallowed in . . . dung . . . the more my frenzy increased"), a masochistic position that is nonetheless inseparable from the sadistic phantasy: " 'I make myself suffer' is always in one way or another 'I make suffer in myself the other that I have placed there.' There is an internal doubling" (Laplanche, p. 724b).[7] In a second phase of the doubling, the sadistic "I" is identified with the superego,[8] that is with the "position of the engineer," that of the "stage director" or the "sadistic position" (Laplanche, "Les Normes morales," p. 726b). The episode just quoted strikingly illustrates how dependent the masochistic position is on the sadistic. Juliette's masochism demands active preparations, and she stages her own humiliation.

The oscillation between belief and knowledge in fetishism, the instability of identifications in the sadistic-masochistic structure, and last but not least the identification with part objects—all these various phenomena give rise to a divided subject, but one fiercely determined to recover its unity. The wish to be wholly conversant with the pre-verbal while at the same time retaining a concept of the person that extends only to lucid thinking, to seize hold of a considerable part of the "representatives of the drive" while at the same time surrendering to them: here is the origin of the text's heterogeneity. The division of the subject is forever on the brink of being controlled, yet it is endlessly disseminated in the tableaux and discourse of the orgy.

## Humor, Laughter

Sade's peculiar sense of humor illustrates on every page the distinction between the subject of the enunciation and the subject of the "énoncé," and it rests upon an implicit dialogue between the ego and the superego. Nonetheless Sade's humor functions within the limits of the conscious.[9] The definition of humor remains uncertain—it may blend in with other forms of the comic, such as irony, and it eludes any rhetorical analysis. It has proved possible to define irony as a figure of style, and even as trope and figure in absentia, at least when it comes close to antiphrasis.[10] Humor too may refer to an absent text, but it does not necessarily invert its language. Above all, humor is a function of situational context. It sometimes uses figures of style such as parallelism. Finally, it often forms one of the ludic ingredients in parody. Discussing the "manifest ludicity of parody and pastiche," Genette notes that in the best cases the game is not "premeditated" and results in humor.[11] He recommends not trivializing the term; humor is a fragile thing and can vanish if named. All the same, some risk must be taken. Sade's humor runs the whole gamut, the "principle of tact" that was so dear to Barthes is not always noticeable, and light tones often shade into dark. We shall need to establish whether black humor is susceptible to the same theoretical explanations as light humor.

As Juliette arrives at the center point of her story, she calls a halt and complacently paints her self-portrait: "I was then embarking upon my twenty-fifth year. As yet I had nothing for which to reproach nature. . . . The delicacy of my waist was perfectly preserved, my bosom, still fresh and round, had held up marvellously well. My buttocks, high and delightfully white, showed no ill effects from the excesses of lust I had inflicted upon them; their hole, it is true, was a little wide . . . ; my cunt too was by no means narrow, but with a little coquetry, some astringents and artful attentions, all of this, at my orders, regained the rosy glow of virginity" (9: 65, 658). Juliette's body both carries and denies the mark of time. It bathes in the oneiric present of orgiastic repetition. Juliette herself is only partly deceived by her own affirmations/disavowals. As for the author—the real subject of the enunciation—and the reader, they *know* that Juliette's libertine life contradicts the fiction of an intact body. The humorous effect results, on the one hand, from this superior knowledge assigned to the target reader (pragmatic value of humor), and on the other from the internal division of the subject, who knows and pretends not to know. Here this division is relayed by Juliette as narrator, that is to say the apparent subject of the enunciation, who establishes a measure of distance from herself at age twenty-five, the subject of the "énoncé."

The hesitation in humor between knowledge and denial of reality, then, recalls the dynamics of fetishism, but this hesitation results from a deliberate and ludic choice, since the subject consciously plays at believing in the existence of a nature attuned to his or her desires. Freud interprets humor as a tension between the pleasure principle and the reality principle,[12] with the narcissistic self, product of an unusually benevolent superego, addressing the subject as parents would a child: "Look! here is the world, which seems so dangerous! It is nothing but a game for children—just worth making a jest about!" (p. 166). The inner division we have detected in Juliette, then, corresponds to a dialectical relation between the superego and the ego, the one being the spectator and the other the object of a comforting humor with which he or she identifies as a subject. All this suggests that the omnipresence of humor, like that of sadism, is linked in Sade to his exceptionally developed superego, which in a mood of pleasantry dictates to him the conscious denial of the real.[13]

When the humorist directs his wit at others, the division is played out between two distinct individuals. The example of Juliette may again serve to illustrate this second situation, once it is realized that the real humorist and subject of the narration is not Juliette the narrator but her creator who, with the reader's complicity, phantasizes the atemporal present of his erotic utopia without ever being deceived by it. In *De l'Essence du rire* (*On the Essence of Laughter*) Baudelaire proposes the opposite path, moving from a division external to the subject to the subject's internal division. Writing from a moral and metaphysical viewpoint, Baudelaire defines this division between the subject and the object of laughter by insisting upon the feelings of superiority felt by the person who laughs and possesses knowledge that escapes the object. We are not far here from Freud's parental superego, if we leave out the indulgence. But Baudelaire is analyzing the comic, and not humor, though his analysis may offer a way of approaching black humor. Moving on to the case of the artist, Baudelaire transposes into an internal and psychological dualism the division of subject and object, and this is where he comes closest to Freud's position.[14] In order to produce laughter, the artist must both know and pretend not to know.[15]

What kind of knowing is involved here? Let us say that humor playfully denies certain truths or some logic accepted by society at large (note that the term "nature" appears in both Freud and Baudelaire). Irony, to the contrary, implies a more intellectual connivance, a particularized knowledge which the reader may not necessarily possess, in which case the ironic effect eludes him or her. Humor pretends to have no knowledge of certain commonplace truths or of a vision of the world that is largely accepted.

On the basis of these fundamental characteristics, which correspond well with Sade's general practice, we can move on to a more refined analysis of his humor. The latter derives in the first place from Sade's relation to the libertine genre. The libertine novel habitually oscillates between two options depending upon whether or not it posits the transgression of the moral consciousness, which in turn entails either the obscene representation of the body or the fiction of innocence.[16] Sade mixes these two points of view. He asserts his innocence, but an innocence founded upon the universality of crime, and he actualizes transgression through the obscenity of his vocabulary. He thereby points to the duplicity of the libertine model, which must always maintain the fiction of innocence. Pretending to be unaware of the demands of conscience or convention, Sade describes all wrongdoing with imperturbable ease and a complete disregard for probability, and in this way we find ourselves in the realm of humor: "If it were necessary to take flight every time one committed a crime, it would be impossible to settle down anywhere" (9: 260, 857). Such humor achieves its effects because, flouting the obstacles of reality, it is almost taken in by its own game. It imposes desire as the ultimate reality, since the plot is driven mainly by the fulfilment of phantasy. Thus, referring to Saint Peter's tomb, "'Oh! what a couch to be sodomized upon,' I said to Sbrigani. . . . 'Now, give me but leave, and, in less than a month, Juliette will receive, upon this magnificent altar, the modest prick of the vicar of Christ'" (9: 64, 657).

Sade's humor will thus go so far as to work uniquely with the multiple reality of desire, opposing one desire to another. Thus, referring to a sodomite: "He forgot himself so far as to frig my clitoris" (8: 259, 271). This humor may rely on other logico-semantic disjunctions. The essential thing is that the utterance should never acknowledge its internal or situational impossibility. One could cite in the register of the obscene the clownish inventions that tend to take the sting out of Sadean violence: "We ended up by tying all the pricks, with silk ribbons, to the ceiling" (9: 365, 962)[17]; "to lick his ass: an operation I commenced by raising the tail of his tigerskin" (9: 502, 1105). We can find here the "something mechanical encrusted on the living," the notion of a "nature that is mechanically tampered with," which Bergson—though remaining on the surface of the phenomenon—uses to explain comedy's denial of the real.[18] Sade loves to reduce the human to the level of the animal, or better still to some inanimate simulacrum. Pursuing this line of analysis, one meets up with the grotesque, which Baudelaire, contrasting creation with imitation, considers to be the source of "the absolute comic." Freed from the demands of mimesis, the grotesque enjoys a wider creative space than other forms of the comic. It expresses "the idea of man's superiority no longer over man, but over nature" (p. 157), a distinction which, by and large, still obeys the rules of mimesis which it seeks to escape. Baudelaire links the monstrous in comedy to the category of the grotesque, and it is in this indirect way that certain forms of Sadean grotesque, humor not excluded, illustrate his distinction between creation and imitation. One is reminded of the anatomical inventions designed to improve sexual performance beyond the norms of the possible: giant clitorises, the monstrous size and peculiarities of male organs, as with the Carmelite monk Claude—"by a miracle, which nature bestows only upon her favorites, Claude was blessed with three testicles" (8: 436, 454)—or the giant Minski who "produces an anchovy eighteen inches long by sixteen around, topped by a rosy mushroom as wide as the butt of a hat" (8: 560, 582).

In his discussion of *black humor*, André Breton noted in particular the parody of the gothic novel, commenting upon those "obviously outrageous" passages by which, he claims, "the author is obviously not taken in."[19] And he illustrates this point with the whole of the Minski episode. This type of humor undoubtedly has an important place in Sade's work, but it is far from the last word on the topic. Black humor still hinges on feigned innocence, which in turn may rely on certain stylistic effects that emphasize breaks in logic—parallelism: "An income *of five hundred thousand livres*, Juliette, and I earn them with *twenty sous of* arsenic" (8: 391, 404); antiphrasis and maxim: " 'Yes, indeed,' the minister went on, 'the laws ought to be stricter; the only countries to enjoy happy governance are those ruled by the Inquisition' " (8: 304, 315); contradiction between two sentences that juxtapose the sacrifice of children and the celebration of man's and nature's fertility: "In the island of Nicaragua, a father is permitted to sell his children for sacrifice. When these peoples consecrate their corn, they water it with semen, and dance around this double product of nature" (8: 184, 189). In these quotations, the symmetries and the nonsense of the juxtaposition carry the disjunctive effect right into the materiality of the sentence. Why do we laugh when someone stumbles against the curb or falls on the ice, Baudelaire asks, and he attributes this effect to the feeling of superiority that the spectator experiences (a comic effect, but outside humor).[20] Yet there is a better explanation. The sudden laughter echoes the unexpected fall, and this allows us to grasp the difference as well as the connexion between the laughter of childhood, and the sense of humor that the child has yet to acquire. Julia Kristeva notes that laughter ties in with (preverbal) "archaic semiotic spatiality" since both share the same "substrate" in the "articulation of mobile and fixed."[21] The acquisition of language—moving into verbalization and the symbolic—enables humor to occur and logical disjunction to take the place of physical disjunction. The way a sentence is put together sometimes retains traces of physical disjunction, just as a laugh punctuates meaning as it totters on the edge of disappearance.

Kristeva is describing a general stage in the evolution of each individual. Bataille, for his part, analyzes Sadean laughter by establishing two parallelisms, one between concrete heterogeneity and intellectual heterogeneity, and the other between anality (physical excretion) and adult laughter (ideological excretion). Based on the alternation of stasis and motility, the connection between the two forms of excretion is reinforced by the fact that "shit can be characterized by the hilarity it provokes."[22] Baudelaire had already made the point that "fabulous creations, beings whose authority and *raison d'être* cannot be drawn from the code of common sense, often provoke in us an insane and excessive mirth" (p. 156). This excretory laughter is a laugh of exclusion: the object of the laughter, "other" and treated as a waste product, occasions rejection. Any alien body not rejected is on the contrary the object of an act of appropriation; this leads us back to black humor.

In the climatic scene when Juliette and Noirceuil execute their respective children, this little sentence, "Marianne is roasted," referring to Juliette's daughter, a seven-year-old child who is thrust into the fire with a few "details," may extract a smile in the reader. It is certainly a humorous effect:

> I assist him, and like him I take up an iron bar to beat back the natural move-
> ments of this unfortunate child who convulsively recoils and moves back
> toward us; we are both frigged, we are buggered; Marianne is roasted [like a
> pullet . . . ] she is burned to a chip. Noirceuil comes, so do I. (9: 580, 1186)

Foreign body, small chicken, meaningless excrement, Marianne raises a
laugh of exclusion. Black humor ignores the norm as much as light humor, and it similarly illustrates the division of the subject, but it does so
with the support of the Sadean superego, and most often at the expense
of others. The pleasure it provides relies on the certainty that evil, not
good, goes beyond the norms of the possible. Pursuing this line of analysis
would lead us to an examination of perverse logic, which at times enrolls
black humor in its attack on moral and political discourse.

## THE PLACE OF THE OBSCENE

The obscene is closer to laughter than to humor, to the preverbal semiotic
than to the symbolic. It thus has less control than humor over its unconscious roots and it offers more evidence of the process of the subject. As
Sade treats it, obscenity immediately challenges our cultural expectations[23]
since it depends on one of the most striking aspects of Sadean idiolect: the
contrast between two registers of language, the coarse and the noble:

> And when we three women were all quite out of our senses, we set to frigging
> ourselves once again like tarts, until at last the daystar in the heavens, coming
> to illumine our saturnalia, finally constrained us to desist. (9: 485, 1088)

This mixing of heterogeneous signifiers from the outset defeats any attempt to reduce the Sadean obscene to mere vulgarity. A constant obstacle
to the unity of tone, it triggers pastiche into parody.[24] It feeds the contrast between two types of description: that of classic beauty, conducted
in a style of conventional elegance, and the enumeration of parts of the
body, named and described in the crudest, and sometimes the most pic-
turesque, of languages. Sade does seem more comfortable, however, with
this second type of description.[25] He emphasizes and systematizes the contrast in linguistic registers which is already common in pornography by
eliminating any euphemistic ornament in his descriptions of the orgiastic body. Inevitably such a practice transforms meaning. It is obvious, in
the first instance, that such a subversion of the linguistic and literary insti-

tution targets society as a whole.[26] The obscene word rends the fabric of language, giving graphic intensity to that part of desire which challenges the conventions and the balance of the community, as well as the control of the rational subject.[27] And it ties up with Sade's ideas on energy:[28] it is not by chance that "energetic" applied to language often means coarse.

The frequency of obscene words, inseparable from naming, is a function of the preponderance of the fragmented body. The obscene is something *in excess*, and "this perception of excess is concentrated on the body."[29] The Sadean novel relies upon obscenity not only in the vocabulary that *clashes* with the elegance of the style but also generally in the display of the body, in which coprophilia holds an unwonted place. It is the obscene word that seals the association of the scatological, the sexual, and the unbridled violence. When spoken, the obscene word conjures up the subject's earliest memories and summons "the popular lexicon of the *mother tongue*" according to the "theory of infantile sexuality which links the excremental to the sexual." This effect is on the contrary "countered" by the use of the "foreign language" of scientific vocabulary. Sade's repetition of obscene words is not unsimilar to repetition in psychoanalytic treatment. "The mnesic image" of the body, including child phantasies of dismemberment, "recur with intensity"[30] during this repetition, released or facilitated by the crudity of the adjacent terms. Nonetheless, in Sade's work, the various kinds of images and their corresponding linguistic registers are sharply delineated. The obscene word is reserved for jouissance whereas torture is described in polished style:

> He puts on a shoe studded with iron spikes, leans on two men, and with all the strength of his back, launches a kick right into the belly of the young woman who, bursting open, torn, bloody, sags under her bonds and lays before us her unworthy fruit, which the ruffian immediately waters with his seed. Very close to this spectacle, fucked at the same time in front and behind, sucking the cock of a young boy who, at this very moment, discharged in my mouth, frigging a cunt with each hand, it was impossible that I should not share in the pleasures of the prince, and I spent my sperm according to the example he set. (9: 409, 1009; Juliette is speaking)

The contrast between the two registers sets apart the scene of pleasure from the dismantling of the mother-child dyad. The contrast is not always quite so clear cut, but it recurs to some extent in every episode of torture, and each time it serves to establish lines of demarcation. That the obscene is muted in this way when confronted with the sadistic act and its excess may be seen as a form of distancing or even censorship. On the other hand, the irruption of the obscene goes along with a process of "desemanticization" which belongs to the order of *signifiance* (i.e., the process of signification before or beyond words).[31] The instinctual charge, repressed in the verbal representation of the perverse act, is invested in the obscene word and, through *its* intervention, becomes actualized in the representation of the jouissance caused by that act. The obscene marks the phantasied realization of desire. All of which supports Barthes's intuition when he writes: "Sade's crude language is the utopian portion of his discourse."[32]

The obscene word keeps with it the mnesic trace of the period in life when playing with the body provides the first representations and when the child makes no clear distinction between thing-representations and word-representations: hence the term organ-word to designate the representations that the obscene word arouses in the adult user, and hence the opposition between "raw affects" and "feelings," just as between primary processes and secondary processes. Polished language, as a place of repression, substitutes *the sentimental for the sexual, the metaphoric for the literal*. Conversely, Sade allows us to see "the sexual which is at the source of language" when language, at the scene of jouissance, is reduced to its simplest expression, the obscenity which short-circuits communication.[33]

Sade not ony demystifies the register of sentiment in his obscene writing, he also attacks it in his speeches. The discourse against love is based throughout upon a strong dichotomy between pleasure and affectivity. Affirming their incompatibility, it reflects a matter-spirit opposition which contradicts Sade's professed materialism: "It seems to me . . . that there is a great difference between loving and taking pleasure, and that not only is it not necessary to love to take pleasure, but that we need only take pleasure to not love" (8: 248, 259). In its most complete form, the argument bases this incompatibility upon a disgust with the sexual organs:

> I do not wish a woman to fancy I owe her anything just because I soil myself upon her. . . . I have never believed that the joining of two bodies resulted in the joining of two hearts; in this physical joining I see great occasions for scorn . . . , for disgust, but none for love. (9: 148, 744)

Thus the fear of physical impurity—the perspective of the abject—unmasks the euphemistic (or "metaphorical") language of love as an imposture and rejects the sentimental register in favor of the crude word. In Sade, this word is almost inseparable from phallic images which conjure up the unity of the subject—often when that unity is about to be lost. Linked to the threat of abjection, which in turn is a substrate for castration anxiety, the phallic obscene is meant to keep the frontiers of the self from being breached, since it is endowed with "the omnipotence of a fetish of the absent organ."[34] Summoned by naming at the moment when conscious-ness is being lost, it appears as a minimal affirmation. In other words, the brutal scission of the mother-child dyad in sadistic violence, the recourse to polished language to describe that scission, and, on the contrary, the use of obscene language at the moment of orgasm, would all three have the same double function: to signify and check the vertigo of the abject and of transgression.

A "masochistic" reversal may, however, occur when the mastery of the Sadean subject takes the form of a victory over his own repugnance, either out of perversion (as we saw in a previous example) or out of finan-cial self-interest, as in the following:

> I did everything this libertine desired: I sucked his balls, I let him knock me around, fart in my mouth, shit on my bosom, spit or piss on my face, tweak my nipples, kick and slap me on the butt, and, definitively, fuck me in the ass, where he merely worked himself up before discharging in my mouth, with the positive order to swallow his sperm. (8: 210, 218)

If the obscene vocabulary in this piece is associated with description of (relatively) brutal abuse, it is from the point of view of the narrator and subject Juliette, who has placed herself in the position of passive victim. Though in this instance Juliette does not orchestrate her own humiliation, she freely consents to it. The mastery she can exercise as subject means that the usual incompatibility between obscene vocabulary and brutality is suppressed.

Need it be said that the agents alone use the language of obscenity? While he associates obscenity too exclusively with the description of the victim, Bataille thereby is better able to see the way it functions to exclude: Sade's "use of coarse language" he writes, "is a way of spurning human dignity," and he stresses that "prostitution, coarse language and every-thing to do with eroticism and infamy play their part in turning the world of sensual pleasure into a world of ruin and degradation."[35] Here Bataille pushes Sade in the direction of "Evil" and sin, but he does not totally mis-represent him. Despite the drollery of some inventions, be they grating and discordant or not, many of Sade's scenes feature only the same dreary words pounded out over and over again:

When all the tools had thus been inserted into my ass, we formed into one single group. I lie flat on my back against a man who thrusts into my ass; another man thrusts into my cunt; with my right hand I assist one man's cock into the ass of Zanetti, who, lying upon another man, receives a cock in her cunt; with my left hand I do the same for Rosetti, who is also fucked in front and behind. A man was thrusting into the ass of the man who was sodomizing me, and each of us had one in our mouths. (9: 485, 1087)

Clearly, a considerable distance separates this compulsive and mechanical routine from Rabelaisian obscenity. For Sade, the corollary of obscenity is the discourse on defilement, and obscenity posits the absolute otherness of the subject vis à vis his own body, or even the wholesale rejection of the body. The Sadean orgy, which ends in the death of the victims, never produces a *becoming* in the executioners. The obscene language merely names fragments of body. Whether this accumulation be considered erotic, grotesque, or wretched, it reveals a body that is reviled as much as it is sollicited and never merges into an acceptance of the physical.[36]

## Written and Oral

The *Histoire de Juliette* dates from a period when the novel genre still carried traces of the oral tradition, traces which were to fade with the crisis of Romanticism.[37] In Sade's work, other, more precise factors also play a part; his subjectivity, his social class, the education he received, his years in prison, his civic activities and political reflection during the years of the Revolution. Thus in his novel a dual relation, both collective and single, exists between the oral and the written.

This relation is not a simple one, since it entails both the written representation of oral speech and the interaction of traits characteristic either of the written or of the oral. The first of these (Juliette's tale) takes up the whole of the text except for a few pages, whose place—at the end—is not devoid of significance. Does the effect of orality continue throughout the narration, or does it yield to the writing effect, despite the presence of Juliette's listeners as minor characters? And what is the significance of this status of orality and its relation to the written? Within Juliette's tale, there are long reported sections—dialogues and harangues in particular— which introduce yet another layer of orality. The same questions arise in regard to this second layer, where the effect of heterogeneity is manifest in blatant ruptures of the narrative texture. These ruptures correspond either to alternations of narration and reported speech, or to different kinds of speech. All the same, this heterogeneity makes sense primarily in relation to the enunciation.

## NARRATIVE VOICES, VOICES OF EROS

Several traits link the text of *Juliette* to story*telling*: the loose plot and the repetition of like episodes; unmotivated encounters, unlikely or fantastic events, evocations of a vague and higher causality that establishes the raison d'être of the actions in a quest for evil and pleasure quite divorced from any psychological connection; recourse to the discourse of the *doxa*—with inverted, parodic content.[38] These same features can be found equally in *La Nouvelle Justine*, which presents itself, at least in this final version of the *Justine*s, as *written* in the third person: they therefore tell us more about the tradition Sade followed, and his way of writing, than they do about the fiction of a first person oral narration. This fiction is most interesting in terms of the enunciation and the point of view of the narrators.

Both the themes of the dissertations and the orgy scene itself feature a confusion between narrative voices and voices of eros. And the confusion of the sexes, and in particular the question of Juliette's sex, contributes to the mixture of voices. What does Sade gain—narratively, textually, psychologically—by choosing a narrator-heroine, and how are we to problematize the privilege thus granted to a woman? And to what extent is Juliette a woman? A study of the various levels of narration will offer us a tentative answer to such questions.

The choice of a narrator-heroine per se does not come out of nowhere. The seventeenth- and eighteenth-century novel often showed a fondness for the female character, and the dominant assumption was that the novel aimed at a female readership—except, perhaps, for the picaresque novel. The first person narrative is a strategy of verisimilitude which dominates the genre in the eighteenth century, and there are many female narrators before Juliette. As for the subgenre of pornography, which, to the contrary, is directed toward a male reader, it too likes using a narrator-heroine, finding that she offers an appreciable erotic bonus. The voice of Juliette, like that of the women historians in *Les Cent-vingt journées*, owes something to this model.

Nonetheless, the presence of these female voices in Sade is overdetermined. As we have seen, Sade seeks to appropriate the feminine, and writing demands a passage through the feminine—be it a phantasy of incest with the mother, a rivalry with the maternal as genitor, or a descent into the Kristevian abject. More profoundly, the choice of women historians or of Juliette as storytellers and spokespersons betrays the survival of a "secret relationship, basically an anal-erotic and anal-sadistic one, between mother and child" introducing the mother as a complicitous witness to the perverse staging,[39] and ending in the phantasy of a phallic writing, which finds its metaphor in the simulacrum and in fetish objects.[40] This hierarchy continues on the level of narration; it is significant that it is a male subject who undertakes the task of transcribing Juliette's oral narrative. However, Juliette's status as narrator is not simple and her value is not limited merely to the art of telling a story aloud, or to the violence of the irrational and the refusal of the law. That value also results, conversely, from her art of reasoning, and it is no less significant that Sade should have transposed his *Justine* into the third person at the very same time that he was creating his Juliette as narrator. This decision arises out of the parodic project and results in having crime narrated and justified by the criminal, and making that criminal a woman philosopher. Finally, given the contradictory aptitudes of the character, the choice of a female narrator forms part of the fetishist structure. On the level of the narration, the text oscillates between two propositions: Juliette has the phallus, and she does not. This privileged woman is a man: she has (almost) all the characteristics of the male, but she lacks writing.

Bisexual eroticism and Juliette's "male" behavior we examined earlier are more or less explicitly connected to the production of the tale. Thus, it is for its supposed richness of invention that Juliette's "tribadism" makes her superior to an ordinary man. She makes this very argument toward the end of the novel, and a note by the author reinforces the point:

> These charming creatures [the tribades], that the opinion of fools chastises so stupidly, carry into society the same qualities that they bring to pleasure; they are always more lively, amiable, and witty than other women; almost all of them have grace, talent, imagination; why then should we reproach them for a sin which belongs only to nature? You ponderous men and devotees of ordinary pleasures blame such women because they refuse you; but if the women who love you were subjected to scrutiny, they would surely be found to be almost as stupid as you yourselves. (9: 542–43, 1147)

If the writer is to know a passage through the feminine, it is a deviant feminine, enriched with a certain familiarity with the masculine. The specular relationship between orgy and narration reappears, emphasized in a dialogue between Juliette and her male friends, in which they congratulate themselves on the fact that confusion between the sexes gives rise to the diversity of the narrative—a purely abstract proposition that is unlikely to convince the reader: " 'Here it is a matter of the corruption of both sexes,' said [Juliette]; for Duvergier provided subjects for the fantasies of both sexes equally: 'Your tableaux, mixed in this way, will be all the more agreeable,' said the chevalier" (8: 107–8, 103). The superiority of the tribadic woman is linked directly to her polymorphous eroticism, for nature, by endowing her with "a more sensitive imagination" has similarly "showered her with all the means for pleasure and voluptuousness" (9: 542, 1147)— a superiority over the male homosexual which is short-lived since, in the great majority of orgiastic figures, sodomy always ends up by bringing female eroticism under the heel of the male Same. Just as Juliette may prostitute herself freely and engage in the exchange of men (with the exception of the masters), so, adopting another prerogative of the male which in no way detracts from her femininity, Juliette is both agent and object of the exchange of the narrative.[41] Reciprocally, in a way exceptional for a female character outside of pornography, she *speaks* her own sexual pleasure, yet only in a register whose choice is significant since it too maintains the fetishist ambivalence.

Indeed, Juliette's privilege most persistently translates into her mastery of sexual vocabulary, be it obscene or technical, but, from this language, which has long been constituted on the basis of a male utterance, her discourse borrows only imprecision as soon as female physiology is involved. Juliette speaks of her sexual pleasure as if she were a man.[42] Likewise she has rational control of it. Hence the following question. Does she speak in this way as much as, or more than, her sisters in pornography? Here one has to compare her language with the pornographic vocabulary of the eighteenth century. Whether out of ignorance or indifference, this vocabulary, when applied to woman, remains vague despite its crudeness. Its reference is to the male since it makes no clear distinction between the two sexes. It habitually refers to female orgasm, as well as male, by the verb "to discharge"[43] and uses for both men and women the nouns "come" ("foutre"), "discharge," and "seed."[44] Sade may be alone in using "sperm" and "ejaculate" for female characters.[45] Even as he lends a voice to a female philosopher, he seems to surpass pornographic and popular usage which lagged far behind contemporary science since the latter had already ceased to attribute sperm to women at the time when he was writing[46] In fact, obscene language and erotic discourse are informed by the relation to desire and ideology rather than to the scientific knowledge of an era. Nonetheless, in *Juliette*, taking command of discourse represents all the other kinds of possession, and obscene language does point to the freedom of the narrator-heroine. But this freedom is uniquely constituted by the appropriation of male prerogatives, in other words by the perfect adhesion to the model of the One. Béatrice Didier shows very clearly that the conquest of libertine language (which includes much more than obscene language) signifies rallying to the side of the fathers.[47] On the other hand, when the text wishes to stress the heroine's female nature, it does so only in order to evoke whatever is instinctual and imaginary. Thus, in many cases, Juliette serves to represent as female whatever is instinctual in man.

So it is scarcely surprising that she appropriates the masculine only to a limited extent and that, despite the precedents afforded by Marivaux's heroine Marianne or Diderot's nun in *La Religieuse*, Juliette never gains access to writing. The relation between telling and writing which determines the two main levels of the narration literally inscribes the equivalence of pen and phallus.[48]

The starting-point for the narrative situation of *Histoire de Juliette* is to be found in the first chapter of *La Nouvelle Justine*. If one begins with the second novel, one assumes for many pages that Juliette is its primary narrator. But it is an intermediate narrator or scriptor, identified in an "editor's note" at the head of *La Nouvelle Justine* as the supposedly posthumous author, who *transcribes* in the third person the story narrated by Justine, then in the first person the tale of Juliette, a thousand-page long quotation which begins with the first word of the *Histoire de Juliette*. By and large the novel respects the fiction that the heroine of the reported events is telling her own story. However, several strategies, and a couple of slips, tend to give the narrative voice a male cast. In the first place, there is the number and length of the reported dialogues and of the harangues, more than half of which are attributed to male characters, and also the importance of embedded stories in which male narrators predominate. In the tale of Borchamps, for example, it is hard to say whether he is speaking, or Juliette. Finally, in the early part of the novel, there are two interventions by the intermediary narrator or scriptor, who makes no further appearance after this point.[49] These two interruptions in the third person remind the reader of the narrative situation and bring him back to the present of the enunciation.

As for the slips which turn Juliette into a male, these are quite rare considering the length of the novel, but they do serve to make the narrator's sex even more problematic. They reveal her voice as contrived, albeit through a well-motivated artifice, rather than as the identificatory projection of the author. On two occasions, the scriptor slips up and Juliette is referred to in the third person.[50] On at least one occasion Juliette forgets she is supposed to be speaking her tale, not writing it: "Two months passed without anything occurring that might add some interest to my writings" (8: 344–45, 357). Here there is a conflation between Juliette and the writing subject.[51]

All such details reintroduce a male narrator whenever Sade abandons or neglects the fiction of an oral narration, even though the female sex of the narrator is the most significant, if not realistic, factor. The end of the novel completely demystifies this fiction. The time of the story and the time of the narration come together five pages before the end. Juliette finishes her tale and the scriptor takes up the thread of the written narrative: the dialogue of Juliette with her friends, the death of Justine who is punished by a thunder bolt for clinging so obstinately to virtue, the summary of the last ten years of prosperity that Juliette enjoys after the end of her tale. The death of Juliette introduces the passage into writing, a truly jubilant moment when a kind of triumphal provocation emerges from the message that someone, this very narrator, has dared to *write* such a work. In fact, Juliette's death occurs almost immediately after Juliette herself makes a reference to the transcribing of her tale:

> Oh, my friends, cries Juliette, drunk with joy, the man who one day writes the story of my life, will make no mistake if he calls it: *The Prosperities of Vice.* . . . Come my friends, [says Noirceuil one page later], let us rejoice; we might perhaps not dare say so were it a novel that we were writing. (9: 585, 1191; 586, 1192)

The final two pages repeat the distinction between oral and written narrative and announce the book which is to come—and already at hand—thus drawing attention to the process of reading. The last sentence of the novel is a web of disavowals. It turns statements upside down, pretending to justify the lack of credibility through the fiction of a spoken autobiography, and suggesting that Juliette herself might be the writer only at the moment when she is made to disappear:

> This woman, unique of her kind, dead without having written the last events in her life, absolutely deprives any writer of the possibility of revealing her to the public. Those who would care to undertake such a task could do so only

by offering us their daydreams as realities, which would make an astonishing difference to people of taste, and especially those who have taken some interest in reading this work. (9: 587, 1193)

The megalomaniac scriptor asserts the uniqueness of his work, forbids anyone else to try and equal him, and wipes out his heroine.

Even before these last five pages, the narrator-scriptor constantly brings himself to the reader's notice by footnotes which unfold their written discourse in parallel and thus form an intrinsic part of the text of the *Histoire de Juliette*.[52] These notes are very frequent—occurring on approximately one to every ten pages in volume 8, and on one to every eight pages in volume 9—and they serve to cement the fact that scriptor and author of *Juliette* are one and the same. Implicitly all the notes are the work of the author, with the exception of the editor's note placed at the head of *La Nouvelle Justine*: this "fictional editorial note"[53] refers to the author as posthumous, an enunciatory device intended to prevent any full identification of the scriptor with Sade. The notes come under the category of an "assumption of authorship" in that they refer to a (fictive) reality and take on the authority of a male judgment standing outside the fiction.[54] It does not follow that they all say the same thing. On the contrary, they give authoritative expression to contradictory opinions and provide either an echo or a counterpoint to Juliette's voice. Often developing some of her favorite themes, they can be divided into two main types according to content, either erotic or metanarrative, which refer in turn to the two main functions Juliette fulfills as erotic subject and narrator. And they either modulate the ideological aspects from an openly male viewpoint or else they maximize the metanarrative strategies of the tale.[55]

The notes with an erotic content are addressed to a presumed female readership and offer comic and provocative advice on how to achieve sexual pleasure. This burlesque discourse, more obviously parodic than that in *La Philosophie dans le boudoir*, habitually adds weight to the self-interested advice of some male character in the novel, and takes on the paternal and paternalistic tone of the moral sermons whose content it inverts. "Copy me," says Saint-Fond, and this gives rise to the following note:

All you lewd and headstrong women, take this advice to heart; it is for you as much as for Juliette, and if you have the wit, you cannot but make the greatest use of it, as she does. Our burning desire for your happiness inspires us to give this advice; never will you achieve the happiness which we strive to afford you, never will you achieve it, if these wise words of counsel do not become the only basis for your conduct. (8: 328, 340) [56]

Sometimes the note affects to rely on a female opinion, but one always endorsed by the voice of the implied author: "Note communicated by a woman of thirty who tried it more than one hundred times during her life" (8: 470, 491); or: "See what the celebrated Ninon de Lenclos, though but a zealot and woman, has to say in this regard" (8: 493, 515).

As this prescriptive discourse continues, a number of notes offer sententious remarks on women's tastes:

> Once women have become accustomed to being aroused to pleasure only when their cruelty has been awakened, the extreme delicacy of their fibres, the prodigious sensitivity of their organs, make them go much further in this vein than men. (9: 201, 797)

At other points, notes address the male reader and revert to male preferences:

> One is always good at doing what one likes; and the reader must not forget that Juliette told us that her greatest passion was to frig pricks. And is there any passion that can give more pleasure? . . . Ah! must one be a woman to taste this pleasure? What man of any sensuality does not understand it? And where is the man who, at least once in his life, has not frigged other men's pricks? (8: 436, 455) [57]

The erotic discourse of the notes serves to inscribe the male model which so often governs Juliette's eroticism, duplicating its arguments and conferring authority upon it, though only selectively, since Juliette refers at several points to her preference for women, whereas the notes express the misogyny characteristic of the orgy and of the masters' statements: "We would be as justified in denying that women are part of our species, as we are in refusing to accept [the monkey of the forests] as our brother, etc." (8: 489, 511) [58]

The metanarrative notes are even more numerous than the erotic ones, and they put the finishing touch on the main text's cavalier treatment of the convention of verisimilitude. In her narrative, Juliette seeks to establish the tale's truth status, beyond the fiction of autobiography, by simply asserting it. She tells us that her storytelling is marked "with the seal of the most exact truth" (9: 381, 978), and she justifies the presence of certain details in terms of her respect for the truth: "No feature is irrelevant to

the artist who unfolds for men the monstrosities of nature" (9: 518, 1122).
The same kind of assertion occurs in the notes, which further exaggerate
the parody of techniques of verisimilitude: she refers to pseudo-learned
sources and attributes them, where need be, to some well-known author
of licentious stories;[59] she refers to literary, philosophical, and historical
works, whose meaning is twisted (8: 173, 177); to unsupported historical or pseudo-historical information recounted in detail, allegedly to lend
authentification: "The reader is warned that the names of the plotters in
this famous affair have all been disguised here" (9: 261, 858), or again: "In
Italy, it is customary to make one's pimp of one's confessor" (9: 383, 980);
there are definitions of foreign words; and notes which seek to strengthen
the fiction of the posthumous author by claiming that the book was written before the Revolution,[60] thus conferring an additional predictive value
upon some of the political speeches. An even more thorough examination
of the novel would no doubt reveal as a factor of heterogeneity those notes
which make a claim to truth value and which undermine the illusion of
the true by juxtaposing the plausible and the extravagant. Even the aberrant historical data are not all confined to the main text of the story. One
detailed note devoted to the marquise de Brinvilliers indicates in passing
that her little chest of poisons "was carried to the Bastille. And its contents served all the members of Louis XVI's family" (8: 251, 262).[61] The
notes do not simply give presence to the narrator-scriptor, or the author,
throughout the novel. With a few exceptions, they share the incongruous
and contradictory nature of Juliette's own discourse, and they support the
logic as it goes astray.

Is Juliette a woman endowed with virile features, or merely a transparent disguise for her creator? The text directs us to the second hypothesis,
but there is little point in deciding one way or the other. What matters, is
that Sade feels the need to distribute his two narrative agencies between
the sexes, with woman telling and man writing. And even though the discourse of authority is constantly being challenged by the contradictions
in the text, the hierarchy between written and oral is not. That hierarchy,
although only implicit, constitutes the unique stable point of reference
in the *Histoire de Juliette*. Now a fully mature novelist, Sade introduces
into his novel a phallocentric theory of writing based in phantasy, and re-
inscribes it constantly in the relationship of the male scriptor and female
storyteller.

The written form, then, accounts for the following elements in the
text. First, the footnotes, a typographic technique which implies a certain

interiorization of the possibilities not only of writing but of printing. Second, the confusion which exists between Juliette and the scriptor—usually one forgets that Juliette is speaking not writing. Then the texture of the narration, which is of such complexity as to suggest the written—variety of tones, richness of connotations, subtle modulations of the division of the subject. Despite those traces of orality that I have indicated, the predominant effect is one of a written text.

At the end of the novel, the implications of the link between the anticipated move to writing and the moment of closure are slightly less apparent, yet even more decisive from the point of view of genre. The scriptor's reemergence is not only a convenient means of using Juliette's death to bring the tale to an end, it really gives the *Histoire de Juliette* its novelistic dimension. No matter how unmotivated the sequence of actions may be, this closure, which foregrounds the scriptural, opens up new possibilities for meaning. Only the written form allows for the reunion of two distinct narrators and for their semantic interaction. The final paragraphs refer us back to the narrative situation at the beginning of *La Nouvelle Justine*—there can be no story other than the one which we have read. This type of ending invites us to "think about the meaning of of an individual life," as Benjamin puts it ("The Story-Teller," p. 101) and it retrospectively puts in place the elements of meaningfulness. In order to be able to say that we are reading a novel, this gesture alone needs to be accomplished, but the book alone can bring this to pass.

## Written and Oral: Dissertation or Harangue?

Strategic moments such as these—the end of the novel, Juliette's reviews of her past—cast some light upon the way the novel as genre is subordinated to writing, but this effect does not hold up entirely. Other novels of the same period, such as *Les Liaisons dangereuses*, make greater and more exclusive use of the possibilities of writing. The *Histoire de Juliette* is heterogeneous not only as a text but as genre. Several of the ways in which the scriptural is made manifest—in the notes, for example—are not exclusively, nor indeed usually, associated with fiction. Certain features, which originate in the oral tradition, affect the narrativity without necessarily being incompatible with the novel, which is an omnivorous genre. The continual juxtaposition of disparate forms only partly parallels the opposition between oral and written. The pseudo-critical apparatus of the notes, as well as the dissertations (to use Sade's own term) or harangues (to use a term more adapted to their oral status) are themselves in part collages of borrowed pieces, and they fragment the reading. In the course of the dissertations, the enumerations of examples give rise to two other effects of heterogeneity: they are an incongruous catalogue in and of themselves, and they interrupt the flow of the argument.

Meanwhile, the harangue lays out some very clear-cut divisions within the text. The dialogue announces a harangue with formulas such as the following: " 'Listen to me, my angel,' said the Mother Superior . . . 'I wish to respond . . . to your frivolous objections.' We sat down. 'As we know the inspirations of nature,' Madame Delbène said to me' " (8: 23, 28). Then the harangue in its turn announces its enumerations of examples: " 'Permit me, dear ladies,' went on Dorval, 'to support my reasoning with some examples; each of you has received an education that will make them less than foreign to you. Theft is given such strong official sanction in Abyssinia' " (8: 122, 120). To be sure, these formulas correspond to the rhetorical models that prevailed in Sade's times, models based in turn upon demands for clarity and upon the notion of a subject master of his discourse. In Balzac's work also the profusion of heterogeneous elements will be channeled in very obvious ways. But Sade carries this technique to the point of caricature, going even further than he had in *La Nouvelle Justine* in his obsession with thresholds.

Passages such as these stand out and the reader can easily work around them, which does not keep the narrative voice from presenting the dissertation as the doublet of the orgy, and indispensable to its economy.[62] Just as Sade regulates the orgy while using it to represent the indistinctness of the bodies, so he marks off the text into different sections while at the same time giving them equivalent meanings. The libertines consider philosophical discourse to be quite as erogenous as the dialogue that describes their excesses. Twisted into an incitement to crime, philosophical discourse becomes an aphrodisiac: a profound insight that both points to the preverbal underpinnings of thought and also holds them in check with clearcut demarcations. The "operation of judgment" is performed by cutting, in a defense against the feminine which itself remains perceptible in and inseparable from the verbal outpouring of the dissertation.[63]

The dissertation is important here in terms of the evolution of the novel genre and of the place of the written and the oral in Sade's own practice. Two factors are usually cited to explain the presence of the dissertation in Sade's work, if not its length: the tight ideological bonds linking novelists and philosophers in the eighteenth century, and the blurred boundaries between genres. However most critics have failed to note that both factors arise out of the written form. It has been argued that only in France did philosophers turn to the novel,[64] and that, for their part, novelists liked "to draw up the balance sheet of philosophy" in their fictions.[65] Already in the work of Prévost "the novel is becoming philosophical."[66] We may recall the complicity, whether acknowledged or not, between philosophers and libertines. *Thérèse philosophe* is probably the first novel in which philosophical discourse and pornographic scenes alternate, but Sade is the only writer to give equal erogenous quality to both. The debt which philosophical and moral discourse owes to writing needs no emphasis here, since "writing is an absolute necessity for the analytically sequential, linear organization of thought," or even to "generate concepts."[67] Distancing itself from the binary oppositions of oral culture,[68] writing is a condition for the development of complex forms of irony[69] and facilitates the drift of argumentation which reaches full flood in the dissertations.

As for the mixture of genres and its corollary, the imprecision of generic distinctions, this did not originate in the eighteenth century. Much earlier fiction had contained long discursive passages. We could go back as far as Jean de Meung, though, in so far as Sade is concerned, the most important precursor is probably *Don Quixote*. Fabre also cites the moral homilies scattered through the novels of Jean-Pierre Camus, the seventeenth-century precursor of gothic novels.[70] When the thief Dorval harangues Juliette and her woman friend (8: 122, 120), he addresses them as "chères filles" ("dear girls" or "dear daughters"), an expression which brings the church to mind as much as the brothel. During the Enlightenment the range of themes becomes wider, and by the end of the eighteenth century, even the popular novel was engaging in scientific and ethnographic commentary. We need only recall the long and obtrusive digressions on the chamois and the marmot to be found in *Coelina, ou l'Enfant du mystère*, a 1798 novel by Ducray-Duminil. An encyclopedic model of fiction had thus been established long before Balzac, George Sand, and Eugène Sue carried it to a higher level in the nineteenth century. Conversely, the philosophical texts of Diderot, for example, included many narrative passages, and even dialogue.

A comparison between Sade's harangues and those of "imaginative" historical discourse suggests the hybrid nature they share as a result of their common roots in classical rhetoric.[71] Both kinds of harangue are coded as "spoken," but both owe some of their characteristics to the written word—a periodic and elevated style and complex organization and modes of reasoning. The dissertation-harangue is a sample of oratorical art—an oral tradition originally, but one that turned to writing early on, even as it kept many traces of orality.[72] From the seventeenth century onward, historians, philosophers, novelists, preachers, and revolutionaries were mostly educated by the Jesuits. Jesuit education gave a central place to rhetoric, and good writing was modeled more or less on good speaking, or at least on classic eloquence, as Barthes notes in his essay on ancient rhetoric (p. 193). One essential detail to note is that this discipline of rhetoric, born in Sicily in the fifth century before Christ from "property lawsuits" (Barthes, p. 175), retained its elitist vocation and secured for the governing classes "ownership of the word" since language is "a power" (p. 173). (Women were excluded from this education, which makes the sex of the women orators in *Justine* and *Juliette* even more problematic.)

When he exploits rhetoric so immoderately, Sade both lays claim to and subverts one of the signs of power, again indirectly through parodic imitation. And he is immediately motivated to do so by revolutionary discourse, a discourse of power that he superimposes on the models of history, philosophy, and preaching. The harangue, which appears discreetly in *Les Infortunes de la vertu* and is almost absent from *Les Cent-vingt journées*,[73] has a forerunner in the discursive pieces in *Aline et Valcour*, though these still do not feature the vehemence of the apostrophes and the series of examples in versicles. At least in the novels, the harangue takes on its ultimate massive form only after Sade had experienced the Revolution. It seems likely that the phenomenon of the Revolution, more than any particular oratorical genre, served as a catalyst for this development.

The increase in length goes along with an increase in bombast and rhetorical techniques, which notably heightens the oratorical or even oral quality of the dissertation in *Justine* and *Juliette*. Although this evolution reflects the overall increase in all the narrative units, it exceeds it because of the immediate influence of revolutionary discourse. A junction seems to occur between the oral character and the oral status, that is to say between the effect of orality and the representation of orality, a change that becomes the most significant feature of the harangue. As Barthes notes ("L'Ancienne rhétorique," p. 198), the harangue bears many traces of the *inventio*, or "search for arguments."[74] Among the units that are rooted, at whatever level, in orality, and that create a fairly pronounced effect of orality, one can single out the *disputatio* and the *altercatio*, the various series of examples, and the words of advice. The *disputatio*, a polemical genre which entails a certain verbal aggressiveness, is an oral exercise long performed in Jesuit schools and still practiced today. It pits two students against one another: the first, called the candidate, defends a thesis and then answers the objections of the second, designated as his opponent. The master then sums up (Barthes, "L'Ancienne rhétorique," pp. 190–91). The *altercatio* is an integral part of the speech: sometimes toward the end it interrupts the *confirmatio* by a "very lively dialogue with the opposing counsel or a witness" (Barthes, p. 217). There is an obvious kinship between *altercatio* and *disputatio*, despite the differences in length and origin.[75] After *Les Infortunes de la vertu*, the dissertation, which already gets longer in the second *Justine*, grows to a length of ten or twenty pages in *La Nouvelle Justine* and *Juliette*, whereas the dialogue devoted to objections remains about two pages long, as in *Les Infortunes de la vertu*. Here we are closer to the *altercatio*, which appears in its purest form not in *Juliette* but in the two *Justines* where the virtuous heroine strives in all good faith to argue with her different mentors. In *Juliette*, on the other hand, where all the discussants, with one or two exceptions, are wholly in agreement, the objections usually seem pro forma. Thus the opinions held by the various characters influence the treatment of the forms adopted. As a counter-example, Saint-Fond does not share the atheism of his partners, and this exception constitutes a complete sampling of the forms I have just listed.[76] Outside of these dialogues, the disquisition itself interiorizes the *disputatio* and/or *altercatio*, lining up the arguments for and against and thus gaining a certain liveliness, despite its length. All these features in different degrees, achieve an effect of orality.[77]

The *exemplum*, a formulaic technique that achieves a maximum of oral effect, "can be of any length . . . a word, a fact, a set of facts, and a narration of those facts," or even consist simply in citing exemplary persons, such as Nero (Barthes, pp. 200–201). This technique provides Sade with a blank slot he can fill with lists of incongruous examples, real or fictitious, that embellish the dissertations and flout logic in a playful mode. Ill-adapted to logical development, the *exemplum* relies on the juxtaposition of detachable pieces and formulas: examples, proverbs, and other "commonplaces or *loci* (topoi)."[78] In most instances, Sade makes a general statement before moving into the "proofs," set out in versicles in such a way as to mark their oral filiation: "Do all peoples have the same respect for these absurd bonds? Let us rapidly review those who have despised them. / In Lapland, in Tartary, in America, it is an honor to prostitute one's wife to a stranger. / The Illyrians, etc. / Adultery was publically authorized by the

Greeks . . . , etc. / Cook discovered a society in Otaiti where . . . etc. / The negroes of the Pepper Coast . . . , etc. / Singha, Queen of Angola . . . , etc." (8: 76–77, 68–69). This series takes up no less than three pages, the normal length in *Juliette*. Violently parodic, the technique caricatures not only the rhetorical model but also the cataloguing that is characteristic of scientific classifications[79] (hinting, incidentally, that these too are distantly rooted in oral culture). The subversive force of this technique is as much a result of the turgid, motley juxtapositions as of the scandalous theses which the orator is illustrating.[80]

The sections offering advice, which often swell into exhortations and admonitions, exemplify a particularly hybrid orality in Sade's work. Here we find classical eloquence at one moment: "O tender creatures, works of the divine hand, created for the pleasures of men! cease to believe that you are fashioned for the sexual pleasure of one man alone" (8: 79, 72), an exhortation followed by three pages of imperatives in the same style; at another moment revolutionary discourse, of which we have already seen examples; at another traditional lore (perhaps turned upside down), which prolongs the practice of the oral narrative:[81] "Never have any children, nothing gives less pleasure; pregnancies ruin the health, spoil the figure, wither the charms, and the uncertainty of such events is the very thing to make a husband surly. There are a thousand ways to avoid pregnancy, the best being to fuck the ass" (8: 86, 79).

The harangue is the supreme form of oratorical art: hence there is a properly tautological reason for the massive dose of oral characteristics which we have just reviewed. That said, the Sadean harangue is so strongly directed toward listening that, without leaving the realm of orality, we can be still more precise about the reasons for its frequency and its extension in *La Nouvelle Justine* and in *Juliette*. If Sade's encounter with revolution- ary discourse has such repercussions in these two works (as well as in *La Philosophie dans le boudoir*), it is, I believe, because that encounter occurred after his years in prison. In the dual practice—both civic and parodic—of this discourse, he found an apt vehicle for all the speeches for the defense and the prosecution which he had been unable to voice during his incar- ceration. The harangue is a reaction to silence and isolation, a response to that frenetic desire to gain a hearing which marks his correspondence (to say nothing of the disputes he had with his jailers, with Mirabeau, who was a fellow prisoner at one period, and with the governor of the prison- castle at Vincennes) and it conjures up the phantasy of a dual communi- cation situation, both internal and external to the novel. Introduced and interrupted toward the beginning by apostrophes to the fictional inter-locutor, the harangue tends to move, in a growing tide of vehemence, to addressing a general audience, a "vous" in the outside world. Already with Delbène's second harangue, which extends over more than twenty pages with a few dialogue interruptions (8: 38–60, 29–52), the woman orator refers to herself by the subject pronoun—"To enlighten me as I make this difficult choice, I have only my reason" (39, 30)—and she apos-trophizes Juliette several times over (8: 38–46, 29–37): "Listen, Juliette! Give me your complete attention"; "O Juliette! let us not doubt"; "Let us not doubt, dear friend," apostrophes which seem to be the equivalent of the gesture that punctuates and reinforces the speech. She then goes on to deal with the objections of imaginary listeners: "Let us grant, if you will, to our antagonists the existence of the *vampire* [God] that makes them so happy" (8: 46, 37) and starts to challenge these external listeners one after another: "If your God is not free"; "Let us continue. I now ask you, o deists" (8: 47, 38). The pope's speech follows exactly the same pattern, though with more moderation (9: 170–202, 765–98). To be sure, there are many more harangues which take place in a situation of internal commu-nication, but they are also shorter.[82] On the whole, when the harangue achieves its maximum development, it tends to create the illusion of a dual communication situation, internal and external.

For it is inded an illusion, and the difference between these two types of harangue is merely superficial. What unites them and contributes most to their oral character is that their only (fictitious) addressee is a single contradictor, and that their development, which interiorizes the *disputa-tio* and the *altercatio*, is determined from beginning to end by alternating objections and refutations. In most cases, it is the haranguer himself who formulates the objections, not in impersonal terms, but by means of a di-rect interpellation. At the end of the harangue, the internal interlocutor declares that he is completely convinced. The "tu" who has been addressed comes to echo the "I," and it is this model of ideal listenership which is laid before the reader, or at least before the implied narratee whom the text sets in the place of the absent and hostile audience—the "deists" or others. This implied narratee whom the writer prefers can, by definition, only be identified with the internal viewpoint. Thanks to him, the harangue makes partisans of the adversaries it collectively apostrophizes. How can we not be reminded of Sade at his window in the Bastille, haranguing the mob—his virtual partisans—and denouncing his enemies? It manifests the same vehemence, the same hysterization of the discourse (the semiotic, gestual value of the apostrophes addressed to the fictional or imaginary listener), and the same lack of response from the real readership, except that Sade is transferred to Charenton.

The harangue offers the instinctual drive the imaginary support of the voice, which is closer to the body than the written word. It is to narrative what the scream is to the description of pain. Although it gives utterance to the discourse of the fictional addressees, alongside that of the haranguer himself, it substitutes for any real communication an oratorical jousting which can only end with the victory of the haranguer. The harangue cannot be separated from the *altercatio* dialogues that surround or interrupt it and distribute shorter series of questions and answers between two characters. More frequent than has sometimes been claimed, dialogues serve to trigger and reactivate the effect of orality. More than Juliette's oral narration, which can rarely be distinguished from the written narrative, the unit formed by harangue and dialogue gives proof of a wish to short-circuit writing; for, in the desire to break away from silence and imprisonment, the escape route offered by writing always seems too deferred. The harangue translates the dream of a direct communication, of a transparent speech which would transform the forthcoming reading into an immediate and perfect listening. This may well explain its centrality in the structuring of the novel. It annexes all the novelistic dialogue, except for those parts devoted to the program and the description of the orgy. It carries into the spoken word of the discourse the movement that Sade fails to imprint upon the scene. The movement of the orgy is transported into the verbal torrent of the dissertation: such is the paradoxical fate of a dream that has failed to find adequate means of expression. Here lies the deepest link between the scene and the dissertation.

Sade's text is a mechanism designed to attack tradition, and it lays to rest any notion of a hierarchy of forms. Whether it be discursive modes (dissertations, dialogues, footnotes), orgy scenes, or narrative, each of these forms destabilizes meaning. This effect is compounded by their juxtaposition. Each aggressively takes its distance from the others, because of their lack of ressemblance as well as the rigidity of their demarcations. Based on the distortion of the models it imitates, heterogeneity can be felt on all levels: between the larger units of the text, which clash with one another thus challenging tradition and laying down the main lines of a parodic organization; within the speeches and descriptions, which provide reversal of the expected meanings, blurring of generic boundaries, mixture of language registers; and in the manifold inscriptions of a divided subject.

# 7. Figures of the Text: Parody and Politics

Our study of the way repetition functions narratively, of the inversion of signifieds (in speeches and action) and of textual heterogeneity has provided us with a sampling of the parodic patterns woven into the *Histoire de Juliette*. It now remains to clarify how they function and to reconsider the figures of the orgy which, as figures of the text, emerge most sharply as figures of parody.

## A Perverse Textual Practice

The prescriptions for libertine living are also models for writing, and the writing moves in step with a sexualization of discourse whereby the sadistic instinct and its various modes of inversion sustain the strategies of the argument. The subject who makes the parodic utterances, at once magisterial and divided, and the subject of the orgy, are one and the same. The relationship between the perversity of the actions and that of the speeches will become even clearer if we look at the forms of repetition and inversion that occur in the sentence or the paragraph. Within the boundaries of the sentence, we find once again the distance between desire and act. It gives rise to well known enumerations of the type "it is in hands defiled by uxoricide, infanticide, sodomy, murders, prostitution, infamies, that heaven saw fit to place these riches" (9: 326, 924). The interchangeable nature of desire and language appears in sentences which pile up incestuous kinship links one on the other: "I had a child by my first cousin: I fucked this child, who was my niece, and by that niece I had this girl who thus is both my great-niece, my daughter, and my granddaughter, since she is the daughter of my daughter."[1] In these sentences verbal juggling is not the only purpose; indeed they demonstrate the tendency to manage heterogeneity through a process of naming which connects incompatible elements and imposes a linear order on them without any real classification. These are anal traits that Sade himself displayed in his mania for collecting. Barthes is right to talk about a "cultural medley" when he discusses the inventory of objects Sade brought back from his journey to Italy: "marbles, stones, a vase or amphora for storing resinated Greek wines, antique lamps, tear vases, all *à la* Greek and Roman, medals, idols, raw and worked stones from Vesuvius, a fine sepulchral urn intact, Etruscan vases, medals"—but there is no need to continue with the list.[2]

More directly tied in with the sadistic instinct are certain syntactic structures which again turn the models upside down but within the unit of the sentence. When one victim protests, "To death? . . . What have I done to deserve death?" the answer that comes back follows the logic of instinctual drives, overturning normal semantic relations in a twist underlined by the parallelism of the two sentences: "if you had deserved death, slut, you would not have been condemned to it" (9: 319, 917).[3] As Jean Clavreul has written, corroborating Sade's case from his own clinical experience as an analyst, "the erotic arousal occasioned by contemplating the suffering of the other is sustained only if one thing is sure: that the other is innocent. Thus the sadist is moved far less by the cries of pain than by the protestations of innocence and pleas for mercy."[4] Hence the chronicle of virtue's misfortunes, in which this perverse motivation overdetermines the inversion:

> I could see . . . an infinite number of ways of redeeming by crimes the gratitude which I owed to this benefactor (9: 238, 834).—Stifle your sobs . . . they arouse our cruelty; the more tears you shed, the more we shall make you suffer. (9: 321, 919)[5]

Hence in turn, within the structuring of the sentence, permutations such as "make vices of all the human virtues, and virtues of all the crimes" (8: 28, 18), and a rhetoric for celebrating vice usually reserved for the praise of virtue.[6] "'Oh! Juliette,' she cried, redoubling her usual blasphemies, 'oh! my darling soul, how delightful is crime! how powerful its effects! What charms they work upon a sensitive soul!'" (9: 393, 991). Heightening the contrast between the grace of the style and the violence of the actions, oxymorons, antitheses, chiasmuses, and syntactic crosses are the rhetorical manifestations of the attack mounted against semantic positions. Stichomythia can achieve the same effect:

> —Bring rods! will you whip, my dear girl?
> —Ah! to the blood, my sweet . . . (8: 275, 286),

as does the reference to the "delicious murmur of the swishes of the rods" (9: 520, 1124), or when Juliette and her companions take over the point of view and the rhetoric of virtue, a technique found throughout Sade's work and which contributes to the blurring of moral values: "Never perhaps had anything so horrible been presented to my eyes" (9: 458, 1060). "At these words, the unfortunate creatures throw themselves at the knees of their relentless tyrant" (9: 460, 1062). Some sentences express the desire which is at the root of this effect of heterogeneity—the desire to reawaken the perception of the indispensable transgression: "Now it was a planned slaying . . . a premeditated murder, a horror, a loathsome infanticide, a jouissance much to our tastes." (9: 117, 712). In other places, a simple possessive adjective serves to convey this need to name the crime while embracing it and thus to establish a complicity between the woman narrator, the criminal, and the reader: "Our villain [inversion of "our hero"] calmly sets about repackaging the torn remains of his daughter" (9: 446, 1047).

Although this simple form of inversion is rarely enough to satisfy the libertine program, it is not wholly lacking in subtlety. Thus crime will be presented as the goal of political activism, not as its accompaniment or its result: "The man who loves murder stirs up people's opinions which in turn will inspire them to commit murder" (9: 194, 790, n. 2). With more complex forms, the most remarkable prescriptions effect a decentering of values that depends entirely on the subject's whim, itself unpredictable: "Your conscience is still not what I would wish; what I demand is that it should become so *twisted* that it can never be straightened" (8: 431, 450, italics in the text). Once all moorings have been cut, the sadistic libertine, identified with his superego, seeks the *reason* for his acts in himself alone: "And what unbelievable injustice will lead you to call *moral* that which issues from you, and *immoral* that which issues from me? Whom shall we consult if we wish to know who is right?" (9: 512, 1116, italics in the text). Sade constantly plays with the different meanings of the word "nature:" in the sense of "humanity" (man is good by his nature) and of "realizable, and therefore to be realized," especially in order to state that nature offers us the means to achieve an anti-nature,[7] which opens the way up for other series of syntactic permutations and semantic slippages (8: 449, 468). Shifting to the idea of nature as the origin of man's worst actions, he uses it as the basis for some provocative syllogisms. Following the *exemplum*, a form of reasoning that, as we saw in the last chapter, is closer to orality and corresponds to "non-scientific" induction, comes the syllogism which corresponds to deduction and is harder to conceive of outside written discourse.

Sade's manner constitutes a singular perversion of the classical conception of the Aristotelian enthymeme (the rhetorical equivalent of a syllogism or, more commonly, a truncated syllogism): Barthes emphasizes its relationship with the doctrine of verisimilitude, itself based upon the *doxa*.[8]

Starting out with an idea that is current if frequently belied by facts, Sade moves on to a proposition diametrically opposed to credibility. Thus he justifies crime on the basis of a premise which goes only slightly beyond the optimistic moralism of his contemporaries—"the character of a good law must consist in making everyone happy": now the law that puts down crime, he goes on, "makes as many men on earth happy as unhappy," and therefore is worthless (9: 516–17, 1120). Or else he pretends to demonstrate that death is a pleasure by linking two premises together that confuse the needs of nature and those of men; that is to say that "our death is nature's sole aim," and that "every need in life is only a pleasure," which leads to the conclusion that "there is therefore pleasure in dying." This procedure completes the demystification of the Rousseauian belief in the happiness inherent in the state of nature. On the transphrastic level, the discourse reworks and complicates the original structure of inversion (innocence/punishment) that, triggered by the sadistic motivation within the limits of the sentence, gathers strength and spreads from paragraph to paragraph in the dialogue and especially in the dissertation. Sade is as systematic as he is skillful. He exploits perverse logic with extraordinary acuteness in order to denounce the contradictions in intellectual productions, and, by setting the scriptor "to contradict himself," he jolts the reader's habitual thought patterns in an "unbearable" way.[9] Sade takes a malicious pleasure in "bringing down" his philosophic and moral adversary in this way. Nonetheless, he does not always emerge from the strife untouched. His parodies of demonstration, for all their absurdity, contain enough ideas he still believes in to blur his voice more than ever, and the faults in this logic risk turning against him. (We may recall the sophism of his opposition between public and private despotisms.) It is true that the reasoning of even his least satiric (or perhaps his most sincere?) flights tends to wander. Yet self-irony is not excluded, so that in many cases the target and the intent remain unclear. This is the consummate form of perverse logic.

If the sado-erotic origins of the procedures of inversion and repetition (as we saw in Chapter 6) are linked to the phallic and sodomic eroticization of the text and its production (as we saw in Chapter 4), it could be argued that this sado-phallic-anal kind of writing bears a certain kinship with the discourse of paranoia. Freud proposed interpreting certain kinds of individual neurosis as a distortion of the "great social institutions of art, religion, and philosophy" and he compared "paranoiac delusion" to a "caricature of a philosophical system."[10] The dissertation, in which Sade's perverse textual practice is most fully evolved, tirelessly distorts the whole philosophical, moral, and political tradition, and Sadean eroticism brings together traits which, according to Freud, are characteristic of paranoia, in particular those he attributes to a phallic-anal type of homosexuality (taste for classification, horror of the maternal body, etc.), associated in turn with an intact intellectual power. There is no need to accept this diagnosis in detail, but its central principle does seem to apply, that is to say the recognition that the Sadean delirium weds sexuality to intellectual elaboration. Sade twists the notion that happiness is grounded in individualism and the satisfaction of desire and turns it into an antisocial dogma. With remarkable tenacity, he sets his sadism at the heart of his moral and philosophical discourse, and his aberrant logic originates in that claim.

## The Orgiastic Body as a Textual Figure: Parricide, Sodomy, and Coprophagia

Whether one speaks of orgiastic textuality or of the combinatory rhetoric of the orgy (without assigning a linear causality or single order to the series of mediations between the body and language), discursive reasoning and orgy rituals share in the same structures. Every practice engaged in during the Sadean scene has its parallel on the purely textual level,[11] but three practices in particular emerge as figures or metaphors of the text and its parodic potential—*parricide*, *sodomy*, and *coprophagia/coprophilia*. Parricide and sodomy have a particularly close semantic relation, the former with the parodic intent, the latter with all the modes of imitation and parodic inversion. Coprophilia/coprophagia is a fairly good figure for the problematic dimension of Sade's relation to his literary models.

Only one passage in the *Histoire de Juliette* introduces parody in the narrow sense of the term. It consists of two poems and names the two models they parody: the "famous sonnet of des Barreaux" (1602–1673) and the *Ode to Priapus* by Piron (1689–1773). These two parodies, attributed to Cardinal de Bernis (one of the "real" characters in the novel) superbly realize the triple alliance of parody-parricide-sodomy. Destined within the novel for Pope Pius VI (Braschi) and recited in his presence, they target Jesus and God the Father (9: 95–96, 690–91).

## PARODY AND PARRICIDE

> —There is nothing I do not allow myself, once my passions speak." — What," I exclaimed, "even murder?" — Even parricide, even the most frightful of crimes if there could be any such for mankind." (9: 486, 1089)

"If divorce were allowed, fewer spouses would die" (9: 487, 1090) goes on the "pleasant Venitian lady" who has not hesitated to put theory into practice, and whose words could be extrapolated in the following way: give up the cult of the father and parricide will occur less often. The eighteenth century was "obsessed with the father"[12] and Sade, a man of his times, places parricide at the very top of the hierarchy of crime. The representation of parricide in the novel of the period accompanies a certain questioning of paternal power and, no doubt as a reaction, its juridical strengthening.[13] Sade takes over this choice form of transgression and theorizes it. As a developed parodic motif and as the implicit metaphor for parody, parricide in the *Histoire de Juliette* forms the theme of one long harangue and one shorter one, as well as of two major episodes (Saint-Fond and Juliette), and several briefer ones (Borchamps, Olympe).

In Sade's day, the term parricide was quite frequently used for the murder of the mother as well as of the father. Sade, however, uses the term in the limited sense, and only rarely do the two crimes have the same significance in his work. He assigns the hatred for the mother's body to the realm of the instinctual drives; the hatred for the father targets the sociopolitical order, with an occasional instinctual component. This distinction characterizes the double crime of Borchamps, who first kills his mother and then his father. His matricide takes the form of an attack on the maternal body, motivated by jouissance and the satisfaction of a primeval hatred. With the assistance of his father, Borchamps slits his mother's abdomen "into four parts," so that he can plunge "into her entrails, an iron burning in his hand," and rip out and cauterize "her heart and viscera" (9: 228, 825). As usual, no sooner is there a hint of incest with the mother than evisceration occurs instead. By contrast, Borchamps's parricide is a matter of pure abstraction. A few months later, Borchamps discovers that his father had encouraged him to commit matricide only because he wished to remarry.

Faced with ruin, Borchamps decides to poison his father, of whom it is reported merely that "he fell down dead at dessert" (9: 229, 826).

Nonetheless, the character of the spouse-mother may on occasion embody patriarchal power and, by extension, literary authority. Juliette loves Noirceuil all the more when he tells her that he has freed her from parental tutelage by having her parents murdered.[14] Thus there are times when Sade includes woman in the representation of hierarchical power recognized by the social order. One particular passage in Belmor's speech even links the respect traditionally accorded to woman with the respect for religion, and condemns both at once (8: 484, 506). The former, he claims, is a sign of decadence that must, like the respect owed to the father, disappear with the progress of free thinking.[15] This type of speech associates family with religious belief, to which the written and cultural tradition is an adjunct.

In this latter domain, a revolt breaks out not only against the literary father, but also the literary mother, even as a manifest or underground intertext continues to take on the function of paternal authority, be it acknowledged, twisted, or denied. On these two counts, the rhetoric in *Reflections on the Novel* is significant, for it assumes different forms with respect to the masculine and the feminine when voicing either admiration or rejection of the parental agency. Curiously, Sade makes no mention of *Les Liaisons dangereuses* in the list of novels he praises in *Reflections on the Novel*—probably a sign of ill-digested envy for his immediate predecessor Choderlos de Laclos[16]—but in general he lavishly praises the great male novelists far more often than he condemns them. His praise of women novelists, on the other hand, is tinged with ambiguity. Sade commends them for their charm, delicacy, and tenderness, and sees them as models for "those who aspire to naught but grace and lightness of touch" (p. 104). He places "Monk" Lewis above Ann Radcliffe (p. 108), a judgment not untypical of his time that critics today would tend to question. Most noticeably, his admiration for *La Princesse de Clèves*, never very warm ("there is nothing more interesting than *Zaïde* nor any work more agreeably written than *La Princesse de Clèves*," p. 103) cools even further as he reminds the reader that Madame de Lafayette may not have been the author: "It has been claimed that . . . La Fayette was aided a great deal, and was able to write her novels only with the help of La Rochefoucauld with what regards the reflections and of Segrais with what regards the style. Be that as it may" (p. 103). Inversely, Sade gives a higher rating to "the vigorous works of Richardson and Fielding," who portray "robust and manly characters" (p. 106), laying out a hierarchy that attempts to raise the value of the novel genre. Without questioning that hierarchy itself, we may yet note the sexed epithets Sade uses in setting it up. Sade places woman in the gallery of literary authorities, but takes away with one hand what he gives with the other. It is the same hierarchy we have already found in the question of who has access to writing, where the written is reduced to the phallic and Juliette lacks the active role of inscription in the symbolic that would give her the privilege of written narration.

As a more direct basis for parody than the matricidal gesture, the parricidal attack unfolds on the socio-political, instinctual, and textual levels all at once. It makes sense to classify the first two rubrics together under the heading of ethno-psychiatry as defined by Pierre Legendre,[17] for the instinctual and the political, closely linked in *Juliette*, work together to produce certain textual procedures which combine and merge the historic and intrasubjective dimensions of the Father's murder—the social and the individual. In fact, the parricidal motif in *Juliette* illustrates the relation between the death of the Father and of parental authority and the death of God. Thus it inscribes itself very precisely within the schema of *Totem and Taboo*, sometimes inverting, sometimes developing the implications of Freud's essay. The parricidal incidents and speeches foreshadow in large measure the Freudian myth whose historicity was emphasized more by Lacan than by Freud himself.[18] While anthropologists have tended to regard the hypothesis of *Totem and Taboo* as both inaccurate and inadequate,[19] the partly retrospective myth it offers is founded on the Oedipus model (itself a myth anchored in history) and does offer some suggestive ethno-psychiatric perspectives. Just as "the mistrust of the father is in direct proportion to the degree of power he is assumed to have,"[20] and just as primitive man uses the totemic meal to commemorate the murder of the father and assimilates his power by consuming the sacrificial animal, so Sade seeks to do away with the father only in order to take over a power he tends to overvalue once it is his. Evidence of this can be found in a letter he wrote to his elder son, who was preparing to join a regiment other than the one his father had destined him for: "I forbid you sir to accept this position . . . and I will not suffer you to enter it. . . . Those who will conceal this order of mine from you will answer with their soul and their conscience for the misfortunes that your disobedience will bring down upon your head and I will visit all my curses upon you if within two months I have not received an assurance in writing that you will carry out my wishes.

The Count de Sade your father." Written from a prison cell, this imperious diatribe with its threat of a father's curse has a desperate ring to it. Lely relates the circumstances that prevented the young Sade from complying.[21]

The last thing Noirceuil does is to immolate his sons. This act is the ultimate, even absurd example of the tyranny of the father which has been explicitly asserted in many other smaller ways.[22] Power speaks *"through blood,"* writes Foucault, "a symbolics of blood" he links to the feudal values of the Ancien Régime.[23] And in more than one instance the violence of parricidal transgression turns out to be the reverse side of the claims to an absolute paternal power (though this is not the final word on the subject, as we shall see). Hence the triple procedure—suppression, identification, appropriation—that characterizes the parricidal gesture. To kill/parody the parent text is also to invest and surpass it.

Apart from a few sacrilegious episodes, the "fathers" reign unchallenged in *Les Cent-vingt journées*. No doubt the Revolution played the decisive role in the development of the parricide motif, since this appears for the first time in the *Histoire de Juliette*. (Even in the dissertations of *La Nouvelle Justine*, there is still no apology for parricide.) It is true that two of the libertines in *Les Cent-vingt journées* have killed their mother and their sister, but none of the four has killed his father, and none has a son. In other words, this first novel does not raise the problem of paternal power or of father-son relations for it does not discuss them, and parricide plays no role. Similarly, Sade has yet to develop or articulate his political thinking. That only happened after his release in 1790, in the wake of his professed pro-revolutionary political activity.[24]

Such an important shift gives us some insight into how Sade lived through the Terror, and, even more important, how he understood it and retrospectively mythified it. Not only did the Terror kill the father and the mother, in the persons of the king and queen, but it condemned Sade to death, since he escaped execution only by sheer luck. In the fiction, everything happens as if the enactment of revolutionary parricide was designed to strengthen the son's power at the expense of the fathers' which had been strained to the limit by the Revolution. It was as an undisciplined son that Sade was imprisoned under the monarchy. Under the Terror, however, as an aristocrat, he could not fail to identify in part with the fathers, and meditate on the fate reserved to them. In other words, Sadean aggression hesitates between the power of the fathers (compromised by the Revolution) and that of the sons (crushed under the monarchy), a sort of dialectic that is resolved by the suppression of any filiation. A rather peculiar triumph of the sons, inscribed in the relation between sodomy and parricide.

A case in point: the murder of Saint-Fond's father is first presented as a political crime, a "ministerial crime," which Saint-Fond, the minister, bids Juliette to perform (8: 241, 251). Saint-Fond's father, "an old man in his sixty-sixth year, commanding universal respect," knows of his son's crimes and depredations and therefore speaks ill of him at court in an attempt to force him out of office before he is unmasked. Thus Saint-Fond needs to kill his father if he is to reinforce his own power. Seeing Juliette somewhat startled by the role she is to play, Noirceuil undertakes to win her over by means of a long speech in defense of parricide, whose first two arguments may be read as an inversion of the Oedipal model. Oedipus's crime transcends objective knowledge and the notion of individual freedom, since Oedipus is guilty despite his ignorance. To the contrary, Noirceuil argues in favor of the negation of filiation and blood ties, and sets up against them a parody of rational thought. His first argument runs like this: My father was not thinking about me when he conceived me, therefore I do not owe him any gratitude (8: 242, 252), and if he reared me, this was because of pride and obedience to the customs of his country (8: 243, 253). His second argument offers a fine example of perverse logic: were I to kill him without knowing him, I should not be committing a parricide. Since I may kill my father without any remorse if I do not know him, the same applies if I do know him. It would suffice to persuade me that the individual I had just killed was my father for me to experience remorse. If my remorse "exists even though the thing does not, it should not legitimately exist when the thing does" (8: 242, 252, my italics).

The end of the tirade suggests that by accepting parricide, and more precisely a political parricide like regicide, which he refrains from naming but which his language connotes, as we shall see, Sade occupies the place of both the tyrant-father and the revolutionary-parricide. He seems initially to salvage the paternal principle, symbolized by the despotism of a single man. Saint-Fond is a "very great minister: he loves blood, his yoke is heavy, he considers murder a useful tool for preserving any government. Is he mistaken? Have Sylla, Marius, Richelieu, Mazarin, or any other great man ever thought otherwise? Does Machiavelli offer any other principles? (8: 244, 254). The decisive moment of the harangue comes when Noirceuil takes up the revolutionary rhetoric and turns its anti-monarchic attack into a positive prescription in favor of monarchy: "Let there be no doubt; blood there must be, especially if monarchic governments are to remain;

the *throne of tyrants* needs the cement of blood, and Saint-Fond is far from shedding as much of it as he should!" (8: 244, 254, my italics). The phrase "the throne of tyrants" encapsulates Sade's oscillation between identifying with the father and with the son. This cliché, so characteristic of revolutionary discourse, inevitably connotes the shedding of blood, not so much by the monarchy as by the Revolutionary Tribunal, and is thus saturated in irony. Such equivocal speaking betrays Sade's doubtful allegiance to the Revolution, motivated in part by the need to survive and probably, in part, by sincere belief. Since the Revolution has killed the symbolic father, it is Saint-Fond-Sade, the aristocrat of the Ancien Régime, who lays claim to the crime and makes it a necessary tool for "preserving any government." How then can one escape the regicidal guillotine without oneself being a parricide? Crowning the defense of parricide, this Janus-faced reasoning sets the son up at the end of the series of substitutive formations God-king-father and confers absolute power on him.

When throne and altar come under attack, writes Freud, the subject feels that his virility is threatened.[25] The fictional enactment of parricide stirs up again all that has been repressed under the ancient taboo. In order to take over the father's power, the Sadean hero turns the taboo into a prescription and represses his obsessive fear of castration behind his thirst for domination. The mark of that obsession is total misrecognition, manifest only in the disavowal, or indeed the refusal, of castration. At stake here is nothing less than everything, in other words power *with* the phallus. This is what accounts for the constant repetition of the act of appropriation and, in discourse, the scandalous extension of naming, the verbalization of the unnameable, and the abusive confiscation of canonic models and their subversion. It is because he is never finished with killing off the father that Sade, despite his singularity, never completely escapes imitation.

Let us look a little more closely at the way the parricidal motif informs the relationship to literary models.[26] No matter how much Juliette may inveigh against the authority of texts—"what man, I pray you, would be stupid enough to embrace such or such an opinion merely because he has found it in a book?" (8: 366, 379)—showing a disrespect which her scriptor ceaselessly buttresses with new evidence, it is as impossible for Sade to completely stray from the conventions of the novel genre or to soften his jarring voice as to yield to the paternal principle or, on the contrary, reject it once and for all. As early as the overture of his harangue in favor of parricide—"Is parricide a crime or not?"—Noirceuil draws upon the parody of classic rhetoric, of the moral debate or of matter of conscience, so many models which he knocks off their pedestals on the same grounds as he does the father figure (8: 241–54, 252–64).[27] More subtly, he both imitates and subverts Pascal's seventh *Lettre provinciale* on the direction of intention, in which the Jesuit father gives the son permission to wish for his father's death in the hope of inheriting, and to "rejoice when this occurs, provided he does so only because of the estate that will befall him, not from any personal hatred." "It would be very simple to hate (one's father)," declares Noirceuil, "but much more natural to seek his life. . . . If self-interest is the general standard of all human actions, there is infinitely less harm in killing one's father than anyone else" (8: 243, 254), since our reasons for doing away with him are far more powerful than with any other man (8: 244, 254). To the justification by self-interest proposed in the seventh *Provinciale*, Sade adds hatred, and there is a flagrant contrast between the placid words of Pascal's Jesuit father and Noirceuil's violent affirmations:

> It is not true that one loves one's father, it is even not true that one might love him; one fears him but does not love him, his existence annoys but it gives no pleasure; self-interest, that most sacred of natural laws, instills in us the invincible wish for the death of a man by which we expect to receive a fortune. (8: 243, 254)[28]

As for Juliette's parricide, it is at once exemplary and problematic in as much as it deviates from the model by substituting the daughter for the son. It first makes a mockery of a stereotyped motif, the scene of recognition between father and daughter. Bernole, whose very name declares him to be a dupe (the French verb *berner* means to dupe), arrives playing the noble father, but he is also needy—and adulterous—and Juliette's first instinct is to send him packing. Her father's reproaches and imprecations seem to echo the topos of the father's curse[29] in which Juliette plays the part usually allotted to the wicked son. Justine, who is one of the women listening to her sister's tale, intervenes exactly at the appointed moment to introduce the character of the virtuous daughter: "Oh heavens! . . . my father was alive, and I did not know it!"[30] But it is the preamble to the parricidal act that carries Juliette's defiance to its paroxysm. Driven to despair by the cruelty of his long-lost daughter, Bernole "throws himself headfirst to the ground, cracks open his skull, and floods of blood gush forth" all over the room. Here is the materialization of the intimate urge to jeer at blood ties (homo-erotic jouissance, masochistic reversal?) as Juliette underscores, using the very words Borchamps spoke when immolating his daughter.[31] "This blood is mine, and it is with rapture that I see it spilled" (8: 449, 468). From this point on, the inventiveness of the details goes beyond a simple formal inversion. Juliette decides to seduce her father before she kills him. The mother is disavowed at the same time as the father. Claiming the mother-daughter likeness, Juliette dethrones her mother and casts out her memory: "You find her again in me, Bernole, here is the woman you loved. . . . She is breathing, you have only to finish bringing her to life" (8: 452, 471). The words describing the seduction, which alternate between padded lyricism and obscene grotesque, harp insistently on Bernole's fatherhood: "Come and give life a second time to one who prides herself on receiving it from you: I owed my first existence to love, let me owe the second one to love also." Juliette refers to "the paternal breeches," "the half-aroused tool" which "gave her life," she "takes pleasure in pumping this first mover of her existence" and receives into "her incestuous entrails the germ of a fruit like unto the one he left one day in her mother's womb" (8: 451–52, 471), a pregnancy designed to end in abortion, thus completing the negation of the paternal principle.

Juliette, furthermore, enjoys "the delicious thought of burying next day the man who joins to the crime of being [her] father," that is to say of holding a symbolic power over her, "the greater crime of intoxicating [her] with delights." Here Juliette's status as a woman assumes its full significance. It exposes the sexual *non-dit* of both family ties and political power, and makes the father's defeat even more shocking because it is brought about by the daughter. Yet this father is too poor and unprotected to have any real power over her. He possesses only his symbolic rights. As a woman enjoying only mediated access to the established power structures, it is Juliette who most clearly embodies the symbolic dimension of parricide, the outright rejection of the law.

Considered as a whole, these different crimes are not characterized only by the eviction of fathers to make way for sons/daughters. They take on their full meaning from the perspective of the absence of sons in the next generation, or, should sons exist, of their elimination. We recall that none of the four libertines in *Les Cent-vingt journées* has a son and that they sacrifice their wives and daughters without the least hesitation. Since this first novel, Sade had experienced an authority conflict with his own sons. After they emigrated, he may even have viewed them as a threat to his own life; he wrote ordering them to return to France, reproaching them for "a situation which holds a sword over the breast of those from whom [you] received [your] lives."[32] At any rate, none of the parricidal agents in the *Histoire de Juliette* is to see his supremacy threatened by a son's existence.

Saint-Fond has no son, and he gives his daughter up to death. Borchamps too has no sons, and will kill his wife and daughters in a series of atrocious tortures. Juliette, even though she plays at best a subordinate part in the exercise of institutional power, also has only one daughter (whom she kills at the end of the novel). Only Noirceuil, the great defender of parricide, has sons, and they make an appearance only at the point when their father is about to execute them. Paternal tyranny culminates with this murder, but it thereby loses its whole point. Parricide sets phallocratic power and sterility in the place of patriarchy and filiation. Of the father and son thus removed, Noirceuil keeps only the fetishized phallus.

## PARRICIDE AND SODOMY

The many associations between parricide and sodomy corroborate this ultimate meaning of parricide: the suppression of any filiation. In Sade, sodomy symbolizes, among other things, a unitary economy of nonreproductive jouissance. It subverts genitality and thus blocks the line of descendance even more effectively. It is the fear of pregnancy that Juliette invokes in order to persuade her father to perform incestuous sodomy with her, an argument that immediately points to the symbolic value of the act since Juliette has already been impregnated. The important thing is that she arranges to be sodomized by her father at the moment she knows they will be interrupted. She then shoots her father while Saint-Fond is sodomizing her: "She who was both sodomist and incestuous can surely be parricidal" (8: 454, 473). Similarly, it is while he is sodomizing his own daughter and being sodomized by Noirceuil that Saint-Fond finishes his father off by strangling him, after Juliette has administered poison (8: 254, 265).

Similar signifieds characterize sodomic holy communion, whose meaning acquires complexity only in *Juliette*. It appears in two episodes, in which the host is designated as "the little God," a phrase that emphasizes its identification with the divine Son (8: 468–69, 489; 9: 161, 766). In terms of the Freudian interpretation of the Crucifixion, however, it is the sodomic communion administered to Juliette by the pope in Saint Peter's of Rome during the sacrifice of the mass that is most clearly linked to the motif of filiation (9: 206, 802). Requested by Juliette, who outlines the scenario, it takes on an ambivalent meaning—a grotesque parody of the parricidal son's triumph and a sacrilegious attack on Christ—while ensuring the symbolic father's survival. Jesus dies on the cross in order to redeem mankind, guilty of an original crime and, in the Freudian interpretation of the Crucifixion, "the crime to be expiated can only be the murder of the father" committed by men, since the son's sacrifice is meant to bring about "atonement with God the Father." By taking communion, "the company of brothers consumed the flesh and blood of the son—no longer the father—obtained sanctity thereby and identified themselves with him." Through this identification of the faithful with the Son, "the Christian communion . . . is essentially a fresh elimination of the father."[33] In Freud's view, then, the dogma of the Eucharist signifies the eviction of the father and the appropriation of his qualities by the sons. Juliette and the pope share respectively the traits of the parricidal son and the filicidal father, and although their sacrilegious act only partially corresponds to the Freudian model, it is singularly illuminated by it. The sodomic communion replays in the burlesque mode both the challenge to the father and the identification of Juliette receiving the host with the parricidal son, along with the derision of this son under his divine hypostasis, a derision in which the pope actively participates. Simultaneously, the pope, the father of Christendom but vowed to nonreproduction, in sacrificing his congregation to his pleasures, represents the father as murderer of his sons. Finally the displacement of the host from mouth to anus turns into total scorn the reverence for the divine Word or the Father's word, and closes the parodic circuit: here the textual and the erotic are joined.[34]

## Parody and Sodomy

The axis of filiation dissolves into the sodomic communion and the eviction of the feminine. Matter is replaced with spirit, and biological production/reproduction with intellectual production. There is no escape from the circle of the One, or the Same, and its textual corollary, the reproduction of models. As a figure for the parodic text, sodomy refers first and foremost to imitation.

In its simple form, which coexists right to the end with its complex forms, Sadean imitation constitutes a variant on the first of Aristotle's four causes, the formal cause. Jean-Joseph Goux defines this as "the form, the idea, the model, the *pattern* . . . the most important cause in the hierarchy," and Goux goes on to show how this definition continues to apply in the realms of production/reproduction, whether intellectual, biological, or economic:

> This is where the preeminence of the *idea*, of the *father*, and of *capital* comes together. . . . What is the reign of the formal cause? It is a certain *paterial-*

*ist* kind of reproduction. It is *homogeneration*. Form that creates form. (*Les Iconoclastes*, pp. 172–73)[35]

This reading of the Aristotelian thesis helps to interpret the meaning of Sadean sodomy, with its "*paterialist* conception of sexual and social reproduction . . . without 'mother' and without 'work,' through desire and form . . . a reproduction by scissiparity, . . . and generation without sexes" (*Les Iconoclastes*, pp. 172–73). In Sade's work, the reproduction of the male Same, though not "without sex," is indeed situated outside of the difference between the sexes and the material, female, bases of production. The discourse and sodomic figures, at any rate, seem to opt for this "conception" and to proclaim it. Spiritualism, as is well known, goes along with the exclusion of the feminine.

It is odd to see how far Sade's materialism[36] remains rooted in idealist and sexed vocabulary and hierarchy:

> There is nothing strange, in fact, in the absolute dominion established by the mind over the body; they compose one same whole, of equal parts, that I will acknowledge, but it is one in which the base parts must, nonetheless, submit to the subtle, just as the flame, which is matter, has dominion over the wax it consumes, which is also matter; and here, in our bodies, is the example of two matters at odds with each other, with the subtle dominating the base. (8: 59, 50–51)

Here we find the very same metaphors which the ancient theories of generation used to contrast the male with the female, and which Sade invoked: woman is wax and base matter, man is breath and contains the Promethean fire that gives life and intelligence to that matter. The lines quoted above are the perfectly coherent complement, within the productions of the mind, of the double equivalence mind-(spirit)-male principle and matter-female principle, which leads to the assertion that the mind has "absolute dominion over the body" (8: 59, 50). The sentence comes very close to setting up as opposites these two "matters at odds with each other," and, despite the materialist profession of faith, it comes very close to spiritualist dualism. On further reflexion, we have here the same Sade who, while continuing to proclaim and demand the supremacy of instinctual desire, puts the body at a distance, imposes on it the discipline of the orgy protocol and declares the necessity of colonizing it through apathy. The simple form of imitation comes out of an idealist, remotely Cartesian, system of reference, in which Sade tries to inscribe his materialist philosophy but which, because the feminine is absent, lacks productivity, that is, the mark of a process of production. Under the sign of the identical, Sade lines up passages of pastiche and casually retreads many worn-out narrative techniques.

Nonetheless, the other representations of sodomy do not stop here. Already the insistent way Sade takes up the term "anti-physis" lays stress on the seme of inversion—the other pole of imitation on the paradigmatic axis of language. Many sodomic figures focus on a simple inversion, emphasized in the commentary and worked out on the lexical level (inversion of good/evil). Sodomy can even be explicitly linked to the word of the traitor, as the man who inverts truth: "I allowed him to take his pleasure, says Juliette, in the manner suited to a man whose profession was treachery" (8: 547, 569–70). In the presence of Cardinal de Bernis, who forgives the fair sex "the error of being women only on the condition that they perform as men" in erotic practice, Olympe guarantees Juliette's "philosophy" (9: 86, 680). The alliance between sodomy and philosophy in the sense of moral and religious libertinism, intellectual daring and heresy, is nothing new. It can be found, to take one example, in Dante's *Inferno*, where the sodomites are philosophers, grammarians, or heretics, and also among the French libertines of the seventeenth century. Henri III is said to have coined the expression "philosophical love," which reveals "the link formed between the love of boys and Greek philosophy after the sixteenth century." This link was "strengthened at the end of the seventeenth century by the introduction of the expression 'philosophical sin.'"[37] In Sade's work, the alliance of philosophy and sodomy, through the rejection of authority, overdetermines the association between sodomy and parricide. If we move on to the examination of figures, we may cite, for grotesque inventiveness, the demands made by the masters who, not satisfied by the Italian-style compliance of their female partners, ask them to wrap their genitals, the better to forget that they are women. This preliminary ritual, which appears first in *Les Cent-vingt journées*, gives rise to several droll and obscene variants.[38] The body of the unfortunate Justine, who dies rent "from end to end" by a lightning bolt, briefly opposes the law of the father to the sodomic rite. Leaning over her body, the libertines note that "the thunder had gone in through her mouth and out by her vagina": "'How justified are those who give praise to God,' said Noirceuil; 'see how decent he is; he respected the ass,'" and all the libertines make haste to sodomize the corpse.

That said, the sodomic figures and their accompanying discourse more usually complicate the forms of inversion, in two ways. In the first place, they imply an uninterrupted mode of repetition-inversion which conceals, but does not erase, the unitary character of the phallic-anal primacy and of parodic specularity. The passage where Clairwil, who has been proclaiming her preference for women and hatred for men throughout the novel, succeeds in getting herself "encunted" by a libertine who detested women and declared he could never manage such a feat, figures rather well this type of parodic reversal set up on the axis of resemblance: "Come and fuck me, you scoundrel! she said to him; come on, on behalf of the cunt of a woman who resembles you, be a traitor to your cult" (9: 387, 984). This game of same and other is the principal schema of the Sadean narrative, and it functions along the infinite series of sodomic variations (in which the praise of the passive position introduces an additional and innovative degree of transgression). Barthes argues that the sodomized woman enjoys transgressive superiority over the boy because she has "two sites." This is how he tries to explain the numerical superiority of female victims, which he reduces to a merely linguistic schema: "The boy, because his body provides the libertine with no opportunity for stating the paradigm of sites (he offers but one), is less *forbidden* than Woman: thus, systematically, he is less interesting."[39] This explanation is inadequate, as we have had numerous occasions to prove, and the argument is at best debatable: is "the boy" really less transgressive, despite the anatomical inferiority that Barthes attributes to him? Jane Gallop is surely right in refusing to decide between the two: "The sodomized man, as counterfeit whore, is in his very falsity a true whore. . . . Integral sodomy brings about not only the metamorphosis of man into woman, but of woman into man . . . the woman whose anus is penetrated plays a man playing a whore/woman. If the man is a false (that is to say, true) whore, then the woman as false man is a false counterfeit (in other words, an authentic) whore. . . . The question, then, of which is the truer whore (the truer essentially false creature) is gaily undecidable."[40] This undecidability is precisely a figure for how difficult it is to put a stop to the specularity of the discourse. As metaphors of parodic reflexivity, serial sodomic inversions make any notion of the norm irrelevant; they destabilize the meaning and position of the model. They nonetheless remain within a self- or "homo-generating" mode of functioning.

## COPROPHAGIA AND PARODY

Coprophagia/coprophilia moves away from the phallic mode of the One, completes the blurring of modes of inversion, and affords the orgy its most scandalous effect of heterogeneity. The ultimate expression of the sadistic superego, it represents Sade's ultimate challenge to the social order, to the authority of texts, and to tradition.

As the American psychoanalyst Sheldon Bach insightfully remarks, the primary narcissism in which coprophagia originates joins up with the masochistic reversal of the sadistic structure.[41] Through a study of *Les Cent-vingt journées*, Bach, like Janine Chasseguet-Smirgel, links coprophagia to the pathological regressions of Sade's narcissism which imprisonment exacerbated, or even triggered, and he concentrates on the hypertrophy of the ego that ensued. Sade uses phantasy to deny the limitations placed upon him in prison, and his denial generates two assertions which between them form a kind of chiasmus: 1) my shit remains idealized (as with a child); 2) not only does my shit remain idealized, but your ideals are nothing but shit.[42] An examination of the example of Saint-Fond will show how the second proposition coincides with the masochistic reversal of sadism and helps to account for it.

Early in the novel Saint-Fond gives Juliette an object lesson in two phases which illustrate respectively these two propositions. The lesson is designed to make her realize the mental agility necessary for a "parodic" mode of living—one organized around the discrepancy of categories. By switching around the objects which merit honor and contempt, Saint-Fond sets up an equivalence between excrement and the highest dignities. He has just received the cordon bleu, and Juliette has hurried over to pay court to him. She begins by kneeling down and kissing his decorations. He then forces her to endure all kinds of physical humiliations, which she contrasts in her tale to the high social situation which he has given her: "If he raised me up high when we were in public, he cruelly demeaned me inside his house . . . he made me adore his prick, his ass; he shitted, I was forced to make a god even of his turd" (8: 227, 236) (*My shit remains idealized*). At the end of this session, Saint-Fond crowns his demonstration by a series of inversions, making Juliette "soil the things which were his greatest source of pride; he demanded that I spit on his order of the Saint-Esprit, and he wiped my ass with his cordon bleu" (8: 227, 236). Juliette is amazed by all this, but he explains that he wishes to show her "that all these rags, made to dazzle fools, have no power over a philosopher" (8: 227, 236) (*Your ideals are nothing but shit*). Far from just figuring the "absolute leveling" of values,[43] this incident inverts extremes. And the lesson goes further. It reveals one of the secrets of sadistic libertinage, which finds a "proud" pleasure in mastering what most gratifies him: "But did you not just make me kiss them?" says Juliette. "That is true," replies Saint-Fond, "but just as these trifles stimulate my pride, so I find a source of astonishing pride in profaning them; such eccentricities of mind are experienced only by libertines like myself" (8: 227, 236). This commentary explicitly makes the masochistic position dependent on the sadistic, and it links the very choice of masochism to the hypertrophy of the ego, or, if one prefers, to the identification of the subject (Saint-Fond) with his superego: a regressive hypertrophy, referring back to the over or under-estimation of "the child's body products" by the mother. She is the essential "public who in the first instance gives to these partial objects *their signifying function as objects of exchange*" (italics in the text).[44]

Coprophagia signifies not only the inversion but also the reconnection of high and low. In order to educate Juliette, Saint-Fond focuses on the need for lucid mastery, and this distinguishes his provocation from mere infantile regression. The mouth is not only the place of oral pleasure and absorption, but also of speech, and the junction of mouth and anus—the second being exclusively devoted to organic function or instinctual satisfaction—can give coprophagia the meaning of a "conscious reclaiming of instincts," which both endorses and goes beyond the analytic viewpoint.[45] Thus the coprophagic figure, that "junction of the fragmentary and the unique," appears as the most accurate representation of the endeavor which the libertine advocates loudly over and again—bringing the drive into discourse and justifying it conceptually, making it a statement directed at others as well as an object of communication. There is no denying coprophagia's significance as a kind of perverse exchange, which, rather than persuade, prefers to deny any disgust on the part of the writing subject and to offer violent forms of swallowing and evacuating.

Thus, for the reader, coprophagia is an exhibition of the drive rather than its sublimation, and of the megalomania of the narcissistic subject rather than of the rationality of the discourse. This understanding leads us on to a third meaning, and brings us again to parodic heterogeneity. Discourse and figure are mutually enlightening, and there should be no minimizing of the disruptive power either of the postures in the orgy or of the perverse logic and paranoiac discourse. Our analysis of sodomy as a figure for parody led us from the notion of simple imitation/inversion, based on the unicity of the model and the exclusion of the feminine, to complex inversion and the destabilization of the model. If coprophagia finally emerges as the ultimate figure for textual heterogeneity, this is because it is the highest realization of what can be called, using Bataille's term, the heterologic function. It "leads to the complete reversal of the philosophical process which ceases to be an instrument of appropriation and now serves excretion; it introduces the demand for the violent gratifications implied by life in society."[46] It is quite obvious that Bataille evolved his notion of "heterology" ("the science of that which is quite other")[47] out of his reading of Sade. His debt to Sade is considerable, but, in return, his theory offers suggestive and seductive insights into the Sadean text which may at times be tendentious, but at other times, as here, are profoundly accurate. Bataille calls attention to the intellectual dimension of coprophagic heterogeneity without isolating it and associates the unleashing of the drive into discourse with what I call generalized parody, which deflects every kind of discourse and pretends to assimilate them by taking possession of them.

Within the category of the heterogeneous, Bataille places any activity whose object "(excrement, shameful parts, cadavers) is found each time treated as a foreign body" (p. 94). This, he remarks, subordinates ingestion to excretion, in that the former merely permits the latter to occur. The object "can just as well be expelled following a brutal rupture as reabsorbed through the desire to put one's body and mind entirely in a more or less violent state of expulsion (or projection)" (p. 94)—a reversal isomorphic to that of the sadistic and masochistic positions. His favorite example is a sentence in *La Nouvelle Justine*: "Verneuil orders shitting, he eats the turd and wishes his own turd to be eaten. The woman who is made to eat his shit vomits it up, he swallows her vomit"—an emblematic sentence indeed, which offers a synthesis of all the scenes of this type.[48]

Let us clarify one point, however. By subordinating absorption to expulsion, Bataille hides the fact that victim and agent have different relations to the phase of ingestion and hence to heterogeneity, and he therefore neglects one of the meanings of coprophagia, in so far as it is a figure for the Same. The denial of disgust on the part of the agent—"the more disgusting the thing is, the more it arouses us" (7: 82****)—links ingestion to those processes of appropriating and reducing the other which define the activity of the masters, and hence, to the idealization of something which, once it has been absorbed, becomes their own. But once it is remembered that the digestive process is never mentioned in Sade, it becomes clear that Bataille is correct in stressing the excretory phase over any other and in finding that it holds the meaning of the whole cycle—nonproductive expenditure, provocation, contempt for the other. In this analysis, Bataille implicitly identifies with the victim. She always experiences the excrement she is forced to swallow as a foreign body. The same goes for the reader. "As soon as your stool appears, I'll eat it. . . . Then all the men come and shit in turn [into my mouth], I swallow their shit, you swallow my fuck, and this is how the scene ends" (9: 480, 1082–83). There is no way coprophagia can be recuperated into a "philosophic system," and the effect of heterogeneity disappears only for the agents. To the variations in the ingestion-excretion cycle corresponds everything in Sade's thought that cannot be incorporated into a system, everything in his writing that obstinately refuses to be assimilated, everything in his discourse that breaks free of repetition/inversion and of games with mirrors.

This irretrievable "remainder" also evades the mode of "paterialist" and "scissiparous" production/imitation, which, together with the eviction of the feminine, characterizes the motifs and figures of parricide and sodomy. But if coprophagia reintroduces the feminine as maternal, it is as a scatological regression, conjuring up that state of abjection Julia Kristeva places at the root of the creative gesture. It is true that Kristeva argues that the Sadean orgy has "nothing abject about it" since "everything is nameable for it,"[49] and naming is the very opposite of the loss of the self. This may be so. However, the scene continues to represent that abjectness even as naming it effects its symbolic negation.

# Conclusion: Which Sade?

*If we admire Sade, we edulcorate his thought.*
　　　　　—Georges Bataille

It is perhaps possible to admire Sade without edulcorating him too much. Yet Bataille's quip is an invitation to reevaluate the many cults that have sprung up around Sade in the twentieth century. These seem to arise either from complacency, the flip side of that boredom Sade so often stands accused of producing, or from self-censorship and denial: the refusal to see or at least acknowledge all the weight and all the representational value owed not only to Sade's brilliant intuitions, but also to the most disquieting implications of the Sadean orgy and its discourse.

The Surrealists set Sade on a pedestal. They saw him as the man of black humor and the revolutionary apostle of the unconscious. Of those who came after the surrealists, Bataille and Klossowski stand preeminent as readers. Unlike Barthes or even Blanchot, they do not take Sade's work in isolation or narrow the extent of its scandalous appeal though Bataille draws Sade towards a mysticism of Evil, and Klossowski toward a mystic religiosity. Beauvoir gives a fine definition of Sade's unique contribution, while perhaps underestimating his importance as a novelist: "The fact is that it is neither as author nor as sexual pervert that Sade compels our attention; it is by virtue of the relationship he created between these aspects of himself. . . . He elaborates an immense system in order to justify [his aberrations]. . . . Sade tried to make of his psycho-physical destiny an ethical choice."[1] During the same period and earlier, Heine and Lely revere, sometimes blindly, the great man who became famous largely through their efforts. "It seems," writes Maurice Heine in an appendix to *La Nouvelle Justine*, "that this word [sadism] was coined in error, to support the inaccurate legend that Sade was a sadist, and at the expense of the historical fact that he was a philosopher who should be honored for being the first man to study, in an objective, methodical, and complete way, one of the great moral forces of man" (7: 428). Surely, it is not Sade's violence that should shock us but the foggy mendacious bigotry which declares the reality of the perversion to be incompatible with the "moral force" of the philosophy, instead of acknowledging that they are inextricably interwoven.

More recently, and especially since 1968, the already well-established image of Sade as a liberator has become *popularized*. This is the only appropriate term even in reference to an intellectual elite which alone can find reasons other than pornographic to get interested in Sade. Sade, it is claimed, sees personal happiness as the primary human need, and the satisfaction of desire as the source of happiness. He frees woman by opening a space for female desire or by preaching in favor of sterility. He is never seen as a pornographer—a "pejorative" term. Sade is untouchable.

Is there any other writer who, on the pretext that he frees us from taboos, gives rise in his turn to such a taboo? Our era is not necessarily wrong to recognize itself in the extreme individualism of Sade, but this recognition may tend to erase other major facets of his thought—such as his nostalgia for the feudal jungle and his absolute submission of the woman libertine to the order of her male masters.

No doubt, Sade is a liberator. With supreme insolence, he casts down the idols and unmasks the pretenses and automatisms of thought. He digs deep to expose the erotic component of the will to power—the link between the instinctual and the political and the power relationships that underpin eroticism. He is tireless in tearing down every romantic illusion, be it social, logocentric, or ethnocentric. But even as he undermines the world by parodying everything and strives to objectivize even perversion, his own illusion, his own prejudice creeps back in. And it is left to the reader, if possible, to maintain the proper distance, as far from rejection as from identification.

# Notes

## Introduction

1. See Naomi Schor's very suggestive essay "Unwriting *Lamiel*," *Breaking the Chain: Women, Theory, and French Realist Fiction* (New York: Columbia University Press, 1985), pp. 135–46.

2. The alliance of orgy and parody recurs in the nineteenth century, after the orgy Balzac describes in his novel *La Peau de chagrin*. See Elisheva Rosen, "Le Festin Taillefer ou les saturnales de la Monarchie de Juillet" ("The Taillefer Banquet or the Saturnalia of the July Monarchy") in *Balzac et La Peau de chagrin*, a collection of essays edited by Claude Duchet (Paris: SEDES, 1979), pp. 115–26. For the parodies this scene immediately inspired, see Lucienne Frappier-Mazur, "Metalanguage and the Book as Model in Romantic Parody: The Example of *Le Bol de Punch*," *Poetics Today*, 5, 4 (1984): 739–51. Claude Duchet has studied the underground influence of Sade at the same period: see "Sade à l'époque romantique" ("Sade in the Romantic Era") in *Le Marquis de Sade*, Colloque d'Aix (Paris: Armand Colin, 1968), and Mario Praz traces his presence through the whole of the nineteenth century in *The Romantic Agony* (New York: Meridian Books, 1957). See also Maurice Regard, "Balzac et Sade," *L'Année Balzacienne* (1971): 3–10, and Claire-Lise Tondeur, "Flaubert et Sade ou la fascination de l'excès" ("Flaubert and Sade or the Fascination of Excess"), *Nineteenth Century French Studies* 10, 1–2 (1981–82).

3. *Carnival in Romans*, trans. Mary Feeney (New York: George Braziller, 1979), pp. 85 ff.: "Bands of young males, journeymen or apprentices . . . wandered the darkened streets . . . ; they literally 'chased skirts' and practiced gang rape. . . . A great many of these juvenile delinquents (. . .) fell heir to the tradition—however diluted—of the fourteenth century's raging *charivaris*; whenever there was a wedding, young and violent practical jokers broke into the church, 'smashed crucifixes, insulted the priest, beat the newlyweds,' then looted the couple's new home. Sometimes they dragged the young couple down to the river for a dunking or took them to the local brothel as a finale to the nuptial festivities" (p. 223). We might be reading the script for one of Sade's "scenes."

4. For example, in *Les Aphrodites, ou fragments thali-priapiques pour servir à l'histoire du plaisir* by Andrea de Nerciat (1793) the inversion of the master-servant relation is replaced by "saturnalia" executed by the lower classes for the benefit of an aristocratic audience.

5. See Jacques Rustin, "Idée sur les romans français de l'année 1760, con-

sidérés du point de vue de l'amour," in *Aimer en France 1760–1860* (Clermont-Ferrand: Université de Clermont-Ferrand II, 1980), 1: 159–67; see 162–63.

6. Michel Foucault, *The History of Sexuality*, Vol. 1, *An Introduction*, trans. Robert Hurley (New York: Vintage Books, 1980), pp. 67–73.

7. See Marcel Mauss, "Les Techniques du corps," *Journal de Psychologie* 32 (March–April 1935): 271–93.

8. Mary Douglas in *Natural Symbols: Explorations in Cosmology* (New York: Vintage Books, 1970) establishes some correlations between cultural variations and symbolic structures. Nonetheless the theoretical implications of her analyses are still marked by the hesitation I am discussing. Thus sometimes Douglas posits the body as the origin of symbolism, but sometimes she posits the perception of the body as the reflection of social organization.

9. See *Civilization and Its Discontents* (New York and London: W.W. Norton, 1961), pp. 80, 88–89, and *Totem and Taboo*, trans. and ed. James Strachey (New York: W.W. Norton, 1950), pp. 146–48.

10. See *Totem and Taboo*, p. 157.

11. On the use of this term, see below, pp. 6–7.

*Part 1 Introduction*

1. Ejaculation was infrequent and painful. Sade himself attributes the pain to the thickness of his sperm and the infrequency to excessive brain stimulation. Annie Le Brun gives the most accurate medical information and commentary on this issue in *Sade: A Sudden Abyss*, trans. Camille Naish (San Francisco: City Light Books, 1990), pp. 17–21.

2. Annie Le Brun has the theory that "there is neither sublimation or (sic) somatization in Sade," because with his exceptional lucidity he subordinates mind to body no more than he does body to mind and objectivizes his experience (*Sade*, p. 21). In fact lucidity is probably irrelevant here. To write is to sublimate, and when Sade consoles himself in prison with preserves, fruit pastes, chocolate, and eel pâté this is already a kind of somatization. See Sade's *Lettres et mélanges litté-raires écrits à Vincennes et à la Bastille*, ed. Georges Daumas and Gilbert Lely (Paris: Editions Borderie, 1980, Vols. 1–2 in 1 vol., 1980), 2, e.g., pp. 126, 172, 207.

3. See Mary Douglas, *Purity and Danger: An Analysis of Concepts of Pollution and Taboo* (London and New York: Ark Paperbacks, 1984), chap. 4, p. 67.

4. See Victor Turner, *The Forest of Symbols: Aspects of Ndembu Ritual* (Ithaca, N.Y. and London: Cornell University Press, 1967), chap. 1, p. 30.

5. *Forest of Symbols*, p. 37.

6. Jean Laplanche and J.-B. Pontalis, *Vocabulaire de la psychanalyse* (Paris: Presses Universitaires de France, 1971), *The Language of Psycho-Analysis*, trans. Donald Nicholson-Smith (New York and London: Hogarth Press, 1973), entry on "Phantasy (Fantasy)," pp. 315–17.

7. Translation of section of the French text, *Vocabulaire*, pp. 153, 152, which is omitted from the English translation.

8. *Vocabulaire*, p. 152 (also omitted from the English version).

9. Quoting a passage from *Three Essays on the Theory of Sexuality*, Laplanche and Pontalis write: "It would seem, therefore, that the Freudian problematic of phantasy, far from justifying a distinction *in kind* between unconscious and conscious phantasies, is much more concerned with bringing forward the analogies betwen them, the close relationship which they share and the transitions which take place between the one and the other" (p. 317). Other theorists take the opposite view, arguing that it is necessary to make this "distinction *in kind*" between conscious and unconscious phantasies. Sée Jean-Pierre Valabrega, "Le Problème anthropologique du phantasme," in *Le Désir et la perversion*, ed. Piera Aulagnier-Spairani et al. (Paris: Editions du Seuil, 1967), pp. 165–72.

10. Turner, *Forest of Symbols*, p. 28.

11. *Natural Symbols*, p. III.

12. *Natural Symbols*, pp. 98–99.

13. *Masochism: Coldness and Cruelty* (New York: Zone Books, 1989), p. 37.

14. *Les Cent-vingt journées de Sodome*, Sade's first major work, was outlined and partially drafted while he was imprisoned in the Bastille, but he lost the manuscript when he was abruptly transferred to a convent in Charenton and was never able to recover it.

## Chapter 1. Indistinction and the Hybrid

1. This fact has been well established in both psychoanalysis and anthropology. The best work to consult in this regard is Janine Chasseguet-Smirgel's *Ethique et esthétique de la perversion* (Paris: Champ Vallon, 1984), pp. 219–20, 225–26, because of the important chapters devoted to Sade.

2. This point is remarkably analyzed by Marcel Hénaff in *L'Invention du corps libertin* (Paris: Presses Universitaires de France, 1978), pp. 209, 212, and in Chapter 7.

3. Hénaff, *L'Invention du corps libertin*, p. 219. Bataille was probably the first to underline the signifying function of shit. See below, Chapter 7, "Coprophagia and Parody."

4. Lacan, "Kant with Sade," *October* 51 (Winter 1989): 64.

5. Janine Chasseguet-Smirgel, *Ethique et esthétique*, chaps. 6, 7. She does not discuss the exchange function of shit.

6. In *Sade: A Biography* (New York: Farrar, Straus, and Giroux, 1993), trans. Arthur Goldhammer, p. 326, Maurice Lever refers to the "prestiges" as Sade's "masturbations with or without accessories," but in fact Sade's letters make it plain that he also used the term specifically for the special dildoes designed for anal masturbation which he had his wife procure for him during his years of imprisonment. See *Lettres et mélanges littéraires*, 1: 275–81.

7. See Julia Kristeva, "Something to be Scared of," chap. 2 in *Powers of Horror: An Essay on Abjection*, trans. Leon S. Roudiez (New York: Columbia University Press, 1982).

8. "Something to be Scared of," p. 61.

9. *Purity and Danger*, chap. 7, p. 121.

10. Such are the implicit questions contained in Mary Douglas's analyses. See Carroll Smith-Rosenberg, "Sex as Symbol in Victorian Purity: An Ethnohistorical Analysis of Jacksonian America," *American Journal of Sociology* (1978): 236.

11. The peasant masses and the rising bourgeoisie were growing increasingly exasperated by the survival of a wasteful and unproductive feudal economy. See Hénaff, *L'Invention du corps libertin*, p. 172, who quotes the research of Soboul; for the precise details on the situation at La Coste (Sade's chateau in Provence), see Jean-Jacques Pauvert's biography, *Une innocence sauvage . . . 1740–1777*, vol. 1 of *Sade vivant* (Paris: Robert Laffont, 1986), pp. 238–39.

12. Quoted by Pauvert, *Sade vivant*, pp. 422–23. Pauvert writes, "it seems that justice no longer worked for him. He was *outside the law*."

13. I shall use the terms "scriptor" or "writing subject" for a textual agency which is to be distinguished from either the author or the narrator and which might be compared to Wayne C. Booth's "implied author." See below, notably Chapter 6.

14. *Sade vivant*, p. 339.

15. Douglas, *Purity and Danger*, pp. 120–24, 139.

16. *Purity and Danger*, p. 132.

17. *Translator's note*. I have translated all the quotations from the works of the Marquis de Sade used in this book. The two page references given after each quotation are (1) to the *Histoire de Juliette*, vols. 8 and 9 in *Oeuvres du Marquis de Sade* (Paris: Cercle du Livre Précieux, 1963); (2) to *The Story of Juliette*, trans. Austryn Wainhouse (New York: Grove Press: 1968).

18. The most memorable example of this is the vampirism of Gernande in *La Nouvelle Justine*. He "phlebotomizes" his victims with a lancet and drinks their blood.

19. One exception occurs in *Juliette* ("I shall grow drunk on the menses that I adore, and once I have started off by devouring them" (9: 478; 1081), and there is another in *Les Cent-vingt journées de Sodome* (13: 321, 541). In her essay "'Frenchwomen' Stop Trying," Luce Irigaray rightly points out that menstrual blood is one of the rare taboos observed in Sade. See *This Sex Which Is Not One*, trans. Catherine Porter with Carolyn Burke (Ithaca, N.Y.: Cornell University Press, 1985), p. 200.

20. See Foucault, *The History of Sexuality*, 1: 147–48.

21. See Joyce McDougall, *Plea for a Measure of Abnormality* (New York: International Universities Press, 1980), pp. 204–5.

22. Lacan has stressed the retroactive phantasy of the fragmented body which accompanies the mirror stage and refers back to the Freudian stage of auto-eroticism. On this issue, the reader can consult Freud, *Three Essays on the Theory of Sexuality*, ed. James Strachey (New York: Basic Books, 1972), pp. 45–49; also Laplanche and Pontalis, *The Language of Psychoanalysis*, entries on autoeroticism, organ pleasure, partial object, and paranoid position; see also Lacan's "The Mirror Stage," in *Ecrits* (New York: Norton, 1977); and *The Ethics of Psychoanalysis, 1959–1960*, trans. Dennis Porter, Seminar of Jacques Lacan 7 (New York: W.W. Norton, 1992): "When one approaches that central emptiness, which up to now has been the form in which access to *jouissance* has presented itself to us, my neighbor's body breaks into pieces." Lacan then quotes this sentence from *Juliette* with Sade's own

italics: *"Lend me that part of your body which will give me a moment of satisfaction and, if you care to, use for your own pleasure that part of my body which appeals to you"* (8: 71, 63–64). Lacan comments that this is "the first considered manifestation of something that we psychoanalysts have come to know as part object" (p. 202).

23. There is one comment, in a note that is not placed on the same phantasy level as the orgy scene, which shows some perception of the erotic object as a whole person: "Those concerned with frigging women are insufficiently persuaded of the extreme need women feel at that moment to have pleasure penetrate through every pore" (9: 104; 698).

24. See 9: 63, 656; 285, 882; 287, 884; 393, 990; 460, 1062; 461, 1063; 463–64, 1064–65. For Sade, who benefited from the mediation of writing, such descriptions no doubt have merely a phantasy referent, but, despite the material impossibility of certain details, this type of torture is well known to be characteristic of sadistic crime.

25. See 9: 27, 618; 30, 620; 146, 742; 248, 844; 401, 1001; 407–10, 1007–10; 497–98, 1100–1; 517–19, 1121–23; 521, 1125. This type of phantasy, which is to be found throughout Sade's work, also haunts the imaginary of science and religion. One may recall the Fragonard pictures of flayed creatures which Annie Le Brun has collected—she refers to the desire to know "what rests in the depths of man"— and which included "Three Human Fetuses" in the flayed category (Catalogue of the Exhibition "Sade's Theatres, Small and Large," Paris Art Center, May 1989, collection of the Alfort Veterinary School). In *Juliette* there is a young girl who is flayed as seven superimposed skins are torn off her (9: 470–71, 1073–74). Similarly, Maurice Heine has made an insightful comparison between Bandol's enthusiasm for "caesarian section" in *La Nouvelle Justine* and the comparable enthusiasm expressed in a religious manual reserved for the clergy (fourth ed., 1868) In this manual, the author explains in lyrical terms that if a priest is forced to perform a caesarian upon a dead woman God will reward him because he has "pulled the child from out of a close prison in which it must needs perish, and above all has baptized it. He will be the child's spiritual father, because he has given it new life in Christ. He will be the child's mother, as Cangiamila says, because he will truly have brought it into the world." Here the desire for motherhood is expressed more openly than in Sade. Heine notes that this "essentially sadistic" practice was still authorized by law at the time he is writing. See "Cent-onze notes pour *La Nouvelle Justine*," 7: 422–23, 440–41. I should add that the desire for progeny was very strong in Sade as a young married man. Pauvert comments on the disappointed hopes of the young Sade couple in the first year of marriage (*Sade vivant*, 1: 107).

26. Janine Chasseguet-Smirgel, *Ethique et esthétique*, p. 206. On p. 204, she cites a passage from *La Nouvelle Justine* (6: 209–10) in which Sade denies that the infant is dependent in any way on the mother. Other such passages exist. Angela Carter has the same Kleinian explanation in the fourth chapter of her book *The Sadeian Woman* (New York: Pantheon Books, 1978), pp. 120–36. She remarks that Nature kills Justine in a parody of the act of birth: "the thunderbolt which had entered her mouth, came out through her vagina" (p. 100).

27. Chasseguet-Smirgel, *Ethique et esthétique*, p. 205.

28. The first sketch of this scene attacks the family trinity: "The father . . .

is whipped first. As soon as his blood runs, his wife is tied to his back; and when, after more than a thousand whip lashes, he has opened the wife's buttocks, the little girl, placed on her mother's shoulders, is immediately given the same treatment" (8: 318, 330). At times womb nostalgia is treated more kindly in Sade's writings, as Jane Gallop shows in *Thinking Through the Body* (New York: Columbia University Press, 1988), pp. 62–64. Gallop further notes that one of the rare instances of son-mother incest is that of Bressac with his mother, whom he sodomizes after he has killed her (p. 57).

29. See Pierre Darmon, *Le Mythe de la procréation à l'âge baroque* (*The Myth of Procreation in the Baroque Era*) (Paris: Editions du Seuil, Collection "Points," 1981), especially chapter 9, "La Rage de faire des mâles" ("The Rage to Produce Males"), and the section entitled "Do women have the right to be born?" pp. 141 ff.

30. Men are far from being spared, but they never suffer evisceration or violent internal rending. Among the many tortures endured by males, a few examples of castration can be noted which again habitually emphasize the crime of incest. Castration is usually performed by a woman—as most notably Juliette castrates Noirceuil's son on his instructions. Clairwil, although claiming to be a specialist in castration, performs only two. Despite their savagery, such scenes are never as inventive, lengthy, or numerous as those when a woman, whether pregnant or not, is torn into pieces. See 8: 455, 474; 9: 524, 1128; 576, 1182.

31. Kristeva, *Powers of Horror*, p. 54.

32. See Janine Chasseguet-Smirgel, "Hubris, Law, Perversion," in *Ethique et esthétique*, pp. 217–40, chap. 7.

33. Freud, "Fetishism," *Standard Edition*, 21: 53: "In later life, a grown man may perhaps experience a similar panic when the cry goes up that Throne and Altar are in danger, and similar illogical consequences will ensue."

34. See Douglas, *Natural Symbols*, p. 114.

35. See Douglas, *Purity and Danger*, chap. 6, p. 95.

36. See Hénaff, *L'Invention du corps libertin*, pp. 244–45.

## Chapter 2. An Ordered Indistinction

1. *Purity and Danger*, chap. 4, p. 69.

2. Similarly, the victims of the orgy in Sade, when they have not been kidnapped from a convent, are bought for a high price, and sold directly by their families or by some female procuress.

3. Roland Barthes, *Sade/Fourier/Loyola*, trans. Richard Miller (New York: Hill and Wang, 1976), p. 168. The example is taken from *La Nouvelle Justine*. Michel Riffaterre comments on this permutation from a linguistic standpoint in his review of Barthes's book "Sade, or Text as Phantasy," *Diacritics* 2 (Fall 1972): 2–9. See also below, pp. 160–64.

4. Pascal Bruckner and Alain Finkielkraut, *Le Nouveau désordre amoureux* (Paris: Editions du Seuil, 1977), p. 101.

5. Barthes may have the same passages in mind when he writes: "When Juliette . . . locks herself away from time to time to count her gold . . . she is

not contemplating the sum of possible pleasures, but the sum of her accomplished crimes; money, therefore, in no way designates what it can acquire (it is not a value) but what it can withhold (it is a site of separation)" (*Sade/Fourier/Loyola*, p. 24). On the contrary, money *is* a value, and a value directed into the future.

6. In *Les Iconoclastes* (Paris: Editions du Seuil, 1978), Jean-Joseph Goux shows that the masturbatory effect is based on the exchange value of wealth, but by generalizing this effect as the representational mode *par excellence* of the Sadean text, Goux gives no representational value to the orgy scene (pp. 180–81). In fact, it is not in Sade but in Balzac that we find misers—such as Gobseck, Grandet, or the antiquarian in *La Peau de chagrin*—for whom the symbolism of abstract jouissance is so powerful that enactment becomes unnecessary. Significantly, a comment in the 1804 edition of Senancour's *Oberman* introduces a link between Sade and Balzac and will be echoed in Gobseck's speech: "I have also seen that there is only one *external* thing which might be worthy of our concern, and that is gold. . . . Gold is a force: it represents all the faculties of man since it opens every door, gives man the right to all pleasures; and I cannot see that gold is any less useful to the good man to fulfill his goals than to the man of pleasure" (*Oberman*, Letter LXXII).

7. See Georges Bataille, *Eroticism, Death, and Sensuality*, trans. Mary Dalwood (London: Boyars, 1987). For the Gide of *The Immoralist*, for the Genet of *The Thief's Journal*, theft has an erotic value linked to homosexuality.

8. The same identification can be found in Balzac's novel *Père Goriot*: "The good man (who is going to see his daughter) led the way down the steps and tossed ten francs to the coachman, with the liberality of a widower who, in the paroxysm of his pleasure, pays nothing any mind." *Translator's note*. I have translated this passage, which corresponds to a section on p. 192 of the English translation by A. J. Krailsheimer (Oxford and New York: Oxford University Press, 1991).

9. The parallel works better for coprophilia: see Goux, *Les Iconoclastes*, pp. 183, 185. While recognizing its pertinence, Hénaff objects that "any unilateral interpretation" is undermined by the "contradictory determinisms" of Sadean phantasies. Hénaff then connects the economy of wastage to the "feudal type of sumptuary consumption" (*L'Invention du corps libertin*, p. 140)—a hypothesis Goux had also entertained (pp. 179–80) and which is by far the more convincing. This archaic model neatly corresponds with the wastage of bodies in the orgiastic crime. Sade in fact theorized it by adducing the example of Nature, to whom it costs nothing to produce human beings (see *La Philosophie dans le boudoir*, 3: 514, 326; 525, 333), but it fails to offer the degree of abstractness necessary to the notion of a pleasure-standard, which substitutes an economy of consumption for an economy of wastage.

10. This is the orthodox order for the Sadean libertine, as critics have often noted. Gilles Deleuze analyses this point in *Masochism: Coldness and Cruelty*: "Sade tried to demonstrate that no passion, whether it be political ambition, avariciousness, etc., is free from 'lust'—not that lust is their mainspring but rather that it arises at their culmination, when it becomes the agent of their instantaneous resexualization" (p. 118). Sometimes the order is reversed: "It is certain, dear madam, that libertinage leads to murder" (8: 298, 309). This is a sign of weakness, showing that Juliette is still a neophyte.

11. Balzac will develop a unitary theory of energy, with a sexual component, that bears strong similarities to the one governing the Sadean universe. (In Balzac this theory can be described as pre-Freudian more correctly than it can in Sade, because it takes sublimation into account.) Furthermore, Balzac at times compares energy, or the life force, to electricity, a notion which links up with the eighteenth century materialist current and is also found in Sade. See below, p. 98.

12. Hénaff among others devotes several pertinent pages to what he calls "arithmetical reduction" and "combinatory reduction," even as he insists on the differential element introduced by numeration in certain instances. See Hénaff, *L'Invention du corps libertin*, pp. 33–39, 40–48. Peter Cryle traces the presence of numbers in pornographic literature, especially multiples of four, from Aretino on and convincingly argues for their metalinguistic function ("this is pornography"). See his *Geometry in the Boudoir* (Ithaca, N.Y.: Cornell University Press, 1994), pp. 54ff. and the whole of chapter 2, "Taking Sade Serially."

13. See J. J. Pauvert, *Sade vivant*, 1: 139–40, for remarks on this playful dealing with numbers, on the fashion for "a kind of numerology" in the eighteenth century, and the very probably medieval origin of these games, however devoid of mysticism they may be.

14. See 9: 35, 626; 316, 914; 378, 975; 509, 1112–13. See also 9: 209, 363–64; 366, 963; 402, 1002; 485, 1087; 519–20, 1123–24.

15. See 8: 550–51, 573–74; 556, 577; 562, 584; 566–67, 588–89.

16. See Hénaff, *L'Invention du corps libertin*, pp. 153–54, 31.

17. Foucault, *The History of Sexuality*, 1: 139.

18. Barthes, *Sade/Fourier/Loyola*, p. 152.

19. See Michel Carrouges, *Les Machines célibataires* (Paris: Editions du Chêne, 1976), p. 156.

20. The term "bachelor machine" chosen by Carrouges is in the direct line of an *anti*-bachelor ideology uncovered by Jean Borie for the nineteenth century in his book *Le Célibataire français* (Paris: Le Sagittaire, 1976). The bachelor machine is itself ambivalent: it combines the challenge that the bachelor poses to familial and social consensus and the corresponding opprobrium. Today, we might expect to find Sade's euphoria in the scientific, or pseudo-scientific, discourse describing marriage and sexuality in terms of system. Based on the notion of productivity, such discourse transforms sexual and affective relationships into a mechanism for producing pleasure and happiness, whose effects can be regulated and relied on.

21. The terms "homosexuality" and "heterosexuality," which according to Robert's dictionary came into the French language in 1907 and 1911, are useful, even if anachronistic. The Hungarian Benkert introduced the term homosexuality in 1869.

22. Pierre Darmon, *Le Mythe de la procréation à l'âge baroque*, p. 23. Sade interprets the clitoris as a little penis, and Freud presents it as "homologous to the masculine genital zone of the glans penis," in *Three Essays on the Theory of Sexuality*, ed. James Strachey (New York: Basic Books, 1962), p. 86.

23. Thomas Laqueur, "Orgasm, Generation, and the Politics of Reproduction," in *The Making of the Modern Body: Sexuality and Society in the Nineteenth Century* (Berkeley and Los Angeles: University of California Press, 1987), p. 14.

24. According to Katharine Park, Renaissance sources document only one case of hermaphroditism per 25,000 people, a proportion hugely at variance with the incidence of hermaphrodites in Sade's novels and in pornography (paper given in 1984 at the Berkshire Conference at Smith College).

25. Foucault, *The History of Sexuality*, 1: 38. Isabelle Vissière, *Procès de femmes au temps des philosophes* (*Trials of Women in the Time of the Philosophers*) (Paris: Des Femmes, 1985), p. 342.

26. See Laqueur, "Orgasm, Generation, and the Politics of Reproduction," *The Making of the Modern Body: Sexuality and Society in the Nineteenth Century*, ed. Catherine Gallagher and Thomas Laqueur (Berkeley and Los Angeles: University of California Press, 1987), p. 13.

27. *The City of God*, XVI.

28. This double sexual malformation is a theme in pornography. Thus, in *Thérèse philosophe*, published in London in 1783, La Bois-Laurier is malformed and so can never be deflowered. Therefore her virginity is sold more than five hundred times. In *Les Cent-vingt journées*, la Martaine is "barred" and Madame Champville has a clitoris more than three inches long (13: 29–30, 220–21).

29. In his book *La Prostitution dans la ville de Paris, considérée sous le rapport de l'hygiène publique, de la morale et de l'administration* (*Prostitution in the City of Paris Considered from the Point of View of Public Hygiene, Morality, and Administration*) (Paris: 1836), Alexandre Parent-Duchâtelet cites cases of women with one malformation or the other, but never with both. He writes for example, "At the time when I was pursuing this research, there were only three prostitutes in Paris known to have an especially great enlargement of the clitoris" (p. 102 of the Paris edition: s.d., Paul Fort, Libraire Editeur, 46, rue du Temple); see p. 96 for the case of the "permanent virgins"). The anatomical description Parent-Duchâtelet goes on to give, though much less detailed, corresponds point for point with the medical observations made on the body of the unfortunate "Herculine Barbin." See Michel Foucault, ed., *Herculine Barbin, Being the Recently Discovered Memoirs of a Nineteenth-Century French Hermaphrodite*, (New York: Pantheon Books, 1980), pp. 133–37.

30. See 8: 513, 535; 9: 431–32, 1033.

31. John Boswell, *Christianity, Social Tolerance, and Homosexuality: Gay People in Western Europe from the Beginning of the Christian Era to the Fourteenth Century* (Chicago: University of Chicago Press, 1980), pp. 74–75. The same point was made by Foucault in his *History of Sexuality*, vol. 2, *The Use of Pleasure*, trans. Robert Hurley (New York: Pantheon Books, 1985), p. 215.

32. This passage recalls Gilbert Lely's commentary on the suspicions and sick jealousy Sade entertained toward his wife: "We can be jealous only of the pleasure that we know, or that we sense in an elective fashion. . . . Bisexual husbands and lovers, or psychic hermaphrodites—and we must place the marquis de Sade in this group—by virtue of the nature and degree of their homosexuality, find themselves not only envious of the pleasure of their rivals, but also, consciously or unconsciously, envious of the pleasure of their wives, which they know, either through having experienced it themselves, or of which they have some inkling, more obscurely, as if through their constitution. They have a terrible knowledge . . . of how their wife's body experiences the foreign penis which they both loathe and

admire, as they both loathe and admire the profligateness of the woman whose betrayal tortures them." See Lely's introduction to *Lettres de madame de Sade*, in Daumas and Lely's edition of Sade's *Lettres et mélanges littéraires*, 2: 68.

33. Pierre Klossowski's remarks on the "androgyne" in Sade betray a certain confusion. See Jane Gallop's book *Intersections: A Reading of Sade with Bataille, Blanchot, and Klossowski* (Lincoln and London: University of Nebraska Press, 1981), pp. 84–89. Gallop refers to Klossowski's *Sade, My Neighbour* (Evanston, Ill.: Northwestern University Press, 1991), pp. 35, 48, and to Klossowski's "Preface to *Aline et Valcour*," in Sade, *Oeuvres Complètes* (Paris: Pauvert, 1963), 9: xvii. The terminological distinction sometimes adopted between androgynous and hermaphrodite helps define the Sadean character. Whereas the hermaphrodite juxtaposes the two sexes within a polarity, the androgyne borrows not the anatomical organs of the two sexes but their respective magico-religious powers, fused into a harmonious and ideal union. For this very reason, the androgyne comes to represent an asexual being, not a bisexual. In this sense there is no androgyne in Sade.

34. See Freud, *Civilization and Its Discontents*, chap. 4, p. 53.

35. There seems to be a mistake in the way this dialogue is printed, but from what follows it seems reasonable to attribute this remark to Durand.

36. See *Les Cent-vingt journées*, 13: 138, 334; 148, 345; 245, 456; 387–88, 643); and *Juliette*, 8: 205, 214; 9: 569–71, 1175–76 (the section dealing with the paroxysms of the Noirceuil marriages, which I discuss later in this chapter).

37. See, among a thousand examples, 8: 64–67, 56–59; 86, 79–80.

38. See Jean Baudrillard, *Pour une critique de l'économie politique du signe* (Paris: Gallimard "Tel," 1972), pp. 110–11, for an analysis of the ideological necessity "of reducing semiologically by means of a large binary opposition between masculine and feminine" the activity/passivity ambivalence characteristic of each sex.

39. Jean Deprun, "Sade et la philosophie biologique de son temps" ("Sade and the Biological Philosophy of His Time"), *Le Marquis de Sade*, pp. 189–205: see pp. 192–95.

40. A variation on this phallocentric theory of generation can be found in the *Memoirs* of Casanova, trans. Arthur Machen, (New York: G. P. Putnam's Sons, 1959), 2: 401–2.

41. See Darmon's historical account, *Le Mythe de la procréation*, chap. 3, pp. 39–40, and Danielle Jacquart and Claude Thomasset, *Sexuality and Medicine in the Middle Ages* (Princeton, N.J.: Princeton University Press, 1985), pp. 61–67. See also Paul Hoffman, *La Femme dans la pensée des Lumières* (*Woman in the Thought of the Enlightenment*) (Paris: Editions Ophrys, 1977), pt. 1, chap. 2.

42. See Jacquart and Thomasset, *Sexuality and Medicine in the Middle Ages*, pp. 84–87, for details on how "female seed" is "systematically devalued in the Aristotelian tradition," and also below, Chapter 6, "Narrative Voices, Voices of Eros" for a few confirmatory quotations.

43. Already noted by Jean Deprun, "Sade et la philosophie biologique," pp. 193–94, 204.

44. See Paul Hoffman, *La Femme dans la pensée des Lumières*, pp. 146–47, and also the critical reading of Michèle Le Doeuff, "Pierre Roussel's Chiasmas,"

*The Philosophical Imaginary* (London: Athlone Press, 1983), pp. 138–90, which brilliantly dismantles the fabrication of a psycho-physiology of woman in Roussel's work.

45. A similar speech appears in *Juliette*, 8: 75; 9: 187, 783.

46. 3: 409, 224. Alice Laborde makes the same point in her essay "The Problem of Sexual Equality in Sadean Prose," in *French Women and the Age of Enlightenment*, ed. Samia I. Spencer (Bloomington: Indiana University Press, 1984), p. 341.

47. "Kant with Sade," trans. James B. Swenson, Jr., *October* 51 (Winter 1989): 75. The French "V....ée" most likely stands for "vérolée" (poxed). J. B. Swenson suggests "violée" and "voilée" (raped and veiled).

48. "No, Eugénie, no; we serve nature just as well through the anus as elsewhere, and perhaps in a more holy fashion. Propagation is merely tolerated by nature. How could she have laid down as law an act that deprives her of her omnipotence, since propagation is merely the product of her early intentions, and new constructions, refined by her hand, were our species entirely erased, would in their turn become the primordial intentions whose act would be far more flattering to nature's pride and power?" (3: 414–15, 230).

49. I have found only one reference, in a note to *Juliette* which bases female inferiority on anatomy, to the most ancient and important isomorphism: that which sees the vagina, the ovaries, and the womb as a hollow inversion of the penis, the testicles, and the scrotum (8: 489n, 511n). Only after the sixteenth century do we find, coexisting with the latter theory, the penis-clitoris isomorphism so apparent in Sade. For a detailed historical account of this issue and its interpretation, see Laqueur, "Orgasm, Generation."

50. See Anne-Marie Jaton, "La Femme des Lumières, la nature et la différence" ("The Woman of the Enlightenment, Nature and Difference," in *Figures féminines et roman* (*Female Figures and the Novel*), ed. Jean Bessière (Paris: Presses Universitaires de France, 1982), pp. 75–87. As she writes, "the new definition is far from splitting radically from Aristotelian discourse or from the theological definition, and the texts clearly show that the notion of difference continues to imply that of inferiority and inequality" (p. 77).

51. Mary Douglas argues that "the most important determinant of ritualism is the experience of closed social groups" (*Natural Symbols*, p. 33), and that a magic character often attaches to organized transgression.

52. See Douglas, *Natural Symbols*, pp. 36, 77.

53. See Foucault, *History of Sexuality*, pp. 37–38.

54. Incest characterizes the orgy of the *Satiricon*, as well as all libertine and pornographic fiction, as Florence Dupont points out in *Le Plaisir et la loi: du "Banquet" de Platon au "Satiricon"* (*Pleasure and the Law: From the "Symposium" to the "Satiricon"*) (Paris: Maspero, 1977), p. 162. The theme of incest recurs over and over again in eighteenth-century fiction, and socio-historical factors, such as the influence of travel narratives, fail to account for this obsession. Nonetheless, incest at that time corresponded to realities very different from our own. For centuries, marriage between cousins was forbidden "within the seventh degree of consanguinity, or blood kinship," which made the prohibition "almost impossible

to observe," as Georges Duby notes in *The Knight, the Lady, and the Priest*, trans. Barbara Bray (New York: Pantheon Books, 1983), p. 35. There were, moreover, many abandoned children, and the girls from this group supplied the brothels.

55. Robin Fox, "*Totem and Taboo* Reconsidered," in *The Structural Study of Myth and Totemism*, ed. Edmund Leach (London: Tavistock Publications, 1967), see pp. 161–78, especially 173–74. The anthropological view suggests that all societies institute a prohibition on some forms of incest, while being lenient to others.

56. Béatrice Didier has made the same point and stressed the anthropological dimension in her general study of incest in Sade, "Inceste et écriture chez Sade," *Lettres Nouvelles* (May–June 1972): 150–58, notably 152.

57. Josué Harari has taken up and developed this Lévi-Straussian analysis in pages which confirm its essential soundness with certain refinements, particularly in regard to *Eugénie de Franval* and *Florville et Courval*. Perhaps, however, Harari is too quick to speak of "the universal character of the incest taboo" (p. 174) and he seems to minimize the function of the exchange of women in Sadean incest. See *Scenarios of the Imaginary: Theorizing the French Enlightenment* (Ithaca, N.Y.: Cornell University Press, 1987), pp. 169–87.

58. See Hénaff, *L'Invention du corps libertin*, pp. 258–62.

59. Hénaff, *L'Invention du corps libertin*, for example pp. 301–14.

60. For example, Saint-Fond gives his daughter to Noirceuil (8: 227–28, 236–37; 457, 477). Similar unions occur in the small group of masters in *Les Cent-vingt journées*.

61. Most of the studies of marriage in the eighteenth century note a strong endogamy, although "among the nobility without profession there are for the first time to be found quite a number of unions with daughters of the bourgeoisie. On the contrary, cases of marriage between bourgeois men and the daughters of the nobility are infinitely rarer." See Marie-Hélène Huet, *Le Héros et son double: essai sur le roman d'ascension sociale au XVIIIe siècle* (*The Hero and His Double: Essay on the Novel of Social Climbing in the Eighteenth Century*) (Paris: Corti, 1975), p. 170. Sade himself married the daughter of a magistrate.

62. Sade certainly was aware of the de facto legality of homosexual marriage in Rome, above all in the wealthy classes, particularly until the year 342 (see Boswell, *Christianity, Social Tolerance, and Homosexuality*, pp. 82, 123), and he seems to extend this legality to incestuous marriage.

63. A significant redundance: Clairwil and Borchamps find each other once again after a long separation and marry a second time. The text stresses their physical resemblance ("It is certain that there is a resemblance between you") and closure ("Hymen has tightened our knots; we now wish for them to become indissoluble") (9: 216, 812). This adelphic marriage is a rosy incest. Clairwil will give her brother/husband up to follow Juliette, but neither brother nor sister will ever harm each other.

64. See 9: 51, 644; 576, 1182.

65. Sade's treatment of incest profoundly differs from the one to be found in Rétif de la Bretonne, who is interested only in immediate sexual pleasure: "Accepting willingly that boys are owed to the State, Rétif claimed that daughters

alone form the delights of paternity and that they are at the service of the fathers. It is now known that he did take some advantage of his own daughters." See Jean-Claude Bonnet, "La Malédiction paternelle," *Dix-Huitième Siècle* 12 (1980): 207.

66. 8: 445–55, 464–74; 501, 522. See below, Chapter 7.

67. This is partly a reminiscence from Roman chronicles according to which Nero supposedly imitated "the cries and lamentations of a maiden being deflow-ered." See Burgo Partridge, *A History of Orgies* (New York: Crown Publishers, 1960), p. 78.

68. Angela Carter, *The Sadeian Woman*, p. 99.

69. This was the name eighteenth-century Jesuit missionaries and French explorers gave to the Indians of the New World who dressed as women and, to use the words of Father Charlevoix, yielded to "infamous passions." "The Persian root 'bardag' refers to a young male slave. Imported into the romance languages, it came to denote men who played a receptive role in homosexual intercourse." See David F. Greenberg, *The Construction of Homosexuality* (Chicago: University of Chicago Press, 1988), p. 41.

70. Mary Douglas, *Natural Symbols*, chap. 7, p. 144.

71. See Roger Lacombe, *Sade et ses masques* (Paris: Payot, 1974), pp. 77–82. Lacombe refers to "the libel by Cadet-Gassicourt, *Le Tombeau de Jacques Molay* (1795)." The second edition, which appeared in 1796, was sub-titled *Histoire secrète et abrégée des Initiés anciens et modernes, des Templiers, Franc-maçons, Illuminés, etc. et Recherches sur leur influence dans la Révolution française, suivie de la Clef des Loges* (*Secret and Abridged History of the Ancient and Modern Intitiates, of the Templars, Freemasons, Illuminati, etc., and Research on Their Influence upon the French Revolution, Followed by the Key to the Lodges*). The date, Sade's interests, and the parallels with his text make Lacombe's hypothesis compelling, though he might be wrong when he concludes: "Following Cadet-Gassicourt, Sade denounced that ambitious syndicate that dreams of universal domination" (p. 82). This is far from clear.

72. Jean Starobinski recalls the link between masonry and the French Revo-lution in his essay "Pouvoir et Lumières dans *La Flûte enchantée*" ("Power and Enlightenment in *The Magic Flute*"), *Dix-Huitième Siècle* 10 (1978): 440. In *Mé-moires pour servir à l'histoire du jacobinisme* (*Memoirs to Assist in the History of Jacobinism*) (1798), Abbé Barruel advances the thesis of the plot concocted by free-masons and the Illuminati of Bavaria, whose "ancient" origins supposedly go back to the order of the Temple. See Simone Vierne and René Bourgeois, "Introduc-tion" George Sand, *Consuelo; la Comtesse de Rudolstadt* (Meylan, France: Editions de l'Aurore, 1983), p. 30. Louis Massignon summarizes this plot scenario thus: "It was Cagliostro, in his trial before the Court of Rome (May 4 to November 12, 1790) who 'confessed' to the 'worldwide' plot of the *Illuminati*, the lodges, and the banks against the sovereign powers, beginning with the Bourbons and ending with the Vatican. He claimed to have read, with 'terror,' his own signature among the twelve signatures of the Templar grand masters who succeeded Jacques Molay on a parchment preserved in a hiding place of the Illuminati." *Parole donnée* (Paris: 10/18, 1970), p. 196.

73. Quoted by Lacombe, *Sade et ses masques*, pp. 113–14.

74. Joan De Jean makes this point in relation to the homosexual libertines of the seventeenth-century burlesque novel. See her *Libertine Strategies* (Columbus: Ohio State University Press, 1981), p. 138.

75. The remarks that follow must be seen in relation to Beatrice Fink's important studies of the sources and meanings of cannibalism in Sade. See in particular "Sade and Cannibalism," *L'Esprit Créateur* 15, 4 (Winter 1975): 403–12, and "Lecture alimentaire de l'utopie sadienne" ("Alimentary Reading of the Sadean Utopia") in *Sade: Ecrire la crise*, ed. Camus and Roger, 175–91. See also in the same volume the more hasty but suggestive reading by Noëlle Châtelet, "Le Libertin à table," pp. 67–83.

76. See Douglas, *Purity and Danger*, chap. 7, pp. 126–27.

77. See Peggy Reeves Sanday, *Divine Hunger: Cannibalism as a Cultural System* (Cambridge: Cambridge University Press, 1986), p. 32.

78. See André Green on "anthropological cannibalism" where "the prisoner is devoured," in "Le Cannibalisme: réalité ou fantasme agi?" ("Cannibalism: Reality or Acted out Phantasy?"), in *Destins du cannibalisme, Nouvelle Revue du Psychanalyse* 6 (Fall 1972): 42 n. 3.

79. See Jean-Bertrand Pontalis, "Preface" to *Destins du cannibalisme, Nouvelle Revue de Psychanalyse* 6 (Fall 1972): 7.

80. The motif of the eaten heart has an ancient and well represented tradition. The treatment it meets at the hands of Sade is one of the intertextuality issues I shall discuss in Chapter 5.

## Chapter 3. The Hierarchy of the Orgy

1. See 9: 557, 1163; 586, 1192.

2. See Laqueur, "Orgasm, generation," p. 18.

3. See above, Chapter 2, pp. 44–45.

4. Douglas, *Purity and Danger*, p. 147.

5. *Purity and Danger*, pp. 147, 151.

6. François Peraldi, "Bouche dégoût" ("Disgust Mouth"), *Traverses* 37 (April 1986): 78.

7. Georges Duby tells us that the sermons which embroider these themes with greatest virulence occur after 1150. See *The Knight, the Lady, and the Priest*, pp. 211–12, 46–47. Preachers condemn "the double monasteries for men and women where male superiority was called into question" (p. 215). Jean Delumeau gives more details of the same kind of discourse, and offers an historical account of the "indictment of women" over the course of the centuries in his book *La Peur en Occident* (*Fear in the Western World*) (Paris: Fayard, 1978), pp. 304–45. "Is it just by chance," he asks, "that hatred of women reaches a kind of climax in Luther's Germany in the years 1560–1620, which were racked by expectations of apocalyptic events?" (p. 337).

8. *Purity and Danger*, p. 142.

9. See Dupont, *Le Plaisir et la loi*, p. 32. Also David Mountfield, *L'Erotisme antique* (Paris: Solar, 1982), and Burgo Partridge, *A History of Orgies*.

10. Hénaff, *L'Invention du corps libertin*, p. 148.

11. See Borie, *Le Célibataire français*, pp. 110, 121. On p. 117, Borie quotes from Proudhon's *De la Justice dans la Révolution et dans l'Eglise, amour et mariage*, 20 (1858): were it not for the necessity to reproduce, says Proudhon, one might entirely do without women in lovemaking, and in fact, if they did not have to bear children, women would thereby win equality.

12. In the same way bodily perfection can symbolize a theocratic ideal. See the Introduction to Douglas, *Purity and Danger*, p. 4.

13. Whether as parodic echo or serious imitation, the influence of Sade can clearly be felt in such passages of Pauline Réage's *The Story of O* as the following: "If the costume we wear in the evening—the one I am now wearing—leaves our sex exposed, it is not for the sake of convenience, for it would be just as convenient the other way, but for the sake of insolence, so that your eyes will be directed there upon it and nowhere else, so that you may learn that there resides your master, for whom, above all else, your lips are intended" Trans. Sabine d'Estrée (New York: Ballantine Books, 1965), p. 16. See the analysis by Anne-Marie Dardigna in *Les Châteaux d'Eros* (Paris: Maspero, 1980), p. 252.

14. Jean-Charles Fougeret de Monbron, *Margot la Ravaudeuse* (circ. 1748) (Cadeilhan: Editions Zulma; Paris: Calmann-Lévy, 1992), p. 67.

15. See Douglas, *Purity and Danger*, pp. 49–56.

16. See Bataille, "L'Homme souverain de Sade" ("De Sade's Sovereign Man") in *Eroticism: Death and Sensuality*, trans. Mary Dalwood (London: Marion Boyars, 1987), pp. 164 ff. as well as "L'Abjection et les formes misérables" ("Abjection and Wretched Forms") in *Oeuvres Complètes* (Paris: Gallimard, 1970), 2: 221: "Sadism is nothing but the direction against *persons* of the force represented by the imperative act of exclusion. . . . Sadism finds its way through simple sexual relations as soon as the impure parts (or at least the vaguely imagined impurity) of *a [female] partner* become the object of a more or less conscious obsession: the general tendency to exclude impurity then takes the form of a tendency to cruelty toward *a person*. . . . The contained erotic pleasure is produced in function of an insurmountable aversion for abject things, merely the moral direction inherent in that aversion disappears" (my italics).

17. See Carter, *The Sadeian Woman*, pp. 142–43.

18. 3: 501–5, 321.

19. In his euphemistic reading, Barthes claims that "the Sadian planner is neither tyrant nor proprietor nor technocrat; he has no permanent hold over his partners' bodies" (*Sade/Fourier/Loyola*, p. 161). We find the same opinions, but in an even more erratic form, in his "L'Arbre du crime," *Obliques* 12–13 (1977): 219–26. This assessment neglects not only the class of the victims, but the submission of women belonging to the class of the masters. Barthes here gives the type of elitist reading the erotic genre so often inspires. See Jacques Rustin, quoted above in the Introduction.

20. These in fact went in tandem in Greco-Roman society. See Boswell, *Christianity, Social Tolerance, and Homosexuality*, pp. 78, 143.

21. See Douglas, *Purity and Danger*, pp. 152–53. It is also useful to refer to the collection made by Isabelle Vissière, *Procès de femmes au temps des philosophes*,

an anthology of the "Famous, Interesting, and Curious Suits in all the sovereign courts in the Kingdom, together with the judgments brought in them," published by Des Essarts from 1773 to 1789, of which Sade certainly read a volume or so (see Hans-Ulrich Seifert, *Sade, Leser und Autor* (*Sade: Reader and Author*) (Frankfurt am Main–Bern–New York: Peter Lang, 1983), pp. 120, 199). The sections entitled "Paternal Authority" and "Women Divorced Without Divorce" bring together examples of paternal and husbandly tyranny which are worthy of Sade's fiction, but which the judicial system tries, albeit imperfectly, to correct or punish. This collection allows us to measure the common points with Sade and the degree to which he may have distorted real cases.

22. Duby says that forcible abductions, whether real or feigned, were common in the ninth century, used by "husbands to get rid of their wives, by brothers to deprive a sister of her inheritance, and by fathers to avoid the burdensome expense of a wedding. But the cause of such violence must sometimes have been the unbridled greed and desire to possess so deplored by Hincmar" (see *The Knight, the Lady, and the Priest*, p. 39). Duby argues further on that in the high society of Europe in the eleventh century, or indeed the ninth, the code of behavior obeyed by the "younger generation" encouraged them to "seize women by violence in the teeth of husbands and matchmaking families" (p. 45).

23. Michel Delon points to this in his essay "Sade thermidorien" in *Sade: écrire la crise*, ed. Camus and Roger, pp. 113–14. The variation on the theme we find in "Yet One More Effort, Frenchmen," comes close to the old cliché of *panem et circenses*: "Every time you fail to offer man a secret way to exhale (through lust) the dose of despotism nature has laid in his heart of hearts, then he will devote himself to applying that despotism to the objects surrounding him, and he will give the government trouble."

24. See for example 9: 194, 790 n and 264, 861 on State despotism; 9: 134–36, 730–31; 237, 833; 8: 124, 122 n, 172, 176 n; as well as 3: 493–94, 521 against the death penalty.

25. See Sarah Maza, "The Diamond Necklace Affair Revisited (1785–86): The Case of the Missing Queen," in *Eroticism and the Body Politic*, ed. Lynn Hunt (Baltimore: Johns Hopkins University Press, 1991), p. 68.

26. The quotation is from Arlette Farge, *Le Désordre des familles: lettres de cachet des Archives de la Bastille*, intro. by Michel Foucault (Paris: Gallimard/Julliard, 1982), pp. 15, 347.

27. See Lynn Hunt, "The Unstable Boundaries of the French Revolution," in *History of Private Life*, gen. ed. Philippe Ariès and Georges Duby, vol. 4, *From the Fires of Revolution to the Great War*, directed by Michelle Perrot (Cambridge, Mass. and London: Belknap Press of Harvard University, 1990), pp. 13–14.

28. *Romanciers du XVIIIe siècle*, ed. René Etiemble (Paris: Gallimard, 1960), 2: 1444, 1451.

29. Interview with Pier Paolo Pasolini by Eugenia Wolfowicz, "Je n'ai jamais abandonné la littérature" ("I never gave up literature"), *Quinzaine Littéraire* 427 (Nov. 1–15, 1984): 10.

30. Citing other examples to support this same point, Michel Delon notes in his *L'Idée d'énergie au tournant des Lumières* (*The Idea of Energy at the Turn of the*

*Enlightenment*) that "Sade . . . dreams of the State making use of criminals and re-cuperating latent energy" (Paris: Presses Universitaires de France, 1988), p. 479.

31. There is no question of assimilating the Sadean phantasy to the reality of the world of concentration camps, or even written representation to visual representation. Pasolini's comments on Sade have an interest quite independent of the success or failure of his film and of his real or avowed aims. Pasolini says elsewhere that he conceived of *Salo* "as a sexual metaphor. . . . In sadism and in power politics, human beings become objects. This point in common is the ideological foundation of my film" Interview by Gideon Bachmann, "Pasolini on de Sade," *Film Quarterly* (Winter 1975–76).

32. The benefits of civilization form no part of this picture, either because Sade doesn't believe in them or has no desire for them. See on this issue Claude Lefort, "Le Boudoir et la Cité," a reading of "Yet one more effort, Frenchmen," in Annie Le Brun, ed., *Petits et Grands Théâtres du marquis de Sade*, pp. 218–21.

33. See 8: 427, 445; 435, 452ff.; 9: 355, 952, etc.

34. 9: 419–21, 1020–22.

35. Juliette emphasizes her privileged position in the torture scene: "The minds were catching fire in a way that made the women tremble. . . . Yet . . . it was apparent that I was in no way included in the conspiracy" (8: 216, 224–25).

36. It is true that she poisons her husband, Monsieur de Lorsange, and later on her male companion Sbrigani. But the former is not one of the agents of the orgy, and the latter is a mere adventurer with no social status.

37. Guillaume Apollinaire, *Oeuvres complètes* (Paris: André Balland and Jacques Lecat, 1966), 2: 231, quoted in Françoise Laugaa-Traut, *Lectures de Sade* (Paris: Armand Colin, 1973), p. 180. Also relevant to this issue are Catherine Claude's essay, "Une Lecture de femme," *Europe* (October 1972): 64–70; Nancy Miller, "*Juliette* and the Posterity of Prosperity," *L'Esprit créateur* (Winter 1975): 413–24; Susan Suleiman, "Reading Robbe-Grillet: Sadism and Text in *Projet pour une révolution à New York*," *Romanic Review* 1 (1977): 43–62 (see 56–57). For a contrasting view, which holds together only when the hierarchy of the orgy, the twists and turns of the plot, and the dominant themes of the speeches (that is to say, essentially the whole work) are ignored, see Maurice Tourné, "Les Mythes de la femme," *Europe* (October 1972). Alice Laborde takes a more tempered view in "The Problem of Sexual Equality in Sadean Prose." For a very sensitive but in my opinion at times inaccurate view, see Béatrice Didier, "Juliette, femme forte de l'écriture sadienne," *Obliques* 14–15 (1977): 271–77. In her "Ambivalence in the Gynogram: Sade's Utopian Woman," *Women in Literature* 1 (Winter 1979): 24–37, Béatrice Fink shows that Léonore in *Aline et Valcour* constitutes an exception to the subordination that even Juliette does not entirely escape.

38. Angela Carter also remarks that the character of Juliette, far from representing the emancipation, that is to say, the secularization of women, remains, in a demonic form, in the service of the "goddess" (the consecrated woman) and thereby continues to cater to male phantasies. See *The Sadeian Woman*, pp. 108–109.

39. Hénaff, *L'Invention du corps libertin*, pp. 279–80. Despite the important differences between these two utopias, he is wrong to contrast them from this angle.

40. *L'Invention du corps libertin*, p. 202.

41. See Ernst Kantorowicz, "La Souveraineté de l'artiste" ("The Artist's Sovereignty") in *Mourir pour la patrie* (Paris: Presses Universitaires de France, 1984), p. 37. The first antecedent of this idea was Roman law, and Kantorowicz explains how this thread was strengthened by the translations of Aristotle that appeared between 1200 and 1250.

## Part 2 Introduction

1. See Joyce McDougall, *Plea for a Measure of Abnormality*, pp. 151–52. The whole fourth chapter of this book could be illustrated from Sade's work.

2. Between *Les Cent-vingt journées de Sodome* and *La Nouvelle Justine* Sade wrote *Les Infortunes de la vertu, Aline et Valcour, Justine, ou les Malheurs de la vertu*, and a certain number of short stories, but the most meaningful comparison is with *Les Cent-vingt journées de Sodome*, in which the orgy is already the narrative kernel.

3. "At first the child . . . is not a whole person. It enters as part object into a series of symbolic equations where, curiously, one finds it next to money, or feces, or even the breast, which are objects, parts of the body, but which are not endowed with what we want to call subjectivity." Jean Laplanche, "Les Normes morales et sociales," p. 272a.

4. "Reflections on the Novel," in *The 120 Days of Sodom and Other Writings*, p. 110.

5. "The writer is someone who plays with his mother's body . . . : in order to glorify it, to embellish, or in order to dismember it, to take it to the limit of what can be known about the body: I would go so far as to take bliss in ("jouir de") a *disfiguration of the language*" *The Pleasure of the Text*, trans. Richard Miller (New York: Hill and Wang, 1975), p. 37.

## Chapter 4. Repetition and Writing

1. See 8: 283, 293–94; 299, 310; 301, 312; 9: 195, 791; 394, 991.

2. "It is the difference in amount between the pleasure of satisfaction which is *demanded*, and that which is actually achieved that provides the driving factor which will permit of any halting at any position attained, but, in the poet's words, 'ungebändigt forwärts dringt.'" Freud, *Beyond the Pleasure Principle*, trans. James Strachey (New York: Norton, 1961), p. 36. Quoted by Peter Brooks in "Machines et moteurs du récit," *Romantisme* 46 (1984): 101.

3. Clairwil, Juliette "become aroused only by imagination" (8: 283, 293; 535, 557): "I worshipped the idea of plunging her into pleasure, before putting her to the torture" (9: 452, 1054); "I should become aroused every day by such delicious ideas . . . and the divine spectacle of the misfortunes I had caused; and in the midst of such delightful pleasures, I would cry out: *Yes, there she is: I have obtained her through crime, that one. . . .* And with your imagination, Juliette, oh how

delightful that complication must be" (9: 557, 1162); "Oh my friend, the Princess went on, strongly empassioned by her narrative" (9: 118, 713). Critics have also noted the lexical permutations, whence the equivalence between erotic and rhetoric systems, such as "Saint-Fond's discharge was brilliant, bold, dashing" (8: 210, 218). See Jean-Claude Bonnet, "La Harangue sadienne," *Poétique* 49 (1982): 43.

4. See 8: 108, 104; 277, 288; 9: 70, 664; 523, 1127: "The imagination alone can cradle sensual pleasures, she alone creates them, directs them; there is but a gross and asinine physicality in anything she does not inspire or embellish."

5. See *Sade/Fourier/Loyola*, p. 164. This extraordinary page did not pass unnoticed by Sade's critics. After Barthes, let us mention Philippe Roger, Marcel Hénaff, Annie Le Brun, Josué Harari. The most recent person to comment on this point is probably Simone Debout in *Petits et grands théâtres de Sade*.

6. The first part of the exercise is reminiscent of Descartes's *Third Meditation*: "I will now shut my eyes, stop my ears, and withdraw all my senses. I will eliminate from my thoughts all the images of bodily things, or rather, since this is hardly possible, I will regard all such images as vacuous, false, and worthless." *Meditations on First Philosophy* (Cambridge: Cambridge University Press, 1986), p. 24. There is the same alienation from the body, in a like—but inverted—search for mastery.

7. Philippe Roger notes, on the basis of other examples, that "the body of the reader enters" into the orgy scene thanks to "the textual set up" *Sade: la philosophie dans le pressoir* (Paris: Grasset, 1976), pp. 119–22.

8. This usage is not included in the dictionaries of erotic vocabulary, those of Pierre Guiraud, *Dictionnaire érotique* (Paris: Payot, 1978); Marie-Françoise Le Pennec, *Petit glossaire du langage érotique aux XVIIe et XVIII siècles* (Paris: Editions Borderie, 1979); Louis de Landes, *Glossaire érotique de la langue française* (Brussels: 1861); or Alfred Delvau, *Dictionnaire érotique moderne* (Basle: 4th ed., n.d.), or in the *Grand Larousse du XIXe siècle*. Sade uses it several times—see 8: 211; 9: 462; 6: 213; 7: 432—but he did not coin this euphemism. It can, for example, be found in *Les Egarements du coeur et de l'esprit*: "I own it: my crime pleased me and my illusion was long, either because the evil spell of my age sustained it, or because Madame de Lursay alone prolonged it" (*Romanciers du XVIIIe siècle*, 2: 186).

9. "Sade," writes Jean Molino, "conceives the sublime to be cut off from nature and God, founded solely upon the creative force of the imagination." See "Sade devant la beauté" ("Sade in Front of Beauty"), *Le Marquis de Sade*, p. 162.

10. "One would expect that the organs or objects chosen as substitutes for the absent female phallus would be such as appear as symbols of the penis in other connections as well. This may happen often enough, but it is certainly not a deciding factor. It seems rather that when the fetish is instituted some process occurs which reminds one of the stopping of memory in traumatic amnesia." The examples Freud gives indeed deal with the last object visually perceived before the discovery, the clothing or pubic hair, which sets up a relationship of contiguity, not similarity ("Fetishism," *Standard Edition*, 21: 155). According to contemporary clinical analysis, any object may serve as a fetish.

11. Jean Baudrillard establishes these distinctions and comes to the opposite conclusion as far as current ideological codes are concerned, in his essay "Fetish-

ism and Ideology: The Semiological Reduction" in *For a Critique of the Political Economy of the Sign* (St. Louis: Telos Press, 1981), pp. 88–101. He recalls that the etymology of the word *fetish* is a *fabrication*, an artifact, a work of appearances and *signs*—a most appropriate etymology for the Sadean dildo.

12. The fetishist venerates his fetish, but "in many cases, he treats it in a way which is obviously equivalent to a representation of castration. This happens particularly if he has developed a strong identification with his father and plays the part of the latter; for it is to him that as a child he attributes the woman's castration" (Freud, "Fetishism," p. 157).

13. See Laplanche's article on castration, "La Castration," *Vocabulaire de la Psychanalyse* pp. 632–33. He accepts the hypothesis that castration anxiety occurs before any threat, and has the value not of a punishment for an actual or intended error, but of a *categorical imperative*: "If you wish to be sexually potent, you must be castrated in relation to your mother" (p. 663b). For Deleuze, hypertrophy of the superego forms part of the sadistic structure (see below, Chapter 6).

14. Michel de Certeau, *The Practice of Everyday Life* (Berkeley: University of California Press, 1984), p. 150.

15. McDougall, *Plea for a Measure of Abnormality*, p. 211.

16. *L'Idée d'énergie au tournant des Lumières, 1770–1820*, pp. 396–97.

17. See the rest of the commentary in chapter 5, in the section entitled "Christianity and the Scriptures."

18. This passage could serve as an illustration for a point made by Leo Bersani and Ulysse Dutoit: "Freud might have found in Sade an explicit argument for the connection between mimetic sexuality and sadomasochistic sexuality." *The Forms of Violence* (New York: Schocken Books, 1985), p. 38.

19. Why seven? One is reminded of the dance of the seven veils of Ishtar or Astarte; the seven veils of Salome appear only in the nineteenth century. I tend rather to see an allusion to Our Lady of Seven Sorrows. In any case, the unveiling is always associated with a woman, and the number seven was sacred long before Christianity. On the other hand, the agonies inflicted on the girl and the many skins she is given can be found in a certain popular saying: Jean Delumeau quotes a sixteenth-century preacher who advises not to "hesitate to administer a good beating to a woman"—"is she not said to have nine skins?" *La Peur en Occident*, p. 315.

20. A few references: for a scene more detailed than the program: 8: 34, 24; 61, 53; 67, 59; program without scene: 8: 66, 58; 96, 90; 515, 537; scene without program: 8: 98, 125; program followed by a scene introducing other details: 8: 281, 290; 9: 318, 916; a long program followed by a long scene with different details: 9: 91, 685. In the second half we find an increase in short programs followed by a summary of a scene, as if, finally, Sade was trying harder to avoid monotony (9: 144, 740: 150–51, 746–47; 342, 940).

21. Without being identical, the works of an artist all carry his or her mark, whereas "perverse sexual scenes are created once and for all and prove little modifiable with regard to their fantasy content or their form of expression," McDougall, *Plea for a Measure of Abnormality*, p. 176. In Sade's case, it is impossible to separate the novelist from his perversion.

22. ". . . his version of the logical culmination of the Classical novelistic heri-

tage," Joan De Jean, *Literary Fortifications* (Princeton, N.J.: Princeton University Press, 1984), pp. 291–92. She further develops this thesis in the following pages. On the metonymic structure, see also Barthes, *Sade/Fourier/Loyola*, 139–40.

23. *Sade: une écriture de désir* (Paris: Denoël/Gonthier, 1976), p. 190.

24. For a definitive analysis of *Juliette* as Bildungsroman, with the inversions of the model occasioned by the heroine's sex and her antisocial values, see Nancy Miller, "*Juliette* and the Posterity of Prosperity," pp. 413–25. Miller shows in particular how much the progress of the plot depends on the struggle of the individual (Juliette) against the power of the family, with Juliette's final liberation achieved with the murder of her daughter.

25. Or again: "I shall inform as to these episodes only by placing them in the context of the action" (9: 450, 1053). Juliette mixes into her tale predictive remarks concerning the plot.

26. Iouri Lotman, "The Origin of Plot in the Light of Typology," *Poetics Today* 1, 1–2 (Autumn 1979): 161–84, see pp. 162, 163.

27. In this sense, Bersani and Dutoit are right to talk about a "complicity between narrativity and violence." See *The Forms of Violence*, pp. v, 47–51.

28. The same device is used at the beginning of the third part (8: 393, 409). Certain tableaux also act as narrative pauses (see 9: 203, 798; 458, 1060; 547, 1152.

29. Freud, "The Uncanny," *Standard Edition*, 17: 238, n. 2, which refers in fact to *Beyond the Pleasure Principle*, and establishes a link between repetition, numeration, and castration anxiety which the first two are designed to stem.

30. Let us also recall the fire in Rome that is set by Juliette and her highly-placed Italian friends—thirty-seven hospitals, more than twenty thousand souls (9: 115, 710; 129–130, 725; 147, 742–743); the example of Genghis Khan who orders the throats of two million children to be slit while he watches (9: 193, 788); see also 400, 1000, 509, 1112; the execution of thirty children (9: 581, 1188); fifteen hundred people killed when Juliette poisons the water of a well (9: 581–82, 1188); twenty thousand people dead in an epidemic started by Durand in Venice (9: 585, 1192).

31. 8: 570–73, 592–96; 9: 202–3, 798.

32. *Don Quixote*, trans. J. M. Cohen (Hammondsworth and New York: Penguin Books, 1950), pt. 1, chap. 43: 393.

33. See pt. 2, chap. 2: 481–85. Foucault has analyzed this extra dimension to the work: "The first part of the hero's adventures plays in the second part the same role originally assumed by the chivalric romances—Don Quixote must remain faithful to the book that he has become in reality." *The Order of Things: An Archeology of the Human Sciences* (New York: Pantheon Books, 1970), p. 48.

34. Here we might make use of René Girard's distinction between external mediation (imitation of a distant model with which the hero has no point of contact) and internal mediation: from Cervantes to Sade, we largely pass from the former to the latter, which from René Girard's point of view would correspond to the disappearance of or retreat from a system of transcendental values. See chapter 1 of *Deceit, Desire, and the Novel: Self and Other in Literary Structure*, trans. Yvonne Freccero (Baltimore: Johns Hopkins University Press, 1966).

35. See *Sade/Fourier/Loyola*, p. 136. We shall probably never know exactly what Sade "did," but his documented acts of violence are significant. Even if such

acts were habitually tolerated in an aristocrat and were merely a pretext for his imprisonment (which is not sure in every case), the denials of his hagiographers, who treat them as innocent pranks and establish a radical distinction between his life and his work, seem naively complacent.

36. The other great period for this type of reading was surrealism. Bataille takes issue with Breton when he writes that the literary men "could essily affirm that . . . only poetry, exempt from all practical applications, permits one to have at his disposal, to a certain extent, the brilliance and suffocation that the Marquis de Sade tried so innocently to provoke," and he sides with those who "refuse to interest themselves in mere verbal conjuring tricks." "The Use-Value of D.A.F. de Sade," in *Georges Bataille: Visions of Excess*, trans. Allen Stoekl (Minneapolis: University of Minnesota Press, 1985), p. 93.

37. *Sade: La Philosophie dans le pressoir*, pp. 190, 209. Roger's opinion here in no way detracts from the value of his analysis of the Sadean procedures for subverting discourse.

38. *L'Invention du corps libertin*, pp. 272, 274. For Sadean quotations that allow one to tone down these views, see above, pp. 17–18, 84.

39. *Sade/Fourier/Loyola*, pp. 129, 133–34.

40. ". . . at first sight sewing frustrates castration: how can sewing . . . be equivalent to: *mutilate, amputate, cut*, create an empty space? . . . Sewing is a secondary castration imposed in absence of the penis." *Sade/Fourier/Loyola*, p. 169.

41. Among those who have criticized the erasure of the representational dimension from Sade's text, let us cite Jean-Pierre Faye: "To reduce to decorousness a text which seeks only to belie, shatter, and overwhelm decorum; even more: to underline that the Sadean tale is a 'text' . . . helps to present it as the medium which makes what Sade narrates 'acceptable', instead of using it to explore the enigma of its acceptability" ("Changer la mort, [Sade et le politique]," *Obliques* 12–13 [1977]: 53); Nancy Huston: "When intellectuals talk about the 'pleasure of the text,' they can insist as much as they want to on the radical break between reality and discourse, they have still not explained why it is *these particular texts* that give them pleasure" (*Mosaïque de la pornographie* [Paris: Denoël-Gonthier, 1982], p. 129); Guy Scarpetta: "Supposedly the only 'good reading' of Sade is one that escapes the representative illusion. But . . . there are *other* Sadean representations (those in fact, that coincide with our phantasies, our perversions, real or imaginary) which clearly produce a physical effect (arousal)" ("Variations," *Traverses* 37 [April 1986]: 25); Josue Harari: Barthes's approach leads him "to resolve the problem of incest in purely formal, linguistic terms, whereas, in fact, the real force of Sade's fictionalization of an incestuous social setting derives from his attempt to test the sexual and only as a consequence the linguistic logic such a situation entails" (*Scenarios of the Imaginary*, p. 185).

42. Thus he demands geographical but not historical accuracy (10: 17–18, "Reflections on the Novel", pp. 111–12) and says that " 'Tis better to invent, albeit poorly, than to copy or translate" (10:21, "Reflections on the Novel," p. 115) — does a note in *Juliette* not guarantee the authenticity of the portraits of all the great Italian personages, including the pope (9: 167, 762)? It is obvious that, even if Sade is not completely indifferent to verisimilitude, it must, in his view, include

everything related to the human, since novels "serve to paint you as you are, you hypocritical men" (10: 15, "Reflections on the Novel," p. 109).

43. "Reflections," pp. 111, 106. A passage of the *Histoire de Juliette* ascribes the same significance to the criterion of "nature": "Only by examining nature even in her most secret lairs will we succeed in eradicating all prejudices" (9: 21, 610).

44. "At this point we cannot escape a suspicion that we may have come upon the track of a universal attribute of instincts and perhaps of organic life in general. . . . *It seems then, that an instinct is an urge inherent in organic life to restore an earlier state of things* which the living entity has been obliged to abandon under the pressure of external disturbing forces; that is, it is a kind of organic electricity" (*Beyond the Pleasure Principle*, p. 30, Freud's italics).

45. *Beyond the Pleasure Principle*, p. 32. The "Introduction" in the *Standard Edition* to "Instincts and Their Vicissitudes," 14: 111 ff. reviews the different definitions that Freud gave of instinct. See below, Chapter 6.

46. *Beyond the Pleasure Principle*, p. 21.

47. See Jean Deprun's masterly summary in "Sade et la philosophie biologique de son temps," *Le Marquis de Sade*, pp. 189–205. Deprun shows that Sade closely follows the theses of D'Holbach, Buffon, La Mettrie, Louis de la Caze, Louis XV's doctor, and Jean-Baptiste Robinet. When these authorities differ, Sade chooses the thesis that nurtures his phantasy. Deprun refers to the speech by the pope (9: 177, 772–73) and also to that by Durand (8: 520, 541–42). In regard to Buffon, see also Pierre Darmon, *Le Mythe de la procréation à l'âge baroque*, pp. 82–84. Other critics have drawn other parallels, for example Antoine Adam compares Sade's ideas with the pantheism of John Toland (quoted by Deprun, p. 199, n. 56). Marcelin Pleynet compares the pope's speech to a quotation from Boulainvilliers. "Sade lisible," *Tel Quel* 34 (1968): 79.

48. Pierre Klossowski was perhaps the first to compare this passage with Freud's ontological theory. See *Sade My Neighbor*, p. 89. Lacan's commentary follows Klossowski quite closely, though of course his analytic point of view is much more developed. See *The Ethics of Psychoanalysis, 1959-1960*, pp. 210–17.

49. See also 8: 398–99, 413–14.

50. On this basis, Freud works out the hypothesis Sade illustrates without developing the theory. The "ego-instincts," insofar as they obey the repetition compulsion, push the being towards death, but also "towards a prolongation of life." These are "conservative" instincts, but they are at one and the same time supportive of life (part instincts, life instinct) and regressive (death instinct). See *Beyond the Pleasure Principle*, pp. 38, 56. In "The Two Classes of Instincts," Freud shows how some of the "ego-instincts" can be tied in with the life instinct and some with the death instinct (*The Ego and the Id, Standard Edition*, 19: 40 ff.). Underlining the hypothetical character of his theory, which yet seems to him to meet the challenge of the facts, Freud continues to illustrate it and gives it more and more psychic content: love-hate opposition and ambivalence, explanation of sadism, masochism, and the tendency to destruction in terms of the death instinct.

51. See Deprun, "Sade et la philosophie biologique de son temps," pp. 197–99, for "the intellectual support" that Sade may have found in Buffon and Robinet for the thesis of "universal inter-devouring." One may easily relate this apology

for a Nature determined to destroy to Sade's attacks against procreation. Deleuze relates it directly to the destructive father with whom the sadistic superego identifies (*Masochism: Coldness and Cruelty*, pp. 55–56). Bataille, for his part, substitutes society for nature when he elaborates his notion of expenditure, but, alongside the debt to Mauss, Sade's direct influence upon Bataille cannot be doubted: "A human society can have . . . an interest in considerable losses . . . , in catastrophes that . . . provoke tumultuous depressions, anxiety crisis and . . . a certain orgiastic state." "The Notion of Expenditure," *Georges Bataille: Visions of Excess*, p. 117.

## Chapter 5. Themes and Motifs

1. See, for example, Jean Deprun, "Quand Sade récrit Fréret, Voltaire et d'Holbach" ("When Sade Rewrites Fréret, Voltaire, and d'Holbach"), *Roman et Lumières au XVIIIe siècle* (Paris: Editions Sociales, 1970), pp. 331–40.

2. *Palimpsestes* (Paris: Editions du Seuil, 1982). Parody (ludic), transvestism (satiric), transposition (serious) are part of the transformation relation; pastiche (ludic), caricature (satiric), forgery (serious) are part of the imitation relation. Genette establishes an additional distinction between parody and transvestism or burlesque, as it is usually known. He defines parody as "diverting the text with minimal transformation, of the *Chapelain décoiffé* type" (p. 33), referring to the 1664 text by Boileau, Racine, et al. Transvestism is defined as "a stylistic transformation whose function is to degrade, of the *Virgile travesti* type," referring to a text by Scarron (1648–52); see p. 37 for the table that summarizes all of this.

3. As an added complication, in North-American criticism the word "parody" also includes Genette's serious transformation or transposition.

4. Hans-Ulrich Seifert, *Sade: Leser und Autor*.

5. "Reflections on the Novel" in The Marquis de Sade, *The 120 Days and Other Writings* (New York: Grove Press, 1967), 91–116, pp. 104–5, 108–9.

6. See "Sade et le roman noir," Colloque d'Aix, reprinted in Jean Fabre, *Idées sur le roman, de madame de Lafayette au marquis de Sade* (Paris: Klincksieck, 1979), pp. 166–94. As Fabre says elsewhere, revolutionary events brought this scion of the gothic novel up-to-date ("L'Abbé Prévost et la tradition du roman noir," *Idées sur le roman*, p. 101). See also Pauvert, *Sade vivant*, 2: 581, who follows Maurice Heine in emphasizing that "Sade came before Lewis and Radcliffe."

7. The history of the fictional genre that Sade traces in "Reflections on the Novel" is not accurate, as Fabre stresses in this conclusion: "Apart from Don Quixote, he seems to have read the authors he discusses only starting with the end of the seventeenth-century" ("Préface aux *Crimes de l'amour*," *Idées sur le roman*, p. 205).

8. Deleuze suggests using the term *pornology* to set Sade and Masoch apart from ordinary pornographers, but, without in any way reducing Sade to their level, it may be that he borrowed too much from ordinary pornographers to justify this distinction. See *Masochism: Coldness and Cruelty*, p. 18.

9. What is more, the *Portier des Chartreux* and the *Académie des dames* are readings recommended to Thérèse by her initiator at the end of *Thérèse philosophe*.

10. This attribution seems to be carrying the day right now; see Alain-Marc Rieu, "La Stratégie du sage libertin" ("The Strategy of the Libertine Sage"), in *Eros philosophe*, ed. François Moureau and Alain-Marc Rieu (Paris: Champion, 1984), p. 57.

11. Elsewhere he cites Brantôme with praise (8: 276, 288).

12. See Henri Lafon, "Machines à plaisir dans le roman français du XVIIIe siècle," *Revue des Sciences Humaines* (1982): 186–87. Mario Praz notes a reference to an armchair designed to conquer female resistance in the *Memoirs* of Casanova, vol. 6, chap. 1 (*The Romantic Agony*, p. 443). *L'Espion anglais* by Pidansat de Mairobert (a chronicle which in fact contains two references to Sade—the Rose Keller and Marseilles affairs) features an armchair designed to rape women (Edition of 1783–84, vol. 2, letter 14, pp. 414–15). Letter 8 of the same volume tells the very Sadean story of a woman persecuted by her brother-in-law and her husband, shut up in prison, and falsely accused of the worst turpitudes. Again we see the marriage of the gothic and pornographic genres; there is no need to continue the list of examples.

13. Jean-Pierre Seguin, "*Les Bijoux indiscrets*, discours libertin et roman de la liberté?" ("*Les Bijoux indiscrets*, Libertine Discourse and Novel of Freedom?") *Eros philosophe*, ed. Moreau and Rieu, p. 41. This collection of essays documents both the link between eroticism and philosophy and the fact that at times it exists only in a state of hidden complicity.

14. See also Jean Leduc, "Le Clergé dans le roman érotique français au XVIIIe siècle," in *Roman et Lumières au XVIIIe siècle*, pp. 341–49.

15. Jean Leduc, "Les Sources de l'athéisme et de l'immoralisme du marquis de Sade," *Studies on Voltaire and the 18th Century* 68 (1969): 9–66, esp. pp. 32–39, makes some very detailed comparisons among *Portier des Chartreux*, *Thérèse philosophe*, and the work of Sade.

16. Nancy Huston, *Mosaïque de la pornographie*, for example, pp. 187–88, in regard to the orphan heroine. As Barthes writes, "The more a story is told in a proper, well-spoken, straightforward way, in an even tone, the easier it is to reverse it, to blacken it, to read it inside out (Mme de Sévigné read by Sade)" (Barthes, *The Pleasure of the Text*, p. 26). Kant had already noted the relation of the sublime and the terrible in literature: "Without the development of moral ideas, that which, thanks to preparatory culture, we call sublime, merely strikes the untutored man as terrifying." *Critique of Judgment* (Oxford: Clarendon Press, 1952), p. 115, quoted by Tania Modleski in "The Terror of Pleasure: The Contemporary Horror Film and Postmodern Theory", Working Paper 8 (Milwaukee: Center for Twentieth Century Studies, 1984), p. 8.

17. Fabre suggests that this literary current begins with the many novels of Jean-Pierre Camus, published in the years after 1621, and he also includes the *Histoires tragiques de notre temps* by Rosset and his successors, "the collection of *Causes célèbres et intéressantes* of the lawyer Gayot de Pitaval: twenty volumes between 1734 and 1745," the novels of Prévost and Baculard d'Arnaud. See "Sade et le roman noir," pp. 176–82.

18. *The Pleasure of the Text*, p. 47. See also Modleski, "The Terror of Pleasure," pp. 7–8. There is one important difference between Sade and the example of

horror movies: the ending, which is open in these movies, is closed in *Juliette*, as we have seen.

19. Jean Fabre has already analyzed these techniques of parodic irony ("Sade et le roman noir," pp. 185–86). Note the swiftness of the flow, the numerical precision, the overturning of viewpoint and the absence of terror which constitute the humor in this paragraph of almost perfect pastiche: "We went downwards. *Two* enormous bronze gates formed the closure of these caves, and we had no tools to break them down. The more difficulties confronted us, the more, as is customary, did our desire to conquer them increase. After much turning around, we discovered *one* small window which gave off this cave, and which was secured by only *two* bars. . . . There, *six* great chests presented themselves to our eyes. . . . My hands fall upon a set of keys, one of which is labelled: *Key to the Treasure*. . . . Oh! my beloved Durand," I exclaimed. . . . Alas! in the first instance we found only *doors without keys*, now here are *keys without doors*" (9: 475, 476, my italics).

20. This is possibly a wink at the *Sylphe*, by Crébillon, a euphemistic narration of an erotic dream.

21. 8: 509, 530; 511, 532; 554, 576.

22. All these heroes in evil constantly make mockery of the laws of gratitude (8: 343, 355) and of hospitality (8: 570–73, 592–95).

23. See 8: 107, 102; 576, 598.

24. See "*Juliette* and the Posterity of Prosperity": "And by widowing herself, she further subverts linguistic patterns, flaunting the need for protection proverbially ascribed to 'la veuve et l'orphelin'" (p. 420).

25. See 9: 325, 922. We find the same subversion of the lyrical and sentimental code when Juliette prepares to sacrifice one of the women she is tenderly attached to: "I undressed her, examined all her charms: and the spirit in which I looked upon her made me nearly to die of voluptuousness. Ah! how sweetly I was moved as I said to myself: in three days this beautiful body will be the prey of worms, and I shall be the cause of that destruction! Divine surge of lust! Inexpressable pleasures of crime! such are the ravages you produce in the organization of a libertine woman! Elise! Elise! you whom I loved, I shall deliver you into the clutches of the executioners . . . and it makes me discharge" (9: 452, 1054). See also 8: 210, 218.

26. There is an additional play with mirrors when, pastiching moral discourse, Juliette pretends to blame the naturalist justification which characterizes all her libertine speeches: "'Oh! monsieur,' I then said to this arrant libertine, as I affected a dogmatic tone, 'it is the passions that have blinded you to this extent, and the passions are not the organs of nature, as you claim, you corrupted men; they are the fruits of God's wrath, and we can be freed from their imperious yoke by praying the Eternal for his grace, but we must ask for it'" (9: 369, 966).

27. *The Romantic Agony*, pp. 107, 113.

28. Sade must have known Boccaccio's story: "Messer Guglielmo Rossiglione feeds his wife the heart of Messer Guglielmo Guardastagno whom he has killed and whom she loved; when she finds this out, she then throws herself out of a high window and dies, and is buried with her lover" (*Decameron* IV, 9). Sade probably also knows *Le Coeur mangé* by Jean-Pierre Camus. The name of the lover in Boccaccio transposes that of the troubadour Guilhem de Cabestanh, the hero

of one of the versions of this tale. Furthermore, lines 835–43 of Thomas's *Tristan* summarize the lai of Guiron, which tells the same story. Many other versions of the story exist.

29. Jules Michelet, *Satanism and Witchcraft: A Study in Medieval Superstition* (New York: Citadel Press, 1971 [1939]), p. 114. The allusion is to a legend set in verse by Jakemon le Vinier at the end of the thirteenth century.

30. Barthes notes that "this portrait (of subjects for debauchery) is purely rhetorical, a *topos*, and that "ugliness is describable, beauty is stated." *Sade/Fourier/Loyola*, p. 22. However this convention of the portrait is not restricted to Sade but is indeed characteristic of the whole tradition of description since the Middle Ages. It is especially a characteristic of classic portraiture, as Michael Riffaterre notes in his review of Barthes's book. "Sade, or Text as Phantasy," p. 6. We may contrast the classic body of beauty with the grotesque body of ugliness which Sade, on the contrary, describes by means of a mortiferous distortion of the grotesque body of carnival.

31. *Reflections*, p. 105.

32. In the same way, the name Dorval refers to Diderot. The name Sbrigani, the man who teaches Juliette to cheat at gambling, refers to a character in *Monsieur de Pourceaugnac* whom Molière describes as a "Neapolitan, and man of intrigue."

33. Already noticed by Jean Leduc, in "Les Sources de l'athéisme," pp. 53–54.

34. *L'Invention du corps libertin*, p. 146.

35. *Literary Fortifications*, p. 293.

36. We may cite Jean-Baptiste Louvet de Couvray, *Les Amours du chevalier de Faublas* in *Romanciers du XVIIIe siècle*, 2: 472, 478–79.

37. Foucault, *Madness and Civilization; A History of Insanity in the Age of Reason*, trans. Richard Howard (New York: Pantheon Books, 1965), p. 283.

38. See in this regard R. F. Brissenden, *Virtue in Distress; Studies in the Novel of Sentiment from Richardson to Sade* (London and New York: Macmillan, 1974).

39. Antoine-François Prévost, *Clarisse Harlowe*, in *Oeuvres Choisies de l'abbé Prévost*, vols. 19–24 (Amsterdam, 1783), 23: 280–442. Prévost's translation expurgates the text. The episode is recounted in letters 257 and 312–13 of *Clarissa* (Tuesday morning June 13 and Thursday night), pp. 883, 898ff. of the Penguin Classics edition, edited by Angus Ross, 1985. Brissenden (*Virtue in Distress*) does not discuss *Juliette* and compares the same incident with *La Philosophie dans le boudoir*, pp. 284–89, even though the resemblance is much less obvious.

40. Fabre, on the other hand, laments the "unfortunately involuntary parody of the great writers whose manner Sade justly admires: Prévost, Richardson, Rousseau" ("Sade et le roman noir," *Idées sur le roman*, p. 184). He goes on to criticize the imitation of the sentimental style in Sade's work which he also judges to be involuntary. In the following pages Fabre does, however, give a very fine analysis of the examples of parodic imitation in *Florville et Courval* (pp. 185–86). One thing is certain: a move into pastiche can never be discounted in Sade's writing.

41. See below, the section entitled "Revolutionary Discourse." Note that the same discourse targets Marie-Antoinette, in the same terms.

42. Witness this "prayer": "Holy and pretty Virgin Mary that Panther . . . finally got with child one night, at the side of that sleeping cuckold, good St

Joseph; from which cuckoldry issued sweet Jesus, the great fucker of that public Whore the fair Madeleine, Marquise de Bethanie, for whom the tramp Jesus also served as procurer, or pimp in other words, though, to the infinite regret of the holy bitch, he still liked to screw his little fairy friend Saint John up the ass." *L'Anti-Justine* (Paris: L'Or du temps, 1969), pp. 238–39.

43. Except in a few pages of pastiche: see 9: 110–11, 704–5.

44. "Sade théologien," *Sade: écrire la crise*, ed. Camus and Roger, pp. 219–20.

45. In the same way, as the exhibition *Petits et grands théâtres de Sade* demonstrated, Sade could borrow some ideas for tortures from the painted representations of the martyrdoms of the saints, whose meaning he twists.

46. See 8: 414, 431; 417, 435; 480–494, 502–16.

47. Quoted above in Chapter 3.

48. See Duby, *The Knight, the Lady, and the Priest*, pp. 27, 50–51, and p. 57 on Johannes Scotus Erigena.

49. *The Knight, the Lady, and the Priest*, p. 212.

50. Note that this prescription of the medieval Church does not appear in the New Testament: neither Jesus nor Saint Paul make procreation the condition of sexuality. See Boswell, *Christianity, Social Tolerance, and Homosexuality*, p. 115.

51. Didier, "Sade théologien," pp. 228–31.

52. See Boswell: "(Moses said) You shall not eat the hare [cf. Lev. 11: 5]. Why? So that, he said, you may not become a 'boy-molester.' . . . For the hare grows a new anal opening each year, so that however many years he has lived, he has that many anuses. . . . And he also rightly despised the weasel(s) [cf. Lev. 11: 29] . . . who commit uncleanness with their mouths, nor shall you be joined to those women who have committed illicit acts orally with the unclean. For this animal conceives through its mouth" (Boswell, pp. 137–38). "The heresiarch Novatian wrote: 'What does the law intend when it says "You shall not eat . . . the hare?" It condemns those men who have made themselves women'" (Boswell, p. 141). Beliefs concerning the hare or the weasel were also found, among other texts, in Pliny the Elder's *Natural History*, in Plutarch's *Isis and Osiris*, and in Ovid's *Metamorphoses* (Boswell, p. 139).

53. The entry in the *Encyclopédie* (1751–1772) on Gnostics notes that "those who might wish to gain more insight into their doctrines and visions have only to consult Saint Irenaeus, Tertullian, Clement of Alexandria, Origen, and Saint Epiphanius, particularly the first who quotes their opinions at length in order to refute them."

54. See Janine Chasseguet-Smirgel, *Ethique et esthétique*, pp. 237–39. She links this phenomenon to the *hybris* that characterizes both mystic and pervert (to know God, to transgress the law).

55. "To come to God, in their view, it was necessary to have accomplished all the works of the world and of concupiscence, which must be completely obeyed; claiming that this was the foe the Gospel orders us to surrender to (Matthew, V, verse 25): they believed that the soul that resisted concupiscence was punished for it after death by passing successively into one body after another, until it had completed all the works of the flesh; and that consequently one could not be in too much haste to shed this debt" (entry on "Carpocratians" in the *Encyclopédie*).

56. *Sade My Neighbor*, pp. 100–102.

57. In the *Bibliothèque ecclésiastique des auteurs des trois premiers siècles* (*Ecclesiastical Library of Authors from the First Three Centuries*) by Dupin, or in the *Histoire ecclésiastique* by Fleury, titles which are referred to in the Gnostics entry in the *Encyclopédie*.

58. Jacques Lacarrière quotes extracts from the narrative of Saint Epiphanus in *Les Gnostiques* (Paris: Gallimard, 1973), pp. 103–5: the Barbelognostics, says Saint Epiphanus, "eat and take in communion their own sperm," which represents the body of Christ, as well as "women's menstrual blood," which represents Christ's blood. They practice *coitus interruptus* and *fellatio*, but their ritual is "strictly heterosexual" (p. 104). "When one of them," goes on Epiphanus, "has, by mistake, allowed his seed to penetrate too deeply into the woman, and she becomes pregnant, hear what even more loathsome thing they do. They tear out the embryo as soon as they can take hold of it with their fingers, take this aborted fetus, grind it up in a kind of mortar, mix it with honey, pepper, and different spices as well as scented oils to dispel revulsion, and they gather together—a true community of pigs and dogs—and each uses his fingers to make communion with this fetus meat paste. . . . In their eyes, this is the perfect Pascal meal" (p. 105).

59. See Barthes, *Sade/Fourier/Loyola*, pp. 44, 49, 52, 70; Hénaff, *L'Invention du corps libertin* pp. 174ff.; Didier, "Sade théologien," pp. 231, 232.

60. We find the same device and the same subversion in the ceremony when Borchamps is admitted to the Swedish senatorial party (9: 265–68).

61. *L'Espion anglais*, vol. 10, letter 9, pp. 179–228. Volume 8 of the *Histoire de Juliette* reproduces a page from this episode, p. 354. Seifert makes no mention of *L'Espion anglais*, but under the heading "Pidansat de Mairobert" (p. 256) he notes that in Naples in 1776 Sade had purchased this author's *Journal historique de la révolution opérée dans la constitution de la monarchie française, par M. de Maupeou, chancelier de France* (London [in fact Amsterdam], 1774–1776). It seems that the anandryne society did exist, as attested by the *Correspondance* of Grimm, according to the *Dictionnaire des oeuvres érotiques* (Paris: Mercure de France, 1971), entry on "Sect of the Anandrynes," p. 654. The existence of erotic societies, for example that of the "Aphrodites," which serves as a title for a work by Andréa de Nerciat, is incontestable. Mlle de Raucourt, as well as Mme Gourdan, the owner of a luxury brothel which Sade may have visited and where the young Sapho (the heroine of "Confession of a Young Girl") is formed, were real people. See above, note 12.

62. See below, Chapter 7, "Parricide and Sodomy," pp. 173–74.

63. Braschi (the pope) has his priests crucify a young man "like saint Peter, upside down" (9: 207, 803).

64. *The Name of the Rose*, trans. William Weaver (San Diego: Harcourt, Brace, Jovanovich, 1983), Sixth day, Terce, pp. 427–35.

65. Mikhail Bakhtin, *Rabelais and His World*, trans. Helene Iswolsky (Cambridge, Mass.: MIT Press, 1968), chap. 4, "Banquet Imagery," p. 286.

66. "Sade théologien," pp. 227–29. Didier notes that in general the favorite targets for Sade's parodies are the sacraments of baptism and marriage, and she points out the frequency of confession (sado-masochistic resources of confession and punishment, comparison of the detailed accounts of debauchery and the examples in the manuals designed for the use of confessors).

67. Klossowski gives too much importance to this speech in relation to the whole of Sade's thought (see *Sade My Neighbor*, pp. 74–78). Notably he tries vainly to fit that speech into a gnostic framework, perhaps in the hope of rescuing Sade from atheism (pp. 100–102).

68. *The Romantic Agony*, chap. 3, addendum to note 27, p. 446.

69. See Michel Maffesoli, *L'Ombre de Dionysos* (Paris: Méridiens/Anthropos, 1982), pp. 133–34. "The bacchanalia which the women unleashed," he goes on, "if we are to believe Euripides, were so cruel and unbridled as necessarily to give us pause."

70. 9: 400–401, 1000 and 15: 469, quoted by Jean-Claude Bonnet, "Sade historien," in *Sade: Ecrire la crise*, ed. Camus and Roger, p. 146.

71. Seifert, *Sade: Leser und Autor*, p. 270.

72. See Boswell, *Christianity*, p. 80, n. 91.

73. Quoted by Jean Leduc, "Les Sources de l'athéisme," p. 45. He also notes that Noirceuil tries to "outdo" Nero with his double marriages at the end of the book: "As Nero wed Tigellinus as a woman and Sporus as a man, I, for my part, do no more than invent the double liaison on the same day" (9: 569, 1175). On p. 46, Leduc shows how Sade shortens and alters a quotation from Tacitus in order to strengthen his attack on the Christians (9: 162–63, note, 758–59).

74. See 9: 148, 744; 151, 747; 519, 1123.

75. According to Bronislaw Baczko, "two works are most commonly quoted in the eighteenth century as examples of utopian texts: More's *Utopia* and Plato's *Republic*." See "L'Utopie et l'idée de l'histoire-progrès" ("Utopia and the Idea of History as Progress"), *Revue des Sciences Humaines* 155 (July–September 1974): 474.

76. Quoted above, Chapter 2, "Holding Women in Conmmon." And Plato: " 'But what of your guardians? Could any of them think or speak of his coguardian as an outsider?' —By no means,' he said, 'for no matter whom he meets, he will feel that he is meeting a brother, sister, a father, a mother, a son, a daughter, or the offspring or forebears of these.' . . . 'Is it not true then, as I am trying to say, that those former and these present prescriptions tend to make them still more truly guardians and prevent them from distracting the city?'" *Republic*, Book 5, 463c, 464c, *Plato: The Collected Dialogues*, ed. Edith Hamilton and Huntington Cairns, Bollingen Series 71 (Princeton, N.J.: Princeton University Press, 1961/1989), pp. 702, 703.

77. Angela Carter sees in the Society of the Friends of Crime both a reminder of the "elitism" of the Platonic republic and a "post-humanist, ironic version of Rabelais' Abbey of Thélème." *The Sadeian Woman*, p. 91.

78. According to Boswell's extrapolation of the *Symposium*, 182b–d, Plato "specifically equated acceptance of homosexuality with democracy." Boswell, *Christianity*, p. 51. In this passage, however, Plato merely associates intolerance of homosexuality with despotism.

79. *Le Plaisir et la loi*, pp. 35, 37, 39.

80. 9: 63, 656, quoted by Jean Gillet, "Sade et la décadence italienne," *Romantisme* 42 (1983): 86.

81. "Sade et la décadence italienne," p. 85. Gillet justly notes that Juliette subverts the notion of decadence: the crimes and debauchery of imperial Rome become signs of energy and greatness (p. 87). See in particular 8: 541, 564; 9: 357, 954.

82. Many critics have devoted important studies to Sade's notion of apathy. See, for example, Hénaff, *L'Invention du corps libertin*, pp. 97ff., and Deleuze who analyses apathy in terms of desexualization and resexualization, in *Masochism*, pp. 117–18.

83. 8: 104, 99; 266–67, 277–78; 370–71, 383–84; 414, 431.

84. Barthes has compared Sadean apathy with the *indifference* of Saint Ignatius of Loyola. This is entirely justified especially because both seek to go "in the direction opposite to that toward which the scale seems spontaneously to tip" (*Sade/Fourier/Loyola*, p. 74).

85. Claude Lefort, "Révolution et parodie," in *The Monkey at the Gate: Toward a Theory of Parody*, ed. "Groupar" (New York: Peter Lang, 1984), pp. 73–95; see p. 84.

86. The dissertations may be compared with the long discursive developments in Sade's earlier work *Aline et Valcour*, but the latter does not have the same formal characteristics, and its structure is not based upon an alternation between orgy and dissertation.

87. Lynn Hunt notes this point in "The Unstable Boundaries of the French Revolution," pp. 29–30.

88. Such interpretations are all too often subjective and, as Pauvert remarks, "moved by passion, empty of any documentary proof, and revelatory above all of the phantasies that have been engendered not only by the work and personality of the divine marquis" but also by the Western myth of the French Revolution (*Sade vivant*, 2: 569). This said, Pauvert's own interpretations, and even his hypotheses, are among the best documented and most convincing, and he devotes fascinating pages to Sade's revolutionary years. Another essential source is Michel Delon, "Sade thermidorien" and *L'Idée d'énergie au tournant des Lumières*, pp. 218–22, 390–91, as well as Claude Lefort, "Le Boudoir et la cité," in *Petits et Grands Théâtres de Sade*, ed. Le Brun, pp. 213–21. Let me sum up what is essential for our purposes here. Sade was opposed to both the Jacobins and the Ancien Régime. He flirted with the idea of a constitutional monarchy that would not harm his own interests, and he was wholly at one with the Revolution as far as anti-clericalism is concerned. He was fascinated by the anarchic potential of the state of revolutionary insurrection, and, a non-negligible detail, before August 10, 1792 he wrote articles for both parties. Finally, one of Klossowski's intuitions is worth remembering. What Sade may have expected from the Revolution is "a complete remolding of the structure of man" which would reflect the "problematic structure" of individuals such as Sade himself. *Sade My Neighbor*, p. 48.

89. François Furet, *Penser la Révolution française* (Paris: Gallimard, 1978), p. 78.

90. Richard Cobb, "Quelques aspects de la mentalité révolutionnaire [avril 1793–thermidor an II]" ("Aspects of the Revolutionary Mentality [April 1793 to Thermidor, Year II]") in *Terreur et subsistances, 1793–1795* (Paris: 1965), pp. 20–21, quoted by Lynn Hunt in *Politics, Culture, and Class in the French Revolution* (Berkeley: University of California Press, 1984), p. 40. This is also stressed by Jean Delumeau, *La Peur en Occident*, p. 178.

91. Hunt, *Politics, Culture, and Class*, p. 46. See also pp. 42, 43.

92. Gilbert Lely, *Vie du marquis de Sade. Oeuvres complètes du marquis de Sade* (Paris: Cercle du Livre Précieux, 1962), 2: 375.

93. Lely believes the denunciation came from his colleagues in the Section (*Vie du marquis de Sade*, 2: 375).

94. Maurice Lever persuasively argues that, in fact, Sade did not escape death by accident, but because "someone in high places wanted him to." This would account for the large sums of money he spent and the debts he incurred during that period. Lever states that Constance Quesnet, Sade's devoted companion, had friends "not only in the Convention but on the Committee of General Security," and that she must have played an active role in saving him. "There can be no doubt that he owed his life to [Constance]," he concludes. *Sade: A Biography*, p. 467.

95. Outside the context of the orgy and its tortures, we find in *Aline et Valcour*, a novel Sade reworked after the Revolution, a dream of decapitation that seems to derive more from the tradition of the gothic novel. The illustration of 1791 would confirm this: "He was holding the head of the darling girl up by the hair . . . , he shook it over my breast . . . , he mingled the blood flowing copiously from the head with the blood spurting from my reopened wounds. . . . I sought to tear the precious head away from him and carry it all bloodied to my lips, but I could seize only a shadow" (5: 361, \*\*\*\*).

96. Sade describes this "earthly paradise" and its contrasts in a letter quoted by Lely, *Vie du Marquis de Sade*, 2: 420.

97. French Revolution and the Printed Word," an exhibition at the New York Public Library, March 1989. In the same serious vein, let me cite Jean-Baptiste Chemin-Dupontès's *L'Ami des jeunes patriotes, ou Catéchisme républicain*, a manual for primary education (Year 2, 1793–1794), and a *Catéchisme français républicain* (1792?) on printed sheet, shown in the same exhibition. For a more detailed study see Frank Paul Bowman, "Les 'Liturgies révolutionnaires': pastiches ou parodies?" *Revue d'Histoire Littéraire de la France* 90 (1990): 599–609.

98. For example, April 6, 1791 in the Palais de l'Egalité. See *Petits et Grands Théâtres de Sade*, ed. Le Brun, engraving p. 210.

99. Hunt, *Politics, Culture, and Class*, p. 105.

100. In oral cultures, the ceremony of insults, which is very common, features "direct and ostentatious hostility." See Walter J. Ong, *Interfaces of the Word* (Ithaca, N.Y.: Cornell University Press, 1977), pp. 288–89. See below, Chapter 6, "The Written and the Oral: Dissertation or Harangue?"

101. *Rehearsing the Revolution: The Staging of Marat's Death, 1793–1797* (Berkeley: University of California Press, 1982), p. 7.

102. For the lettres de cachet, see, for example, 8: 213, 226.

103. Quinet, quoted by Lefort, "Révolution et parodie," pp. 81–82. To this second vein can be traced the truculence of certain striking examples of revolutionary discourse, for example the nicknames that Juliette lavishes upon the King of Sardinia, "king of the chimney sweeps," "emperor of the marmots," and that, according to Michel Delon, are derived from the *Jugement dernier des rois*. "Sade thermidorien," p. 113.

104. "La plus grande joie du *Père Duchesne*," in *Ecrire la Révolution, 1789–1799* (Paris: Presses Universitaires de France, 1989), pp. 103–18.

105. See Lynn Hunt, "The Unstable Boundaries of the French Revolution," p. 22. Jean-Pierre Faye grafts an interesting Bakhtinian reading upon this comparison between Sade and *Le Père Duchesne*, but his essay does not sufficiently mark the differences between Sade and the carnival tradition. See Camus and Roger, *Sade: Ecrire la crise*, "Juliette et *Le Père Duchesne*, Foutre," ed. Camus and Roger, pp. 289–302.

106. Quoted by Lynn Hunt, "The Unstable Boundaries of the French Revolution," p. 22. Let me also choose from many examples the seven page antimonarchist poem in alexandrines called *Les Orgies du Gros Louis et des sans-culottes. Journées du 20 juin et du 10 août, Poème civico-bernesque (The Orgies of Fat Louis and the Sans-Culottes. Days from June 20 to August 10, A Civic-Bernesque Poem*, De l'imprimerie des Révolutions de Paris, s.d.). Louis XVI in this poem is presented as a glutton, but "Antoinette" and "Elisabeth" are treated as Messalinas who "lose control of themselves" when they see the ragged republican guardsmen march past.

107. See for example Chantal Thomas, *La Reine scélérate (The Villainous Queen)* (Paris: Editions du Seuil, 1989). Let us also recall that Sade turns "proscribes" into "prescribes" when he borrows his epigraph for *La Philosophie dans le boudoir* from "a revolutionary pamphlet: *Fureurs utérines de Marie-Antoinette, femme de Louis XVI (Uterine Frenzy of Marie-Antoinette, Wife of Louis XVI*, 1791), in which is found the following sentence: 'The mother will proscribe her daughter from reading it.'" See Lely, *Vie du Marquis de Sade*, 2: 498, n. 2.

108. Another common theme is a trust in nature, inspired by Rousseau. This argument was constantly invoked by the revolutionaries and Sade reduces it to an absurd caricature.

109. As Lynn Hunt says in "The Unstable Boundaries of the French Revolution," p. 15.

110. Quoted by Hunt to illustrate the bond asserted by the republicans to exist between public virtue and private morality. "Unstable Boundaries," p. 15.

111. Delon studies certain contradictions within "Français, encore un effort," "Sade thermidorien," pp. 105–6, 108, 109–10.

112. "Without mentioning Plato, he invokes the theory of the sharing of women, but perverts it while deriving from it the legitimacy of incest. Without mentioning Machiavelli [this is in regard to "Français, encore un effort"] he remarks after him that Rome was founded upon crime . . . ; but he fails to recall what the Florentine writer considered the greatness of the Romans, that is to say the fecundity of the law when it is wedded to the desires of a free people. . . . Without mentioning Hobbes, he takes for his own the thesis that the state of nature is one in which all fight against all, but he is careful not to note that civilization is born out of man's inability to withstand the test of that struggle. Without mentioning Rousseau . . . he puts civilization on trial, but with an opposite purpose, since he denies the natural goodness of man." Claude Lefort, "Le Boudoir et la cité," p. 215a.

113. *L'Enjeu et le débat: l'invention intellectuelle* (Paris: Denoël/Gonthier, 1979), p. 141.

114. *L'Enjeu et le débat*, p. 144.

115. Perhaps because of Sade's irony, Deleuze does not believe that he has any pedagogic intent: he claims that it is not a matter of convincing but of dem-

onstrating "that reasoning itself is a form of violence." *Masochism: Coldness and Cruelty*, p. 18. Such a component seems more than probable, but how are we to distinguish Sade's "intentions"?

116. *Ethics of Psychoanalysis*, p. 199 (trans. modified).

117. See also 9: 14, 604, 467–68, 488–89.

118. A term that Genette, on the final page of *Palimpsestes*, borrows from Lévi-Strauss in order to designate the patchwork of the hypertext.

*Chapter 6. Voicing the Hybrid*

1. See Bataille, *Eroticism, Death, and Sensuality*, trans. Mary Dalword (London: Marion Boyars, 1987), p. 194.

2. This formulation refers to Freud's final conception of the drive or instinct; the drive itself would, in this definition, be a *somatic force* and its "psychic representative," to which "a certain quantity of psychic energy (libido, interest)" was attached, would be unconscious, but potentially able to become conscious. See the Introduction to "Instincts and Their Vicissitudes," *Standard Edition*, 14: 113.

3. Jean Laplanche, "Les Normes morales et sociales," 726a. While making it quite clear that "sado-masochism" does not form a single perversion, Laplanche follows Freud in insisting that sadism and masochism share interlocking structures like the dialectical relation between active and passive. See Freud, "Instincts and Their Vicissitudes," pp. 126 ff.

4. *Masochism: Coldness and Cruelty*, pp. 105–6, 133–34.

5. Janine Chasseguet-Smirgel, *Ethique et esthétique de la perversion*, p. 210.

6. For example, "It is possible to find as much pleasure in the role of patient as in that of agent."

7. Deleuze gives precise definitions of the Sadean identifications: the sadist "can only find an ego in the external world," for the sadistic superego "expels the ego along with the mother-image," it identifies the ego with the other, the external victim that it internalizes, which explains its "pseudomasochism." *Masochism: Coldness and Cruelty*, p. 124.

8. "And not only the 'myself' of 'I make myself suffer' is an other, but it must be understood—*and this the theme of the superego*—that the 'I' is also an other" Laplanche, "Les Normes morales et sociales," p. 724b (my italics).

9. Freud sees in humor "the contribution made to the comic through the agency of the superego," and in the joke the contribution of the unconscious ("Humour," *Standard Edition* 21: 165).

10. See Catherine Kerbrat-Orecchioni, "L'Ironie comme trope" ("Irony as a Trope"), *Poétique* 41 (1980): 108–27.

11. Gérard Genette, *Palimpsestes*, pp. 452, 53.

12. Freud, "Humour," pp. 161–62. It is by displacing "large amounts of cathexis" from his ego to his superego" (p. 164) that the humorist spares himself suffering. The ludic reaction of the listener or reader constitutes an attenuated replica of this transfer of affect.

13. The social marginalization which Sade suffered may have exacerbated his

sense of humor. Béatrice Didier notes Juliette Stora's definition of Jewish humor, "a defense reaction by a minority group." "La Plus grande joie du *Père Duchesne*," p. 117.

14. "The dominant idea of superiority is found in the absolute [i.e., the grotesque], no less than in the significative comic; . . . in order to enable a comic emanation, explosion, or, as it were, a chemical separation of the comic to come about, there must be two beings face to face with one another; . . . the special abode of the comic is in the laugher, the spectator; . . . an exception must nevertheless be made in connection with the 'law of ignorance' for those men who have made a business of developing in themselves their feeling for the comic. . . . This last phenomenon comes into the class of all artistic phenomena which indicate the existence of a permanent dualism in the human being—that is, the power of being oneself and someone else at one and the same time." Charles Baudelaire, "On the Essence of Laughter," in *The Painter of Modern Life and Other Essays*, trans. Jonathan Mayne (London: Phaidon Press, 1964), p. 164.

15. "The essence [of the absolute comic] is that it should appear to be unaware of itself, and that it should produce in the spectator, or rather the reader, a joy in his own superiority and in the superiority of man over nature. Artists . . . know that such and such a being is comic, and that it is so only on condition of its being unaware of its nature, in the same way that, following an inverse law, an artist is only an artist on condition that he is a double man and that there is not one single phenomenon of his double nature of which he is ignorant." *The Painter*, pp. 164–65.

16. Claude Reichler, "La Représentation du corps dans le récit libertin," in *Eros philosophe*, ed. Moureau and Rieu, pp. 73–82.

17. Sade may not be the only author of this invention; in any case, on an "Illustration for the Aretin François, by a member of the Academy of Ladies, in London, 1767, engraved by Elluin, after Moreau" is to be found a garland of male organs, bedecked with a set of female genitalia. See Le Brun's catalogue of *Petits et grands théâtres du marquis de Sade*, p. 119.

18. Henri Bergson, *Laughter: An Essay on the Meaning of the Comic*, trans. Clondesley Brereton and Fred Rothwell (New York: Macmillan, 1917), pp. 37, 43.

19. André Breton, *Anthologie de l'humour noir* (Paris: Pauvert, 1966), p. 53.

20. "On the Essence of Laughter," p. 152.

21. *Polylogue* (Paris: Editions du Seuil, 1977), p. 482. In the same vein: "Children laugh readily when motor tension is linked to sight . . . , when an adult shifts the child's body too abruptly . . . ; when some movement stops suddenly (someone stumbles, falls)." *Polylogue*, p. 482.

22. "Probably the only satisfactory interpretation of laughter is to see it as a spasmodic process of the sphincter muscles of the buccal cavity, analogous to that of the anal sphincter during defecation. . . . Thus, when laughter bursts out, we should hypothesize that the nervous discharge which would habitually be performed by the anus (or the neighboring sexual organs) is being performed by the buccal cavity. But in laughter excretion ceases to be positively material; it becomes ideological." Bataille, "La Valeur d'usage de D.A.F. de Sade," *Oeuvres complètes*, 2: 71 (part 2 of "The Use Value of D.A.F. de Sade," not translated).

23. Here there is perhaps a "fact of language" that partly eludes us. Noting

that Sade's "enumerations of debauchery reproduce rather precisely the enumeration of the sinner's failures to obey the commandments" detailed in confession manuals, Béatrice Didier reminds us that "crudity of expression" was common in such manuals right into the seventeenth century. See "Sade théologien," in *Sade: Ecrire la crise*, ed. Camus and Roger, p. 232 and note 43.

24. We can see this in the sermon which Juliette jokingly embarks upon, in a register notably lacking in homogeneity: "It is not by having three or four hundred cocks stuck up your ass every day, not by never approaching the holy tribunal of confession, not by never partaking in the graces of the holy treasury of the eucharist . . . that you will succeed in amending your faults or erasing them in the eyes of others" (9: 369, 966).

25. Jacques Proust noticed this when studying the manuscript of *Florville et Courval*, "Discussion," *Le Marquis de Sade*, p. 99. Michael Riffaterre analyzes one of the sources of this "polarization." A maximum of feminine grace must be contrasted with a maximum of masculine brutality, just as obscenity is much more striking in a stylistic context "which still conforms to the elegance of literary convention." See "Sade, or Text as Phantasy," p. 7.

26. "Sade was clearly aware of the equation between classical rhetoric and the discourse of power" (police, *Encyclopédie*), writes Philippe Roger, quoting certain letters Sade wrote to his wife. Dumarsais, Roger reminds us, condemns the "incongruities" Sade is so fond of. See *Sade: La Philosophie dans le pressoir*, the chapter entitled "La Guerre des tropes," especially pp. 200–204.

27. See Julia Kristeva, *Polylogue*, p. 166.

28. Michel Delon, *L'Idée d'énergie au tournant des Lumières*, pp. 134–36.

29. Marc Guillaume, "Délivrez-nous du corps," *Traverses* 29 (1983): 59.

30. See Pierre Fédida (who is basing his ideas upon Ferenczi), "L'amour muqueux," *Traverses* 29: 98.

31. See Julia Kristeva: "The obscene word mobilizes the subject's signifying resources, takes him across the layer of meaning in which his consciousness keeps him, connects him up with the gestual, the kinesic, the instinctual body, with the movement of rejecting and appropriating the other. . . . Around the object denoted by the obscene word, as a meager limit, unfolds more than a context—the drama of a process heterogeneous to the meaning that preceeds and exceeds it." *Polylogue*, pp. 168–69.

32. Barthes, "Crudity," *Sade/Fourier/Loyola*, p. 134.

33. See Fédida, "L'amour muqueux," pp. 95–96.

34. See Fédida, "L'Amour muqueux," pp. 102–3.

35. *Eroticism*, pp. 138, 170 (trans. slightly modified).

36. The plays on words and cratylism of names are also tied in with the division of the subject. This ludic category has been the object of much commentary. Sade's use of it has verve and talent, but is in no way idiosyncratic.

37. See in this regard Walter Ong, *Interfaces of the Word*, p. 203.

38. See Walter Benjamin, "The Story-Teller," *Illuminations*, trans. Harry Zohn (New York: Schocken Books, 1969), pp. 86–89, 90, 95–97.

39. See Joyce McDougall, *Plea for a Measure of Abnormality*, p. 210.

40. See above, pp. 78–81.

41. See Hénaff, *L'Invention du corps libertin*, p. 311.

42. In his *Dictionnaire érotique*, p. 113, Pierre Guiraud notes as a "notable cultural fact" that "this representation of sexuality and the language it gives rise to is, in its dual tradition (popular and literary), entirely male in its origins," and that "this language—if we are to judge by the number of words and images, by their relevance and originality—is very poor and often inadequate as far as the description of female sexuality is concerned."

43. The article devoted to "Orgasm" in Diderot's *Encyclopédie* does not include the sexual connotation of the word, which appeared only in the twentieth century, but gives as synonyms "irritability, violent oscillation, mobility, crispation."

44. Only "foutre" ("fuck" as noun) as applied to woman as well as man is listed in Alfred Delvau's *Dictionnaire érotique moderne* and in Louis de Landes's *Glossaire érotique de la langue française*. The word is also found in *Les Cent-vingt journées* in relation to a lesbian couple.

45. This comparison is based upon *L'Académie des dames* (1660); Alexis Piron, *Ode à Priape* (1710); *Histoire de Dom Bougre, portier des Chartreux* (1741); Jean-Baptiste de Boyer, marquis d'Argens, *Thérèse philosophe* (1748); Fougeret de Monbron, *Margot la Ravaudeuse* (1748); Andrea de Nerciat, *Félicia ou mes Fredaines* (1775) and *Le Diable au corps* (posthumous, 1803); Mirabeau, *Le Rideau levé ou l'Éducation de Laure* (1785); Rétif de la Bretonne, *L'Anti-Justine* (1797). (Only a partial verification was carried out for *Le Rideau levé*, *Thérèse philosophe*, and *L'Académie des dames*.) Juliette refers to her "sperm" (9: 405, 502) and her "ejaculation" (9: 566), and Clairwil to the "ejaculation" of her "sperm" (8: 276).

46. The *Encyclopédie* entry on "semen" ("seed," synonymous with "sperm") asserts that this view is wholly discredited and gives a historical survey of the uses of the term since antiquity. It still advances the thesis that woman is like man, but with a minus sign attached to her (see above, Chapter 2, "The Male Monopoly on Generation"). "Hippocrates says that the woman's seed is weaker than the man's; but that it is necessary. Aristotle . . . believes that the libidinous fluid women exude in coitus is not a seed, and has no role to play in conception. Galen admits women have seed, but less than men; according to Galen women's seed is more imperfect, etc." In this same article there is an example of the word "sperm" applied to women: "The liquor in the prostate contains no animalcules, nor does the sperm of women." Thus Sade's usage is not wholly unique to him. The entry on "ejaculation" refers only to man, but the following sentence is found in the entry on the adjective "ejaculative": "This word is also applied to two muscles of the clitoris, which go from the sphincter to the anus, stretch laterally, and are attached alongside the clitoris."

47. "Sade et le dialogue philosophique," *Cahiers de l'Association Internationale des Etudes Françaises* 24 (May 1972): 49–74, see p. 72.

48. "Oral history is not an art; a voice is not a signature," "From the phallus to the pen and the word, culture transcodes for us." "The subject of *parole* is not the subject of *écriture*, Juliette's voice is narrated," writes Nancy Miller, who appears to have been the first to latch onto this fundamental distinction. See "*Juliette* and the Posterity of Prosperity," p. 424 and note.

49. 8: 107, 102; 160, 162. Both scriptorial interventions describe, between Juliette and her audience, a priapic interlude directly programmed by the episode that Juliette has just narrated: we are very close to the model of the women historians of the *Cent-vingt journées*.

50. "So we are agreed, said Juliette" (9: 371, 969) and "And now, the rascal, served by Juliette" (9: 461, 1063). *Translator's note*. In both these examples, the English translation by Waynhouse corrects this slip, changing "Juliette" to "I."

51. Without amounting to real slips, certain remarks with a metanarrative value conjure up reading rather than listening: Juliette comments ironically on the virtuous speeches made by one of the victims: "Oh! said I, we have the hero of a novel here!" (8: 347, 359), or contemplates the publication of her story: "If these tales were ever to appear in print" (9: 381, 978).

52. On this question of the notes, see Philippe Roger, *Sade: La Philosophie dans le pressoir*, pp. 75 ff., and Andreas Pfersmann, "L'Ironie romantique chez Sade" in, ed. Camus and Roger, *Sade: Ecrire la crise*, pp. 85–98, especially pp. 89–94.

53. That is to say that the note is attributed to a fictional editor. See Gérard Genette, *Seuils* (Paris: Editions du Seuil, 1987), p. 298.

54. Genette, *Seuils*, pp. 298, 305 (on text and paratext), 312 (on fictional notes), 296 (on assumptive authorial notes). For his part, Barthes comments that the notes represent "the real" (*Sade/Fourier/Loyola*, p. 167). In his view, the notes contradict Juliette's speech, but we shall see that this is not the case, at least on the level of the content.

55. The opinions contained in the notes can be categorized, in order of decreasing importance, as anticlerical and atheistic, moral (in favor of vice), political, and philosophical.

56. The same device can be found in 8: 414, 431 ("oh you women voluptuaries and philosophers"), 468, 488.

57. See also, among many such examples, 8: 183, 189; 9: 463, 1065.

58. Elsewhere, it is the man of the people who "is only the species which forms the first rung after the monkey of the forests" (8: 311, 322). See above, Chapter 3, p. 72.

59. For example, the *Histoire des flagellants* by the Abbé Boileau, which is linked to the "excellent translation of Meibomius by Mercier de Compiègne," a pornographic author (9: 288, 885).

60. 8: 74, 66; 9: 20, 610; 328, 926.

61. In the first half of the novel, the scriptor's notes offer a more generous development of the subversive themes that have already been treated. In the second half, the notes refer to earlier passages in *Juliette*, and even in *Justine* (8: 242, 252; 297, 308; 448, 468; 9: 373, 971; 555, 1160).

62. Sade himself condems the "distasteful motley" quotations introduce into a text (8: 276, 288), while taking care to make no mention of his own dissertations. The criticism is relegated to a footnote which, in actual fact, cuts up the reading, but which the reader is free to avoid.

63. See Wladimir Granoff, *La Pensée et le féminin* (Paris: Editions de Minuit, 1976), "The feminine and the conditions of thought," pp. 248–67. For example:

"to entertain a process in oneself which, by its very nature, allows one not to think of the mother, like any thought process, and which yet ceaselessly leads back to her" (p. 265).

64. Especially, of course, Rousseau and Diderot. See Jean Fabre, *Roman et Lumières au dix-huitième siècle*, discussion p. 457.

65. Fabre, preface to *Aline et Valcour*, in *Idées sur le roman*, p. 219.

66. Fabre, "Sade et le roman noir," *Idées sur le roman*, p. 114.

67. See Walter J. Ong, "Literacy and Orality in Our Times," *Profession 79*, PMLA (1979): pp. 2a,b.

68. Ong, "Literacy and Orality," p. 3b.

69. Ong, *Interfaces of the Word*, p. 287.

70. See the section on "Fictional Models" in Chapter 5 above. At times, the *Histoire de Juliette* parodies religious preaching.

71. A certain aesthetic of historical narrative restores the harangue's oral dimension; hence it could be argued that the harangues in *Juliette* not only annex philosophy but imply that history and fiction are one and the same. See Jean-Claude Bonnet, "La Harangue sadienne."

72. For the major stages in this evolution, and their meaning, see Barthes, "L'Ancienne rhétorique," *Communications* 16 (1970): 172–229.

73. In *The 120 Days of Sodom*, p. 249, there begins a three-page parody of a sermon addressed to woman. Pages 426–27: a one-page outline reduced to the thesis and a few arguments, which changes into a philosophical dialogue; pp. 475–76: a half-page harangue on the hatred owed by child to mother. On the other hand, two sentences are enough to sum up what in *Juliette* would form the subject of a whole dissertation.

74. Such as the *exemplum* and the *enthymeme*, a form of syllogism I shall be discussing in Chapter 7.

75. A rather rapid dialogue, which in Sade's work may include more than two characters, seems to follow the model of the *altercatio*. When the objection is as long as a dissertation, we are closer to the *disputatio*.

76. In a brief series of statements, Saint-Fond puts forward the thesis that God exists, which Juliette and Clairwil oppose, first in the course of a dialogue discussion with Saint-Fond (*altercatio*) (8: 356–57, 366–67), and then in a 23-page harangue by Clairwil (*disputatio*). Saint-Fond refutes this line of argument over five and one half pages, and then follow two pages of objections in dialogue.

77. For other examples of *altercatio* in *Juliette*, see 8: 307–8, 318–19; 9: 337–38, 935–36; 371–75, 968–72. On pp. 514–17, 1119–21 we are closer to the *disputatio*.

78. Ong, "Literacy and Orality," pp. 2b, 3b. In Aristotle "the example is the equivalent of induction in formal logical operations. Rhetorical examples and logical induction both move from individual instances to generalizations. . . . Orality sometimes provides nonanalytic shortcuts into the depths of human issues" (p. 4b).

79. See Foucault, *The Order of Things*, pp. 125–65.

80. As Philippe Roger has emphasized, the facts related are mutually contradictory, or else contradict the thesis they are supposed to be proving. See *Sade: La Philosophie dans le pressoir*, p. 139.

81. "Counsel woven into the fabric of real life is wisdom. The art of story-telling is reaching its end because the epic side of truth, wisdom, is dying out". Walter Benjamin, "The Story Teller," pp. 86–87.

82. Juliette's harangue to Ferdinand is addressed to him alone (9: 329–36, 927–35) and soon turns into an animated dialogue (336–38, 935–37). The first and last harangues by Noirceuil are also addressed exclusively to Juliette (8: 167–80, 170–85, and 9: 548–57, 1154–62).

## Chapter 7. Figures of the Text

1. *La Nouvelle Justine* (Sceaux: Pauvert, 1954) 2: 227, quoted by Béatrice Didier in her essay "Sade: du conte philosophique au roman épique et romantique" ("Sade: From the Philosophical Short Story to the Epic and Romantic Novel") in *Le Préromantisme: hypothèque ou hypothèse?* (Paris: Klincksieck, 1975), p. 215. Barthes was probably the first critic to remark on this type of phrase from a linguistic perspective. See *Sade/Fourier/Loyola*, pp. 32–33.

2. Barthes, *Sade/Fourier/Loyola*, p. 176 (translation modified.)

3. Similarly, in the plans for the *The 120 Days of Sodom*: "She greatly bemoans the injustice of the proceedings. — 'If it were just,' said the duke, 'it would not arouse us'" (p. 642).

4. "Le Couple pervers," in Piera Aulagnier-Spairani, Jean Clavreul, François Perrier, Guy Rosolato, and Jean-Paul Valabrega, *Le Désir et la perversion* (Paris: Editions du Seuil, coll. "Points," 1967), p. 100.

5. Michael Riffaterre has underlined the interdependence and parallel functioning of these various structures of semantic opposition and of the erotic imagination in Sade. "Sade, or Text as Phantasy," p. 7a.

6. In *De Sade's Quantitative Moral Universe of Irony, Rhetoric, and Boredom* (The Hague-Paris: Mouton, 1976), Roberta J. Hackel draws up statistical tables and makes a detailed study on the level of the single word of the vice-virtue inversion in *Eugénie de Franval, Florville et Courval, Faxelange, Dorgeville*, and *La Comtesse de Sancerre*.

7. "Even if you were to disturb and overturn the order of nature in every possible direction, you would merely have used the faculties she herself endowed you with" (8: 460, 480). Sade rarely fails to exploit this antinomy. All the same, he attributes to the libertine life Juliette's failure to have *natural* maternal feelings when she sees her daughter again: "She could not have been prettier; but nature was dumb within me, the libertine life had stifled it" (9: 547, 1152).

8. "Rhetorical syllogism" founded on "verisimilitudes and signs, not on the real and the immediate, . . . developed on the basis of the *probable*, that is to say upon what the public believes; it is a deduction with a concrete value. . . . The enthymeme secures persuasion, not demonstration; for Aristotle, the enthymeme is adequately defined by the probable character of its premises" (Barthes, "L'Ancienne rhétorique," pp. 201–2).

9. Barthes, "L'Ancienne rhétorique," p. 191, in relation to the Greek and the Westerner in general.

10. Freud contrasts the "decisive role" played by the sexual drives in neuroses to the process of socialization that gives rise to "the great social institutions," socialization which, despite "a combination of egoistic and erotic components," permits a flight from the sexual and the private. *Totem and Taboo*, pp. 73–74 (here Freud seems to classify paranoia among the neuroses).

11. Some critics have already suggested this, for example Michael Riffaterre, quoted above, note 5. See also Beatrice Fink, "Sade and Cannibalism" and Béatrice Didier, "Inceste et écriture chez Sade."

12. See Jean-Claude Bonnet, "Naissance du Panthéon" ("Birth of the Pantheon"), *Poétique* 33 (February 1978): 46–65, and "La Malédiction paternelle." While commenting in this second article that "legally, the power of the father had continued to grow from the fourteenth century on" (p. 195), Bonnet posits that "in a certain way, the father is an invention of the Enlightenment, and [that] one could use this fact as a basis for an archeology of Freud's research since he defined the Oedipus complex in a culture and a society whose origins lay in the eighteenth century" (p. 208). In a similar vein, Michel Delon notes that "the reverses suffered by religious faith and the divine right of kings" made men seek out "new, lay, agencies of spirituality: the philosophers imagine avenues bordered with the statues of great men," etc. (*L'Idée d'énergie au tournant des Lumières*, p. 521). On the first point, see also Régine Pernoud, *Histoire de la bourgeoisie en France* (Paris: Editions du Seuil, 1962), 2: 26–30: she notes the legal aggrandizement of the father at the expense of the woman and the child in the seventeenth and eighteenth centuries. See also Farge, *Le Désordre des familles: lettres de cachet des Archives de la Bastille au XVIIIe siècle*, especially p. 159 and all the last section, pp. 343–65. This last work illustrates how often in real life conflicts of interest did flare up between parents and children.

13. Bonnet, "La Malédiction paternelle," pp. 198, 196.

14. Sade had less freedom than Juliette. He married the woman his father had chosen for him and, as Pauvert remarks, by entering into a family of "representatives of the preservation of social order" belonging to the magistrature, he chose his mother-in-law, Mme de Montreuil, as "*Mother—representative of authority* and as scapegoat" (*Sade vivant*, 1: 223, 337). Sade's correspondence suggests that as an adult he got along well with his father.

15. "In the family environment," writes Georges Gusdorf, "humanitarian needs move toward a lessening, or even an elimination, of the father's transcendence, and this must be set in the context of the retreat of God-the-Father from philosophical reflexion." *Les Sciences humaines et la Pensée occidentale* (Paris: Payot, 1967), 4: 389. Thus two currents run in parallel: in law, an increase in paternal powers, and in philosophical thinking, a decrease (see above, note 12). Here Sade interprets in his own way this "humanitarian discourse."

16. Georges May was probably the first critic to have emphasized this. See his essay "Novel Reader, Fiction Writer," *Yale French Studies* 35 (December 1965): 5–11, pp. 9–10.

17. *L'Amour du censeur* (Paris: Seuil, 1974), p. 200.

18. "It is as a function of the death of God that the murder of the father that represents it in the most direct way is introduced by Freud as a modern myth." *The Ethics of Psychoanalysis*, p. 143.

19. See, for example, the very balanced critique by Robin Fox, *"Totem and Taboo* Reconsidered."

20. *Totem and Taboo*, p. 73.

21. Lely, *Vie du marquis de Sade*, 2: 145–46.

22. "A king from the North . . . immolated nine of his children with the unique purpose, he said, of prolonging his own life at their expense" (9: 190, 786). Similarly, the murder of the father by the son is less recommended than that of the son by the father, for the second "breaks off more," interferes with the line of descent (9: 180, 776).

23. "[Blood] flowed through the whole dimension of pleasure—the blood of torture and absolute power, the blood of the caste which was respected in itself and which nonetheless was made to flow in the major rituals of parricide and incest." *The History of Sexuality*, 1: 148–49.

24. *Aline et Valcour* (drafted in 1788 and published in 1793) does touch on politics, particularly on the theme of despotism, but this does not have the same degree of actuality as the political passages in the *Histoire de Juliette*, except for additions made *after* the Revolution. This is the argument outlined by Jean-Marie Goulemot in his "Lecture politique d'*Aline et Valcour, Le Marquis de Sade*, pp. 115–19.

25. Freud, "On Fetishism," *Standard Edition*, 21: 153.

26. Let us also take note of the treatment Sade reserves for two other eighteenth-century literary topoi that maintain an obvious relationship to the cult of the father: the praise of great men and the visit paid to great men. In both cases, Bonnet says, those great men were orators, philosophers, and writers, both past and present. See Bonnet, "Naissance du Panthéon," pp. 47ff, 59ff. Such sanctification was often serious, at times ironic, and always theatrical. Sade attacks it in two parodic sections: in the praise of pornographic authors, and then in Juliette's tour, visiting Italian leaders, each more criminal than the last, and all of whom she crushes with her cynical superiority even as she preaches an ideal of revolutionary freedom.

27. "Do animals know their fathers? Nature gives us absolutely no indication thereof," and furthermore nature incites us to carry out her wishes by killing someone who has ceased to be useful (8: 243–44, 254).

28. The second half of the novel contains, as a counterpart to the speech by Noirceuil which is specifically referred to, a fine pastiche sermon against parricide; this internal inversion takes on the value of self-parody since it reaffirms several of the traditional arguments that Noirceuil had perverted. But this game of mirrors does not blur the hierarchy of values; a few reassuring words at the end of the sermon set things in their proper place and Olympe's parricidal plan is only confirmed (9: 110, 706).

29. In the eighteenth century, this scene was often portrayed in words and pictures (by Greuze, for example); see Bonnet, "La Malédiction paternelle," pp. 198 ff.

30. "My God! why did you not send him to me? I would have eased his sorrows, shared his misery, and, sister, he would have found in my sensitive heart the comfort that yours doubtless rudely refused him" (8: 447, 466).

31. 9: 309, 907 quoted above, p. 000.

32. Letter of August 17, 1792, quoted by Pauvert, *Sade vivant*, 2: 628.

33. *Totem and Taboo*, pp. 154–55.

34. In the other scene of sodomic communion, the host is very roughly treated before insertion. Performed on Easter day but without the patronage of the pope, this episode complicates the above schema without contradicting it (8: 468–69, 489–90). There has been a development in the meaning of the act since *Les Cent-vingt journées*, where a passage in the plans notes several profanations of the host with the conclusion that "the already depucelated sultanas are all fucked with hosts," *The 120 Days*, p. 583.

35. Goux gives a historical dimension to his homology by linking it to capitalist economy.

36. "The mind is matter, since it is composed of parts. Let us accept that it is absolutely impossible for the mind to exist without the body, or the body without the mind" (8: 58, 50).

37. Claude Courouve, *Vocabulaire de l'homosexualité masculine* (Paris: Payot, 1985), p. 181. Yet philosophical love may often have been a platonic love (p. 183).

38. See for example 8: 133–34, 132; 9: 87, 681; 387, 985; and *The 120 Days*, pp. 298, 306, 340–41, 376.

39. *Sade/Fourier/Loyola*, p. 124.

40. *Intersections: A Reading of Sade with Bataille, Blanchot, and Klossowski*, pp. 83–84.

41. See above, Chapters 1 and 6, for related comments.

42. Sheldon Bach, *Narcissistic States and the Therapeutic Process* (New York: Jacob Aronson, 1985), pp. 129–50, esp. pp. 145–46.

43. This is how Janine Chasseguet-Smirgel interprets it, pp. 209–10. Furthermore, coprophagia does not escape Sade's tendency to organize disorder, especially in *Les Cent-vingt journées*, where the diet of the victims is planned to ensure various qualities of stool.

44. Joyce McDougall, *Plea for a Measure of Abnormality*, p. 208.

45. See Jacques Lacarrière for the sexual deviations of the Gnostics: "Where exactly do we find the cycle's point of departure . . . which shuttles the unconscious drive and its conscious demand from one to the other? If we take up that revealing image of the snake biting its tail . . . it is where the mouth joins up with the anus, place of junction for the fragmentary and the unique . . . or . . . for the fragmented unconscious and the totalizing consciousness" (*Les Gnostiques*, pp. 106–7).

46. "The Use Value of D.A.F. de Sade," p. 97.

47. But not, for all that, a "science of the heterogeneous," since "heterology is opposed to any homogeneous representation of the world, in other words to any philosophical system," *Visions of Excess*, p. 9.

48. In fact this sentence comes from Sade's notes for *La Nouvelle Justine* that Maurice Heine collected and published in an appendix to the text. The note is recognizably developed in one of the scenes in the novel (7: 199–200).

49. Kristeva, *Powers of Horror*, p. 21. She claims that the Sadean orgy scene has "nothing heterogeneous." Coprophagia, however, includes and takes charge of the heterogeneous, while the linguistic operation saves the subject from abjectness.

*Conclusion*

1. Simone de Beauvoir, "Faut-il brûler Sade?" ("Must We Burn Sade?"). This essay, first published in 1951, has been reproduced many times, and is included as part of the introduction to the paperback edition of the English translation of *The 120 Days of Sodom and Other Writings* by Austryn Wainhouse and Richard Seaver (New York: Grove Press, 1966 reprint 1986), pp. 3–64; see p. 4.

# Bibliography

*L'Académie des dames* [1660]. *L'Enfer de la Bibliothèque Nationale.* Vol. 7. *Oeuvres éro-tiques du XVIIe siècle*. Paris: Fayard, 1988.

Apollinaire, Guillaume. *Oeuvres complètes.* Vol. 2. Paris: André Balland and Jacques Lecat, 1966.

Argens, Jean-Baptiste, marquis d'. *Thérèse philosophe* [1748]. London: 1783.

Ariès, Philippe and Georges Duby, general eds. Vols. 3, 4. *A History of Private Life*, Cambridge, Mass. and London: Belknap Press of Harvard University, 1990.

Aulagnier-Spairani, Piera, Jean Clarveul, François Perrier, Guy Rosolato, and Jean-Paul Valabrega, *Le Désir et la perversion*. Paris: Editions du Seuil, 1967.

Bach, Sheldon. *Narcissistic States and the Therapeutic Process*. New York: Jacob Aronson, 1985.

Baczko, Bronislaw. "L'Utopie et l'idée de l'histoire-progrès." *Revue des Sciences Humaines* 155 (July–September 1974).

Bakhtin, Mikhail. *Rabelais and His World*. Trans. Helene Iswolsky. Cambridge, Mass.: MIT Press, 1968.

Barbin, Adélaïde Herculine (also known as Alexina Barbin, Abel Barbin). *My Memoirs*. Michel Foucault, ed. *Herculine Barbin. Being the Recently Discovered Memoirs of a Nineteenth-Century French Hermaphrodite*. New York: Pantheon Books, 1980. 1–115.

Barthes, Roland. "L'Ancienne rhétorique." *Communications* 16 (1970): 172–229.

———. "L'Arbre du crime." *Obliques* 12–13 (1977): 219–26.

———. *The Pleasure of the Text*. Trans. Richard Miller. New York: Hill and Wang, 1975.

———. *Sade/Fourier/Loyola*. Trans. Richard Miller. New York: Hill and Wang, 1976.

Bataille, Georges. "L'Abjection et les formes misérables." *Oeuvres complètes*, Vol. 2. Paris: Gallimard, 1970.

———. *Eroticism, Death, and Sensuality*, trans. Mary Dalwood. London: Marion Boyars, 1987.

———. "The Notion of Expenditure." *Georges Bataille: Visions of Excess*, trans. Allen Stoekl. Minneapolis: University of Minnesota Press, 1985.

———. "The Use-Value of D.A.F. de Sade." *Georges Bataille: Visions of Excess*, trans. Allen Stoekl. Minneapolis: University of Minnesota Press, 1985.

———. "La Valeur d'usage de D.A.F. de Sade. Part 2." *Oeuvres complètes*, Vol. 2. Paris: Gallimard, 1970.

Baudelaire, Charles. "On the Essence of Laughter." *The Painter of Modern Life and Other Essays*. Trans. Jonathan Mayne. London: Phaidon Press, 1964.

Baudrillard, Jean. *For a Critique of the Political Economy of the Sign*. St. Louis: Telos Press, 1981.

———. *Pour une critique de l'économie politique du signe*. Paris: Gallimard "Tel," 1972.

Beauvoir, Simone de. "Must We Burn Sade?" *Sade: The 120 Days of Sodom and Other Writings*. Trans. Austryn Wainhouse and Richard Seaver, 3–64.

Benjamin, Walter. "The Story-Teller." *Illuminations*, trans. Harry Zohn. New York: Schocken Books, 1969.

Bergson, Henri. *Laughter: An Essay on the Meaning of the Comic*. Trans. Clondesley Brereton and Fred Rothwell. New York: Macmillan, 1917.

Bersani, Leo and Ulysse Dutoit. *The Forms of Violence*. New York: Schocken Books, 1985.

Bonnet, Jean-Claude. "Naissance du Panthéon." *Poétique* 33 (1978): 46–65.

———. "Sade historien." Camus and Roger, *Sade: Ecrire la crise*, 133–48.

———. "La Harangue sadienne." *Poétique* 49 (1982): 31–50.

———. "La Malédiction paternelle." *Dix-Huitième Siècle* 12 (1980): 195–208.

Borie, Jean. *Le Célibataire français*. Paris: Le Sagittaire, 1976.

Boswell, John. *Christianity, Social Tolerance, and Homosexuality: Gay People in Western Europe from the Beginning of the Christian Era to the Fourteenth Century*. Chicago and London: University of Chicago Press, 1981.

Bowman, Frank Paul. "Les 'Liturgies révolutionnaires': pastiches ou parodies?" *Revue d'Histoire Littéraire de la France* 90 (1990): 599–609.

Breton, André. *Anthologie de l'humour noir*. Paris: Pauvert, 1966.

Brissenden, R. F.. *Virtue in Distress: Studies in the Novel of Sentiment from Richardson to Sade*. London and New York: Macmillan, 1974.

Brooks, Peter. "Machines et moteurs du récit." *Romantisme* 46 (1984): 97–104.

Bruckner, Pascal and Alain Finkielkraut. *Le Nouveau désordre amoureux*. Paris: Editions du Seuil, 1977.

Camus, Michel and Philippe Roger, eds. *Sade: Ecrire la crise*. Colloque de Cerisy. Paris: Belfond, 1983.

Carrouges, Michel. *Les Machines célibataires*. Paris: Editions du Chêne, 1976.

Carter, Angela. *The Sadeian Woman*. New York: Pantheon Books, 1978.

Casanova, Giacomo. *Memoirs*. Trans. Arthur Machen. New York: G. P. Putnam's Sons, 1959.

Certeau, Michel de. *The Practice of Everyday Life*. Berkeley: University of California Press, 1984.

Cervantes, Miguel de. *Don Quixote*. Trans. J. M. Cohen. Harmondsworth and New York: Penguin Books, 1950.

Chasseguet-Smirgel, Janine. *Ethique et esthétique de la perversion*. Paris: Champ Vallon, 1984.

Châtelet, Noëlle. "Le Libertin à table." Camus and Roger, *Sade: Ecrire la crise*. 67–83.

Claude, Catherine. "Une lecture de femme." *Europe* (October 1972): 64–70.

Clavreul, Jean. "Le Couple pervers." Aulagnier-Spairani, et al. *Le Désir et la perversion*. 91–126.

Cobb, Richard. "Quelques aspects de la mentalité révolutionnaíre [avril 1793–thermidor an II]." *Terreur et subsistance, 1793–1795*. Paris: 1965.

Courouve, Claude. *Vocabulaire de l'homosexualité masculine*. Paris: Payot, 1985.

Cryle, Peter. *Geometry in the Boudoir*. Ithaca, N.Y.: Cornell University Press, 1994.

Dardigna, Anne-Marie. *Les Châteaux d'Eros*. Paris: Maspero, 1980.

Darmon, Pierre. *Le Mythe de la procréation à l'âge baroque*. Paris: Editions du Seuil, Collection "Points," 1981.

De Jean, Joan. *Libertine Strategies*. Columbus: Ohio State University Press, 1981.

———. *Literary Fortifications*. Princeton, N.J.: Princeton University Press, 1984.

Deleuze, Gilles. *Masochism: Coldness and Cruelty*. New York: Zone Books, 1989.

Delon, Michel. "Sade thermidorien." Camus and Roger, *Sade: Ecrire la crise*. 99–117.

———. *L'Idée d'énergie au tournant des Lumières*. Paris: Presses Universitaires de France, 1988.

Delumeau, Jean. *La Peur en Occident*. Paris: Fayard, 1978.

Delvau, Alfred. *Dictionnaire érotique moderne* [1864]. Basle: 4th ed.: no date.

Deprun, Jean. "Quand Sade récrit Fréret, Voltaire et d'Holbach." *Roman et Lumières au XVIIIe siècle*. Paris: Editions Sociales, 1970.

———. "Sade et la philosophie biologique de son temps. *Le Marquis de Sade*. 189–205.

Descartes, René. *Meditations on First Philosophy*. Cambridge: Cambridge University Press, 1986.

Didier, Béatrice. "Inceste et écriture chez Sade." *Lettres Nouvelles* (1972): 150–58.

———. "Juliette, femme forte de l'écriture sadienne." *Obliques* 14–15 (1977): 271–77.

———. "La Plus grande joie du *Père Duchesne*." *Ecrire la Révolution, 1789–1799*. Paris: Presses Universitaires de France, 1989.

———. "Sade: du conte philosophique au roman épique et romantique." *Le Préromantisme: hypothèque ou hypothèse?* ed. Paul Viallaneix. Paris: Klincksieck, 1975.

———. "Sade et le dialogue philosophique." *Cahiers de l'Association Internationale des Etudes Françaises* 24 (1972): 49–74.

———. "Sade théologien." Camus and Roger, *Sade: Ecrire la crise*. 219–40.

———. *Sade: une écriture du désir*. Paris: Denoël/Gonthier, 1976.

Douglas, Mary. *Natural Symbols: Explorations in Cosmology*. New York: Vintage Books, 1970.

———. *Purity and Danger: An Analysis of Concepts of Pollution and Taboo*. London and New York: Ark Paperbacks, 1984.

Duby, Georges. *The Knight, the Lady, and the Priest*. Trans. Barbara Bray. New York: Pantheon Books, 1983.

Duchet, Claude, ed. *Balzac et* La Peau de chagrin. Paris: SEDES, 1979.

———. "Sade à l'époque romantique." *Le Marquis de Sade*.

Dupont, Florence. *Le Plaisir et la loi: du "Banquet" de Platon au "Satiricon."* Paris: Maspero, 1977.

Eco, Umberto. *The Name of the Rose*. Trans. William Weaver. San Diego: Harcourt, Brace, Jovanovich, 1983.

Etiemble, René, ed. *Romanciers du XVIIIe siècle*. Vols. 1–2. Paris: Gallimard, 1960.

Fabre, Jean. "L'Abbé Prévost et la tradition du roman noir." *Idées sur le roman de madame de Lafayette au marquis de Sade*. Paris: Klincksieck, 1979. 100–119.

———. "Préface aux *Crimes de l'amour*." *Idées sur le roman de madame de Lafayette au marquis de Sade*. 195–216.

———. "Sade et le roman noir." Colloque d'Aix. Reprinted in *Idées sur le roman de madame de Lafayette au marquis de Sade*. 166–194.

Farge, Arlette. *Le Désordre des familles: lettres de chachet des Archives de la Bastille*, Introduction by Michel Foucault. Paris: Gallimard/Julliard, 1982.

Faye, Jean-Pierre. "Juliette et *le Père Duchesne*, Foutre." Camus and Roger, *Sade: Ecrire la crise*. 289–302.

———. "Changer la mort (Sade et le politique)." *Obliques* 12–13 (1977): 47–57.

Fédida, Pierre. "L'Amour muqueux." *Traverses* 29 (1983).

Fink, Béatrice. "Ambivalence in the Gynogram: Sade's Utopian Woman." *Women in Literature* 1 (Winter 1979): 24–37.

———. "Lecture alimentaire de l'utopie sadienne." Camus and Roger, *Sade: écrire la crise*. 175–91.

———. "Sade and Cannibalism." *L'Esprit Créateur* 15, 4 (Winter 1975): 403–12.

Foucault, Michel, ed. *Herculine Barbin: Being the Recently Discovered Memoirs of a Nineteenth-Century French Hermaphrodite*. New York: Pantheon Books, 1980.

———. *The History of Sexuality*. Vol. 1, *An Introduction*. Trans. Robert Hurley. New York: Vintage Books, 1980.

———. *The History of Sexuality*. Vol. 2, *The Use of Pleasure*. Trans. Robert Hurley. New York: Pantheon Books, 1985.

———. *Madness and Civilization: A History of Insanity in the Age of Reason*. Trans. Richard Howard. New York: Pantheon Books, 1965.

———. *The Order of Things: An Archeology of the Human Sciences*. New York: Pantheon Books, 1970.

Fougeret de Montbron, Louis Charles. *Margot la Ravaudeuse*. Ed. Michel Delon. Cadeilhan, France: Zulma, 1992.

Fox, Robin. "*Totem and Taboo* Reconsidered." *The Structural Study of Myth and Totemism*, ed. Edmund Leach. London: Tavistock Publications, 1967. 161–78.

Frappier-Mazur, Lucienne. "Metalanguage and the Book as Model in Romantic Parody: The Example of *Le Bol de Punch*." *Poetics Today* 5, 4 (1984): 739–51.

Freud, Sigmund. *Beyond the Pleasure Principle*, trans. James Strachey. New York: W. W. Norton, 1961.

———. *Civilization and Its Discontents*. New York and London: W. W. Norton, 1961.

———. *The Ego and the Id*. *Standard Edition*, Vol. 19. London: Hogarth Press, 1953.

———. "Fetishism." *Standard Edition*, Vol. 21.

———. "Humour." *Standard Edition*, Vol. 21.

———. "Instincts and Their Vicissitudes, preceded by 'Editor's Note'." *Standard Edition*, Vol. 14. 111–40.

———. *Totem and Taboo*. Trans. James Strachey. New York and London: W. W. Norton, 1950.

———. *Three Essays on the Theory of Sexuality.* Ed. James Strachey. New York: Basic Books, 1972.

———. "The Uncanny." *Standard Edition*, Vol. 17. 219–56.

Furet, François. *Penser la Révolution française.* Paris: Gallimard, 1978.

Gallop, Jane. *Intersections: A Reading of Sade with Bataille, Blanchot, and Klossowski.* Lincoln and London: University of Nebraska Press, 1981.

———. *Thinking Through the Body.* New York: Columbia University Press, 1988.

Genette, Gérard. *Palimpsestes.* Paris: Editions du Seuil, 1982.

———. *Seuils.* Paris: Editions du Seuil, 1987.

Gillet, Jean. "Sade et la décadence italienne." *Romantisme* 42 (1983): 77–89.

Girard, René. *Deceit, Desire, and the Novel: Self and Other in Literary Structure.* Trans. Yvonne Freccero. Baltimore: Johns Hopkins University Press, 1966.

Goulemot, Jean Marie. "Lecture politique d'*Aline et Valcour.*" *Le Marquis de Sade.* 115–39.

Goux, Jean-Joseph. *Les Iconoclastes.* Paris: Editions du Seuil, 1978.

Granoff, Wladimir. *La Pensée et le féminin.* Paris: Editions de Minuit, 1976.

Green, André. "Le Cannibalisme: réalité ou fantasme agi?" *Destins du Cannibalisme. Nouvelle Revue de Psychanalyse* 6 (Fall 1972): 27–52.

Greenberg, David F.. *The Construction of Homosexuality.* Chicago: University of Chicago Press, 1988.

Guillaume, Marc. "Délivrez-nous du corps." *Traverses* 29 (1983).

Guiraud, Pierre. *Dictionnaire érotique.* Paris: Payot, 1978.

Gusdorf, Georges. *Les Sciences humaines et la pensée occidentale*, Vol. 4. Paris: Payot, 1967.

Hackel, Roberta J. *De Sade's Quantitative Moral Universe of Irony, Rhetoric, and Boredom.* The Hague and Paris: Mouton, 1976.

Harari, Josué. *Scenarios of the Imaginary: Theorizing the French Enlightenment.* Ithaca, N.Y.: Cornell University Press, 1987.

Hénaff, Marcel. *L'Invention du corps libertin.* Paris: Presses Universitaires de France, 1978.

*Histoire de Dom Bougre, portier des Chartreux* [1741]. *L'Enfer de la Bibliothèque Nationale*, Vol. 3. *Oeuvres anonymes du XVIIIe siècle.* Paris: Fayard, 1985.

Hoffman, Paul. *La Femme dans la pensée des Lumières.* Paris: Editions Ophrys, 1977.

Huet, Marie-Hélène. *Le Héros et son double: essai sur le roman d'ascension sociale au XVIIIe siècle.* Paris: Corti, 1975.

———. *Rehearsing the Revolution: The Staging of Marat's Death, 1793–1797.* Berkeley: University of California Press, 1982.

Hunt, Lynn, ed. *Eroticism and the Body Politic.* Baltimore: Johns Hopkins University Press, 1991.

———. *Politics, Culture, and Class in the French Revolution.* Berkeley: University of California Press, 1984.

———. "The Unstable Boundaries of the French Revolution." *History of Private Life*, gen. ed. Philippe Ariès and Georges Duby, Vol. 4, *From the Fires of Revolution to the Great War*, directed by Michelle Perrot. Cambridge, Mass. and London: Belknap Press of Harvard University, 1990.

Huston, Nancy. *Mosaïque de la pornographie*. Paris: Denoël/Gonthier, 1982.

Irigaray, Luce. *This Sex Which Is Not One*. Trans. Catherine Porter with Carolyn Burke. Ithaca, N.Y.: Cornell University Press, 1985.

Jacquart, Danielle and Claude Thomasset. *Sexuality and Medicine in the Middle Ages*. Princeton, N.J.: Princeton University Press, 1985.

Jaton, Anne-Marie. "La Femme des Lumières, la nature et la différence." *Figures féminines et roman*, ed. Jean Bessière. Paris: Presses Universitaires de France, 1982.

Kantorowicz, Ernst. "La Souveraineté de l'artiste." *Mourir pour la patrie*. Paris: Presses Universitaires de France, 1984.

Kerbrat-Orecchioni, Catherine. "L'Ironie comme trope." *Poétique* 41 (1980): 108–27.

Klossowski, Pierre. "Preface to *Aline et Valcour*." *Oeuvres complètes du marquis de Sade*, Vol. 9. Paris: Pauvert, 1963.

———. *Sade, My Neighbor*. Trans. Alphonse Lingis. Evanston, Ill.: Northwestern University Press, 1991.

Kristeva, Julia. *Polylogue*. Paris: Editions du Seuil, 1977.

———. *Powers of Horror: An Essay on Abjection*. Trans. Leon S. Roudiez. New York: Columbia University Press, 1982.

Laborde, Alice. "The Problem of Sexual Equality in Sadean Prose." *French Women and the Age of Enlightenment*, ed. Samia I. Spencer. Bloomington: Indiana University Press, 1984.

Lacan, Jacques. *The Ethics of Psychoanalysis, 1959–1960*. Trans. Dennis Porter. Seminar of Jacques Lacan. 4. New York: W. W. Norton, 1992.

———. "Kant with Sade," trans. James B. Swenson, Jr. *October* 51 (1989): 55–104.

———. "The Mirror Stage," *Ecrits*. New York: W. W. Norton, 1977.

Lacarrière, Jacques. *Les Gnostiques*. Paris: Gallimard, 1973.

Lacombe, Roger. *Sade et ses masques*. Paris: Payot, 1974.

Lafon, Henri. "Machines à plaisir dans le roman français du XVIIIe siècle." *Revue des Sciences Humaines* (1982).

Landes, Louis de. *Glossaire érotique de la langue française*. Brussels: 1861.

Laplanche, Jean. "Les Normes morales et sociales, leur impact dans la topique subjective." *Bulletin de Psychologie* 306–8 (1972–74): 705–28.

Laplanche, Jean and J.-B. Pontalis. *The Language of Psycho-Analysis*. Trans. Donald Nicholson-Smith. New York and London: Hogarth Press, 1973.

———. *Vocabulaire de la psychanalyse*. Paris: Presses Universitaires de France, 1971.

Laqueur, Thomas. "Orgasm, Generation, and the Politics of Reproduction." *The Making of the Modern Body: Sexuality and Society in the Nineteenth Century*, ed. Catherine Gallagher and Thomas Laqueur. Berkeley and Los Angeles: University of California Press, 1987.

Laugaa-Traut, Françoise. *Lectures de Sade*. Paris: Armand Colin, 1973.

Le Doeuff, Michèle. "Pierre Roussel's Chiasmas." *The Philosophical Imaginary*. London: Athlone Press, 1989. 138–90.

Le Brun, Annie, ed. *Petits et Grands Théâtres du marquis de Sade*. Exhibition Catalogue. Paris: Paris Art Center, 1989.

———. *Sade: A Sudden Abyss*. Trans. Camille Naish. San Francisco: City Light Books, 199.

Leduc, Jean. "Le Clergé dans le roman érotique français au 18e siècle." *Roman et Lumières au XVIIIe siècle*.

———. "Les Sources de l'athéisme et de l'immoralisme du marquis de Sade." *Studies on Voltaire and the 18th Century* 68 (1969): 9–66.

Lefort, Claude. "Le Boudoir et la cité." Le Brun, *Petits et Grands Théâtres du marquis de Sade*. 218–21.

———. "Révolution et parodie." *The Monkey at the Gate: Toward a Theory of Parody*, ed. "Groupar." 73–95. New York: Peter Lang, 1984.

Legendre, Pierre. *L'Amour du censeur*. Paris: Editions du Seuil, 1974.

Lely, Gilbert. *Vie du marquis de Sade. Oeuvres complètes du marquis de Sade*, Vols. 1, 2. Paris: Cercle du Livre Précieux, 1962.

Le Pennec, Marie-Françoise. *Petit glossaire du langage érotique aux XVIIe et XVIIIe siècles*. Paris: Editions Borderie, 1979.

Leroy-Ladurie, Emmanuel. *Carnival in Romans*. Trans. Mary Feeney. New York: George Braziller, 1979.

Lever, Maurice. *Sade: A Biography*. Trans. Arthur Goldhammer. New York: Farrar, Straus and Giroux, 1993.

Lotman, Iouri. "The Origin of Plot in the Light of Typology." *Poetics Today*, 1–2 (Autumn 1979): 161–84.

Maffesoli, Michel. *L'Ombre de Dionysos*. Paris: Méridiens/Anthropos, 1982.

*Le Marquis de Sade*. Colloque. Centre Aixois d'Etudes et de Recherches sur le Dix-huitième Siècle. Paris: Armand Colin, 1968.

Massignon, Louis. *Parole donnée*. Paris: 10/18, 1970.

Mauss, Marcel. "Les Techniques du corps." *Journal de Psychologie* 32 (March–April 1935): 271–93.

May, Georges. "Novel Reader, Fiction Writer." *Yale French Studies* 35 (December 1965): 5–11.

Maza, Sarah. "The Diamond Necklace Affair Revisited (1785–86): The Case of the Missing Queen." *Eroticism and the Body Politic*, ed. Lynn Hunt. Baltimore: Johns Hopkins University Press, 1991. 63–89.

McDougall, Joyce. *Plea for a Measure of Abnormality*. New York: International Universities Press, 1980.

Michelet, Jules. *Satanism and Witchcraft: A Study in Medieval Superstition*. Translation of *La Sorcière*. New York: Citadel Press, 1971, circa 1939.

Miller, Nancy. "*Juliette* and the Posterity of Prosperity." *L'Esprit Créateur* (Winter 1975): 413–24.

Mirabeau, Honoré-Gabriel de Riquetti, comte de. *Le Rideau levé ou l'éducation de Laure* [1785]. *L'Enfer de la Bibliothèque Nationale*, Vol. 1. Paris: Fayard, 1984.

Modleski, Tania. "The Terror of Pleasure: The Contemporary Horror Film and Postmodern Theory." Working Paper 8. Milwaukee: Center for Twentieth Century Studies, 1984.

Molino, Jean. "Sade devant la beauté." *Le Marquis de Sade*. 141–70.

Mountfield, David. *L'Erotisme antique*. Paris: Solar, 1982.

Moureau, François and Alain-Marc Rieu, eds. *Eros philosophe*. Paris: Champion, 1984.

Nerciat, Andrea de. *Les Aphrodites, ou fragments thali-priapiques pour servir à l'histoire du plaisir*. Vols. 1–4. 1793. Reprint edition 1864.

———. *Le Diable au corps, oeuvre posthume du très recommandable Docteur Cazzoné, membre extraordinaire de la joyeuse Faculté Phallo-coito-pygo-glottonomique*. Vols. 1–2. Posthumous. Paris: 1803.

———. *Félicia ou mes fredaines* [1775]. Paris: Nouvelles Editions Françaises, 1929.

*Obliques* 12–13 (1977). Special double issue on Sade.

Ong, Walter. *Interfaces of the Word*. Ithaca, N.Y.: Cornell University Press, 1977.

———. "Literacy and Orality in Our Times." *Profession* 79, PMLA (1979): 1–7.

Parent-Duchâtelet, Alexandre. *La Prostitution dans la ville de Paris, considérée sous le rapport de l'hygiène publique, de la morale et de l'administration*. Paris: 1836.

Partridge, Burgo. *A History of Orgies*. New York: Crown Publishers, 1960.

Pasolini, Pier Paolo. "Je n'ai jamais abandonné la littérature." Interview by Eugenia Wolfowicz. *Quinzaine Littéraire* 427 (November 1–15, 1984): 10.

———. "Pasolini on de Sade." Interview by Gideon Bachmann. *Film Quarterly* (Winter 1975–76).

Pauvert, Jean-Jacques. *Sade vivant*. Paris: Robert Laffont, 1986–90. 3 vols. Vol. 1, *Une innocence sauvage . . . 1740-1777*; Vol. 2. *"Tout ce qu'on peut concevoir dans ce genre-là . . ." 1777-1793*.

Peraldi, François. "Bouche dégoût." *Traverses* 37 (April 1986).

Pernoud, Régine. *Histoire de la bourgeoisie en France*. 2 Vols. Paris: Editions du Seuil, 1962.

Pfersmann, Andreas. "L'Ironie romantique chez Sade." Camus and Roger, *Sade: Ecrire la crise*. 85–98.

Pia, Pascal, ed.. *Dictionnaire des oeuvres érotiques: Domaine français*. Paris: Mercure de France, 1971.

Pidansat de Mairobert, Matthieu-François. *L'Espion anglais*; Vols. 2, 10. Paris: 1783–84.

Piron, Alexis. *Ode à Priape*. 1710.

Pleynet, Marcelin. "Sade lisible." *Tel Quel* 34 (1968): 75–85.

Pontalis, Jean-Bertrand. "Avant-Propos." *Destins du cannibalisme. Nouvelle Revue de Psychanalyse* 6. Paris: Gallimard, 1972. 5–7.

Praz, Mario. *The Romantic Agony*. New York: Meridian Books, 1957.

Prévost, Antoine-François. *Clarisse Harlowe: Oeuvres choisies*, Vol. 23. Amsterdam: 1783. Translation of Samuel Richardson, *Clarissa*.

Proust, Jacques. "Discussion" [on the ms. of *Florville et Courval*]. *Le Marquis de Sade*. 99.

Réage, Pauline. *The Story of O*. Trans. Sabine d'Estrée. New York: Ballantine Books, 1965.

Regard, Maurice. "Balzac et Sade." *L'Année Balzacienne* (1971): 3–10.

Reichler, Claude. "La Représentation du corps dans le récit libertin." Moureau and Rieu, *Eros philosophe*. 73–82.

Rétif de la Bretonne, Nicolas-Anne-Edme. *L'Anti-Justine [1797]*. Paris: L'Or du Temps, 1969.

Rieu, Alain-Marc. "La Stratégie du sage libertin." Moureau and Rieu, *Eros philosophe*.

Riffaterre, Michael. "Sade, or Text as Phantasy." *Diacritics* 2, 3 (Fall 1972): 2–9.

Roger, Philippe. *Sade: la philosophie dans le pressoir*. Paris: Grasset, 1976.

*Roman et Lumières au XVIIIe siècle*. Colloque. Paris: Editions Sociales, 1970.

Rosen, Elisheva. "Le Festin Taillefer ou les saturnales de la Monarchie de Juillet." Duchet, *Balzac et* La Peau de chagrin. 115–126.

Rustin, Jacques. "Idée sur les romans français de l'année 1760, considérés du point de vue de l'amour." *Aimer en France 1760–1860*, Vol. 1. Clermont-Ferrand: Université de Clermont-Ferrand II, 1980. 159–67.

Sade, Donatien-Alphonse-François. *Lettres et mélanges littéraires écrits à Vincennes et à la Bastille, avec des lettres de Madame de Sade, de Marie-Dorothée de Rousset et de diverses personnes*. Ed. Georges Daumas and Gilbert Lely. Paris: Editions Borderie, 1980.

———. *Oeuvres du marquis de Sade*. Vols. 1–15. Paris: Au Cercle du Livre Précieux, 1962–64.

———. *The 120 Days of Sodom and Other Writings*. Comp. and trans. Austryn Wainhouse and Richard Seaver. New York: Grove Press, 1966.

———. "Reflections on the Novel." *The Marquis de Sade: The 120 Days and Other Writings*. 91–116.

———. *The Story of Juliette*. Trans. Austryn Wainhouse. New York: Grove Press, 1968.

Sanday, Peggy Reeves. *Divine Hunger: Cannibalism as a Cultural System*. Cambridge: Cambridge University Press, 1986.

Scarpetta, Guy. "Variations." *Traverses* 37 (April 1986).

Schlanger, Judith. *L'Enjeu et le débat: l'invention intellectuelle*. Paris: Denoël/ Gonthier, 1979.

Schor, Naomi. "Unwriting *Lamiel*." *Breaking the Chain: Women, Theory, and French Realist Fiction*. New York: Columbia University Press, 1985. 135–46.

Seguin, Jean-Pierre. "*Les Bijoux indiscrets*, discours libertin et roman de la liberté?" Moureau and Rieu, *Eros philosophe*.

Seifert, Hans-Ulrich. *Sade: Leser und Autor. Quellen, Kommentare und Interpretationen zu Romanen and Romantheorie von D.A.F. de Sade*. Frankfurt am Main-Bern-New York: Peter Lang, 1983.

Smith-Rosenberg, Carroll. "Sex as Symbol in Victorian Purity: An Ethnohistorical Analysis of Jacksonian America." *American Journal of Sociology* (1978).

Starobinski, Jean. "Pouvoir et Lumières dans *La Flûte enchantée*." *Dix-Huitième Siècle* 10 (1978): 435–49.

Suleiman, Susan. "Reading Robbe-Grillet: Sadism and Text in *Projet pour une révolution à New York*." *Romanic Review* 1 (1977): 43–62.

Thomas, Chantal. *La Reine scélérate*. Paris: Editions du Seuil, 1989.

Tondeur, Claire-Lise. "Flaubert et Sade ou la fascination de l'excès." *Nineteenth Century French Studies* 10, 1–2 (1981–82): 75–84.

Tourné, Maurice. "Les Mythes de la femme." *Europe* (October 1972).

Turner, Victor. *The Forest of Symbols: Aspects of Ndembu Ritual*. Ithaca, N.Y. and London: Cornell University Press, 1967.

Valabrega, Jean-Pierre. "Le problème anthropologique du phantasme." Aulagnier-Spairani et al., *Le Désir et la perversion*. 163–206.

Vierne, Simone and René Bourgeois. "Introduction" to George Sand, *Consuelo; La Comtesse de Rudolstadt*, Maylan (France): Editions de l'Aurore, 1983.

Vissière, Isabelle. *Procès de femmes au temps des philosophes*. Paris: Des Femmes, 1985.

# Index